Vi[a] ...li

Via del Babuino

Via ...li

Via Boncompagni

Piazza Augusto Imperatore
P. Cavour

Via del Corso

Via Condotti

Via Frattina

Viadel Trifone

Via XX Settembre

Via della Scrofa

Via Stamper

V.Quirinale

Via Ag. Depretis

Piazza Rotonda

V. Seminario

Via Nazionale

Via Panisperna

Via Plebiscito

Via d. Botteghe Oscure

Via dei Fori Imperiali

Via Giovanni

Via Arrenula

Piazza Venezia

Teatro Marcello

V. Consalazione

Lung. d. Ceci

V.

Via S. Gregorio

Via Claudia

Lung. Ripa

Aventino

Via del Cerchi

ITALIAN

AT A GLANCE

PHRASE BOOK & DICTIONARY FOR TRAVELERS

BY MARIO COSTANTINO
Assistant Principal, M.A., Foreign Languages and English as a Second Language
Tottenville High School, New York
Adjunct Professor of Italian and Spanish, Metropolitan College, St. John's University
Staten Island, New York

Editorial Consultants

GIOVANNA M. PIDOTO-REIZIS, M.A.
Tottenville High School, New York
Adjunct Professor of Italian
St. John's College, St. John's University
Staten Island, New York

HEYWOOD WALD,
Coordinating Editor
Former Chairman, Department
of Foreign Languages
Martin Van Buren High School, New York

Third Edition

BARRON'S

All inquiries should be addressed to:
Barron's Educational Series, Inc.
250 Wireless Boulevard
Hauppauge, New York 11788
http://www.barronseduc.com

Library of Congress Catalog Card No. 99-80140

International Standard Book No. 0-7641-1256-2

Cover and Book Design Milton Glaser, Inc.
Illustrations Juan Suarez

PRINTED IN HONG KONG
9 8 7 6 5 4 3 2

CONTENTS

PREFACE

So you're taking a trip to one of the many fascinating countries of the world. That's exciting! This phrase book, part of Barron's popular *At a Glance* series, will prove an invaluable companion.

In these books we present the phrases and words that a traveler most often needs for a brief visit to a foreign country, where the customs and language are often different. Each phrase book highlights the terms particular to that country, in situations that the tourist is most likely to encounter. This revision includes dialogues using words and expressions for each situation. Travel tips found throughout the book have been updated. With a specially developed key to pronunciation, this book will enable you to communicate quickly and confidently in colloquial terms. It is intended not only for beginners with no knowledge of the language, but also for those who have already studied it and have some familiarity with it.

Some of the unique features and highlights of the Barron's series are:

- Easy-to-follow *pronunciation keys* and complete phonetic transcriptions for all words and phrases in the book.
- Compact *dictionary* of commonly used words and phrases—built right into this phrase book so there's no need to carry a separate dictionary.
- Useful phrases for the *tourist*, grouped together by subject matter in a logical way so that the appropriate phrase is easy to locate when you need it.
- Special phrases for the *business traveler*, including banking terms, trade and contract negotiations, and secretarial services.
- Thorough section on *food and drink*, with comprehensive food terms you will find on menus.
- *Emergency phrases* and terms you hope you won't need: legal complications, medical problems, theft or loss of valuables, replacement or repair of watches, cameras, etc.
- *Sightseeing itineraries*, shopping tips, practical travel tips, and regional food specialties to help you get off the

beaten path and into the countryside, to the small towns and cities, and to the neighboring areas.

■ A *reference section* providing: important signs, conversion tables, holidays, abbreviations, telling time, days of the week and months of the year.

■ A brief *grammar section*, with the basic elements of the language quickly explained.

Enjoy your vacation and travel with confidence. You have a friend by your side.

ACKNOWLEDGMENTS

We would like to thank the following individuals and organizations for their assistance on this project: Giuseppe Abbatangelo, Italian Government Travel Office, New York, New York; Professor Alvino Fantini, School for International Training, Brattleboro, Vermont; Jim Ferri, managing editor, *Travel-Holiday* magazine; Robert Fisher, Fisher Travel Guides, New York, New York; George Lang, George Lang, Inc., New York, New York; Professor Joseph Tursi, SUNY Stony Brook, New York; Professor Henry Urbanski, chairman, Department of Foreign Languages, SUNY New Paltz, New York; Robert Brainerd; and Hedy Giusti-Lanham.

Also Alitalia, the Association of American Travel Writers, the Italian Cultural Council, the Italian Government Travel Office, the *New York Times*, *Signature* magazine, *Travel-Holiday* magazine, *Travel and Leisure* magazine, U.S. Tour Operators, and U.S. Travel Data Center.

Also, we wish to thank Biagio Coluccio, M.D., Padre Saverio Corradino, S.J. (Istituto Biblico di Roma), Lawrence Gambella, Assistant Principal at Tottenville High School in New York, and Dr. Emanuela Costantino (Rome) for their suggestions and review of various stages of manuscript.

QUICK PRONUNCIATION GUIDE

Although all the phrases in this book are presented with an easy-to-use key to pronunciation, you will find speaking Italian quite a bit easier if you learn a few simple rules. Many vowels and consonants in Italian are pronounced as they would be in English. There are some exceptions, however, which are given below. Since these sounds don't usually vary, you can follow these guidelines in pronouncing all Italian words. Note: When pronouncing the words in the following examples, stress the vowels that appear in CAPITAL letters.

ITALIAN LETTER(S)	SOUND IN ENGLISH	EXAMPLE
VOWELS		
a	ah (y<u>a</u>cht)	**casa** (*kAH-sah*), house
è	eh (n<u>e</u>t)	**lèggere** (*lEH-jeh-reh*), to read
e	ay (h<u>ay</u>)	**mela** (*mAY-lah*), apple
i	ee (f<u>ee</u>t)	**libri** (*lEE-bree*), books
o	oh (r<u>o</u>pe)	**boccone** (*boh-kOH-neh*), mouthful
u	oo (c<u>oo</u>l)	**tutto** (*tOOt-toh*), everything
CONSONANT SOUNDS		
ci	chee (<u>chee</u>se)	**cinema** (*chEE-nay-mah*), movies
ce	chay (<u>ch</u>air)	**piacere** (*pee-ah-chAY-reh*), pleasure
ca	kah (<u>c</u>ot)	**casa** (*kAH-sah*), house
co	koh (<u>c</u>old)	**cotto** (*kOHt-toh*), cooked
che	kay (<u>k</u>ent)	**perché** (*pehr-kAY*), because
chi	key (<u>k</u>ey)	**pochi** (*pOH-key*), few
gi	jee (<u>jee</u>p)	**giro** (*jEE-roh*), turn

ITALIAN LETTER(S)	SOUND IN ENGLISH	EXAMPLE
ge	jay (<u>ge</u>neral)	**generale** (*jay-nay-rAH-leh*), general
gh	gh (spa<u>gh</u>etti)	**spaghetti** (*spah-ghAYt-tee*)
gli	ll (mi<u>lli</u>on)	**egli** (*AY-ly-ee*), he **bottiglia** (*boht-tEE-ly-ee-ah*), bottle
gn	ny (ca<u>ny</u>on)	**magnifico** (*mah-ny-EE-fee-koh*), magnificent
qu	koo (<u>qu</u>iet)	**àquila** (*AH-koo-ee-lah*), eagle
sce	sh (fi<u>sh</u>)	**pesce** (*pAY-sheh*), fish
sci		**sciòpero** (*shee-OH-peh-roh*), strike
z or zz	ts (ea<u>ts</u>)	**pizza** (*pEE-tsah*), pizza **zero** (*tsEH-roh*), zero

Travel Tips There are many theories and much research on how to survive jet lag—the adjustment to a long trip into a different time zone. Some multinational corporations take jet lag so seriously they do not allow employees to make business decisions on the first day abroad. Most experts agree on several techniques: avoid alcohol but drink plenty of other fluids while flying to avoid dehydration; take frequent strolls around the plane to keep your blood circulating; if possible, get some rest on the flight; ear plugs, an eye mask, and an inflatable neck collar make sleep easier; if you arrive early in the morning, take an after-lunch nap, get up for some exercise and dinner, then go to bed at the regular new time; if you arrive at your destination in the afternoon or later, skip the nap and let yourself sleep late the next morning; in countries where massage or saunas are standard hotel service, indulge yourself on the evening of your arrival to help you sleep soundly that night.

THE BASICS FOR GETTING BY

GENERAL INFORMATION

ITALY

Shape: A boot in the midst of the Mediterranean Sea, crowned by the Alps in the North with the Apennines running down its dorsal spine toward Sicily. Sardinia and other islands are like gems about its contours.

Area: 116,303 square miles (approximately the combined sizes of the states of Pennsylvania, New York, New Jersey, Connecticut, Rhode Island, and Massachusetts).

Population: 56,778,000.

Population Density: 487 per sq. mile.

Capital: Rome (2,775,000 inhabitants).

Language: Italian. French, German, Slovene, and Ladino are also spoken by minorities.

Climate: Temperate.
  Winter: Mild/warm in Sicily and on the Neapolitan and Ligurian coasts. Cold in the Alps, cold and foggy in the Po Valley and Central Apennines. Ideal for skiing in mountain areas.
  Summer: Hot and dry. The coasts are mitigated by sea breezes. The Alps and Apennines are pleasantly cool. Ideal for camping, excursions, and hiking. Beaches and lake resorts are packed with tourists.
  Spring and Fall: Temperatures are mild. It is an optimal time to visit the cities rich in artistic treasures.

Currency: The Italian **lira(e)** *(lEE-rah)(eh)* will be replaced by the **euro** in the year 2002. Tourists have to declare any amount exceeding 20 million **lire** (about U.S. $12,000) imported into the country. A similar amount can be exported out of the country.

Documents: A visa is *not* required for citizens of the U.S. or Canada, Australia, and New Zealand holding valid passports. A **permesso di soggiorno** (*pehr-mAYs-soh dee soh-jee-Ohr-noh*) or permit to stay is required for stays after 90 days. You must go to the **Questura** (*koo-ehs-tOO-rah*), the Main Police Station, to apply for either a **permesso di lavoro** (*payr-mAYs-soh dee lah-vOH-roh*), a permit to work, or a **permesso di studio** (*payr-mAYs-soh dee stOO-dee-oh*), a permit to study.

Valid driving licenses and other traffic documents from other countries are recognized in Italy.

Vaccination certificates are *not* required to enter Italy or to reenter the United States.

Electric Appliances: The voltage is 220 volts and the cycle is 50. Tourists should carry a transformer. Usually, Italian plugs have two round-pronged plugs. An adapter is a must.

Gasoline: Fuel prices per liter are very high. The use of **la benzina verde** (*lah behn-tzEE-nah vAYr-deh*), the green fuel that contains less lead, is recommended for the protection of the environment. On the motorways, service stations are open 24 hours a day. Carrying fuel in gas containers is strictly prohibited.

Hotels: There are more than 38,000 hotels in Italy. Rates include air-conditioning, heating, service, and taxes. The current value-added tax (IVA) is 10%. In cities, towns, and resort centers, November to March, hotels offer low rates. At ski resorts, during April, May, and September through November, hotel rates are lower. Accommodations are also available in private homes, youth hostels, day hotels, and rural cottages and farmhouses (agriturism).

Motels along the roads are modern and comfortable. They offer parking facilities and delicious food. Gardens, small parks, swimming pools, private beaches, and tennis courts are also provided in many motels. **AGIP** is the main motel chain on **L'Autostrada del Sole** (*lah-oo-toh-strAH-dah dAYl sOH-leh*), the Italian superhighway network.

Medical Insurance: U.S. citizens traveling in Italy are not covered by Italian medical programs and should either buy insurance before visiting the country or check with their insurance provider/company for proper coverage before departing.

Papal Audiences: In Vatican City, Wednesday at 11 A.M. is usually the time for the general audiences with His Holiness either inside St. Peter's Basilica itself or in the Hall of the Papal Audiences, **Aula Paolo VI**, with a seating of 7,000.

In summer, they take place either in Saint Peter's Square or at Castel Gandolfo, the papal summer residence.

MOST FREQUENTLY USED EXPRESSIONS

The following are expressions you'll use over and over—the fundamentals of polite conversation, the way to express what you want or need, and some simple question tags that you can use to construct all sorts of questions. We suggest you become very familiar with these phrases.

Yes	**Sì**	*see*
No	**No**	*noh*
Maybe	**Forse**	*fOHr-seh*
Please	**Per piacere**	*pehr pee-ah-chAY-reh*
Thank you (very much)	**(Mille) grazie**	*(mEEl-leh) grAH-tsee-eh*
You're welcome	**Prego**	*prEh-goh*
Excuse me	**Mi scusi**	*mee skOO-see*
I'm sorry	**Mi dispiace**	*mee dee-spee-AH-cheh*
Just a second	**Un momento**	*oon moh-mEHn-toh*
That's all right, okay	**Va bene**	*vah bEH-neh*
It doesn't matter	**Non importa**	*nohn eem-pOHr-tah*
*Good morning (afternoon)	**Buon giorno**	*boo-Ohn jee-Ohr-noh*

*NOTE: Generally, **buon giorno** is used throughout the day until about 4–6 P.M. The expression **buon pomeriggio** ("good afternoon") is generally not used in conversation but might be heard on the radio.

*Good evening (night)	**Buona sera (notte)**	*boo-Oh-nah sAY-rah (nOHt-teh)*
Sir	**Signore**	*see-ny-OH-reh*
Madame	**Signora**	*see-ny-OH-rah*
Miss	**Signorina**	*see-ny-oh-rEE-nah*
Good-bye	**Arrivederci**	*ahr-ree-veh-dAYr-chee*
*See you later (so long)	**A più tardi (ciao)**	*ah pee-OO tAHr-dee (chee-AH-oh)*
See you tomorrow	**A domani**	*ah doh-mAH-nee*

COMMUNICATING

Do you speak English?	**Parla inglese?**	*pAHr-lah een-glAY-seh*
I don't speak Italian.	**Io non parlo italiano.**	*EE-oh nohn pAHr-loh ee-tah-lee-AH-noh*
I speak a little Italian.	**Parlo poco l'italiano.**	*pAHr-loh pOH-koh lee-tah-lee-AH-noh*
Is there anyone here who speaks English?	**C'è qualcuno qui che parla inglese?**	*chEH koo-ahl-kOO-noh koo-EE kay pAHr-lah een-glAY-seh*
Do you understand?	**Capisce? (ha capito?)**	*kah-pEE-sheh (ah kah-pEE-toh)*
I understand.	**Capisco (ho capito).**	*kah-pEE-skoh (oh kah-pEE-toh)*
I don't understand.	**Non capisco (non ho capito).**	*nohn kah-pEE-skoh (nohn oh kah-pEE-toh)*
What does that mean?	**Che cosa significa (quello)?**	*kay kOH-sah see-ny-EE-fee-kah (koo-Ayl-loh)*

*NOTE: **Buona sera** is used when meeting people in the late afternoon and throughout the evening. **Buona notte** is used when leaving at the end of the evening. The casual expression **ciao** ("Hello," "Bye," "So long") is used only with friends and family.

What? What did you say?	**Che? Che cosa ha detto?**	*kAY kay KOH-sah ah dAYt-toh*
What do you call this (that) in Italian?	**Come si chiama questo (quello) in italiano?**	*kOH-meh see key-AH-mah koo-AYs-toh (koo-Ayl-loh) een ee-tah-lee-AH-noh*
Please speak slowly.	**Per piacere parli lentamente.**	*pehr pee-ah-chAY-reh pAHr-lee lehn-tah-mEHn-teh*
Please repeat that.	**Lo ripeta per favore.**	*loh ree-pEH-tah pehr fah-vOH-reh*

INTRODUCTIONS

I'm American (English) (Australian) (Canadian).	**Sono americano(a) (inglese) (australiano [a]) (canadese).**	*sOH-noh ah-meh-ree-kAH-noh (nah) (een-glAY-seh) (ah-oos-trah-lee-AH-noh [nah]) (kah-nah-dAY-seh)*
I'm a(n) ____.	**Sono un (una) ____.**	*sOH-noh oon (OO-nah)*
▦ accountant	**ragioniere**	*rah-jee-oh-nee-EH-reh*
▦ artist	**artista**	*ahr-tEE-stah*
▦ banker	**banchiere**	*bahn-kee-EH-reh*
▦ businessperson	**uomo (donna) d'affari**	*oo-OH-moh (dOHn-nah) dahf-fAH-ree*
▦ computer programmer	**programmatore**	*proh-grahm-mah-tOH-reh*
▦ dentist	**dentista**	*dehn-tEE-stah*
▦ doctor	**dottore**	*doht-tOH-reh*
▦ hairdresser	**parrucchiere(a)**	*pahr-rook-kee-EH-reh(ah)*
▦ jeweler	**gioielliere**	*jee-oh-ee-ehl-lee-EH-reh*

▓ lawyer	**avvocato (avvocatessa)**	*ahv-voh-kAH-toh (ahv-voh-kah-tAYs-sah)*
▓ merchant	**commerciante**	*kohm-mehr-chee-Ahn-teh*
▓ nurse	**infermiera**	*een-fehr-mee-EH-rah*
▓ police officer	**agente di polizia**	*ah-jEHn-teh dee poh-lee-tzEE-ah*
▓ secretary	**segretario(a)**	*seh-greh-tAH-ree-oh(ah)*
▓ student	**studente (studentessa)**	*stoo-dEHn-teh (stoo-dehn-tAYs-sah)*
▓ teacher	**professore (professoressa)**	*proh-fehs-sOH-reh (proh-fehs-soh-rAYs-sah)*
▓ technician	**tecnico**	*tEH-knee-koh*

I'm retired. **Sono pensionato(a).** *sOH-noh pehn-see-oh-nAH-toh(ah).*

My name is _____. **Mi chiamo _____.** *mee kee-AH-moh*

What's your name? **Lei, scusi, come si chiama?** *lEH-ee skOO-see kOH-meh see key-AH-mah*

How are you? **Come sta?** *kOH-meh stAH*

How's everything? **Come va?** *kOH-meh vAH*

Very well, thanks. And you? **Molto bene, grazie. E lei?** *mOHl-toh bEH-neh grAH-tsee-eh Ay lEH-ee*

LOCATIONS

Where is _____? **Dove si trova _____?** *dOH-veh see trOH-vah*

▓ the bathroom **un gabinetto (una toilette)** *oon gah-bee-nAYt-toh (OO-nah too-ah-lEHt)*

▓ the dining room (restaurant) **un ristorante** *oon rees-toh-rAHn-teh*

▦ the entrance	**l'ingresso**	*leen-grEHs-soh*
▦ the exit	**l'uscita**	*loo-shEE-tah*
▦ the telephone	**un telefono**	*oon teh-lEH-phoh-noh*

I'm lost.	**Non so dove mi trovo.** *nohn sOH dOH-veh mee trOH-voh*
We are lost.	**Non sappiamo dove ci troviamo.** *nohn sahp-pee-AH-moh dOH-veh chee troh-vee-AH-moh*
Where are _____?	**Dove sono _____?** *dOH-veh sOH-noh*
I am looking for _____.	**Sto cercando _____.** *stOH chehr-kAHn-doh*

Which way do I go?	**In che direzione devo andare?** *een-kAY dee-reh-tsee-OH-neh dAY-voh ahn-dAH-reh*
▦ to the left	**a sinistra** *ah see-nEE-strah*
▦ to the right	**a destra** *ah dEH-strah*
▦ straight ahead	**sempre diritto** *sehm-preh dee-rEEt-toh*

▨ around the corner	**all'angolo (della via)**	*ahl-lAHn-goh-loh (dAYl-lah vEE-ah)*
▨ the first street on the right	**la prima strada a destra**	*lah prEE-mah strAH-dah ah dEH-strah*
▨ after (before) the second traffic light	**dopo il (prima del) secondo semaforo**	*dOH-poh eel (prEE-mah dAYl) say-kOHn-doh say-mAH-foh-roh*

SHOPPING

How much is it?	**Quanto costa?**	*koo-AHn-toh kOH-stah*
I'd like ____.	**Vorrei ____.**	*vohr-rEH-ee*
Please bring me ____.	**Per piacere mi porti ____.**	*pehr pee-ah-chAY-reh mee pOHr-tee*
Please show me (please let me see) ____.	**Per piacere mi mostri (per piacere mi fa vedere) ____.**	*pehr pee-ah-chAY-reh mee mOH-stree (mee fah veh-dEH-reh)*
Here it is.	**Eccolo(a).**	*EH-koh-loh(lah)*

MISCELLANEOUS

I'm hungry.	**Ho fame.**	*oh fAH-meh*
I'm thirsty.	**Vorrei bere (ho sete).**	*vohr-rEH-ee bAY-reh (oh sAY-teh)*
I'm tired.	**Mi sento stanco(a).**	*mee sEHn-toh stAHn-koh(ah)*
What's that?	**Che cos'è quello(a)?**	*kay ko-sEH koo-AYl-loh (lah)*
What's up?	**(Che) cosa succede?**	*(kay) kOH-sah soo-chEH-deh*
I (don't) know.	**(Non) lo so.**	*(nohn) loh sOH*

QUESTIONS

Where is _____?	**Dov'è _____?**	*doh-vEH*
When?	**Quando?**	*koo AHn-doh*
How?	**Come?**	*kOH-meh*
How much?	**Quanto?**	*koo-AHn-toh*
Who?	**Chi?**	*key*
Why?	**Perchè?**	*pehr-kAY*
Which?	**Quale?**	*koo-AH-leh*

EXCLAMATIONS, COLLOQUIALISMS

Ouch!	**Ahi!**	*AH-ee*
Wow! Gosh!	**Eh! Càspita!**	*AYh kAH-spee-tah*
Darn it! (expressing annoyance)	**Maledizione!**	*mah-leh-dee-tsee-OH-neh*
How beautiful!	**Che bellezza! (che bello!)**	*kay behl-lEH-tsah (kay bEHl-loh)*
That's awful!	**Non va! Non si fa così!**	*nohn vAH nohn see fAH koh-sEE*
Great! Wonderful!	**Magnifico! Splendido!**	*mah-ny-EE-fee-koh splEHn-dee-doh*
That's it!	**Proprio così!**	*prOH-pree-oh ko-sEE*
My goodness!	**Per l'amor del cielo!**	*pehr lah-mOHr dayl chee-AY-loh*
Good Heavens!	**Grazie a Dio!**	*grAH-tsee-eh ah DEE-oh*
Bottoms up! Cheers!	**(Alla) salute! Cin-cin!**	*(Ahl-lah) sah-lOO-teh cheen-chEEn*

Quiet!	**Silenzio!**	*see-lEHn-tsee-oh*
Shut up!	**Zitto!**	*tsEEt-toh*
That's enough!	**Basta!**	*bAH-stah*
Never mind!	**Non importa!**	*nohn eem-pOHr-tah*
Of course!	**Naturalmente!**	*nah-too-rahl mEHn-teh*
With pleasure!	**Con piacere!**	*kohn pee-ah-chAY-reh*
Let's go!	**Andiamo!**	*ahn-dee-AH-moh*
What a shame (pity)!	**Peccato!**	*pehk-kAH-toh*
What a nuisance! (showing annoyance)	**Che seccatura!**	*kay sayk-ah-tOO-rah*
Nonsense! No way!	**Ma che! Impossibile!**	*mah kay eem-pohs-sEE-bee-leh*
Don't be stupid.	**Non faccia lo stupido (la stupida).**	*nohn fAH-chee-ah loh stOO-pee-doh (lah stOO-pee-dah)*
Are you crazy?	**È pazzo(a)?!**	*EH pAH-tsoh(ah)*
What a fool!	**Che sciocco(a)!**	*kay shee-OH-koh(ah)*
Good luck.	**Buona fortuna. (In bocca al lupo!)**	*boo-OH-nah fohr-tOO-nah (een bOHk-ah ahl lOO-poh)*
God bless you!		
▪ (sneeze)	**Salute!**	*sah-lOO-teh*
▪ (congratulations)	**Dio ti (vi) benedica!**	*dEE-oh tee(vee) beh-neh-dEE-cah*

PROBLEMS, PROBLEMS, PROBLEMS (EMERGENCIES)

Watch out! Be careful!	**Attenzione! Stia attento(a)!** *ah-tehn-tsee-OH-neh stEE-ah aht-tEHn-toh(ah)*
Hurry up!	**Si sbrighi!** *see sbrEE-ghee*
Look!	**Guardi!** *goo-AHr-dee*
Wait!	**Aspetti un momento!** *ah-spEHt-tee oon moh-mEHn-toh*
Fire!	**Al fuoco!** *Ahl foo-OH-koh*

ANNOYANCES

What's the matter with you?	**Ma che cosa ha?** *mah kay kOH-sah ah*
Stop bothering me!	**Non mi stia a seccare!** *nohn mee stEE-ah ah sayk-kAH-reh*
Go away!	**Se ne vada!** *say nay vAH-dah*
Leave me alone!	**Mi lasci in pace!** *mee lAH-shee een pAH-cheh*
Help, police!	**Aiuto, polizia!** *ah-ee-OO-toh poh-lee-tsEE-ah*
I'm going to call a cop!	**Adesso chiamo un poliziotto!** *ah-dEHs-soh key-AH-moh oon poh-lee-tsee-OHt-toh*
Get out!	**Via! Se ne vada!** *vEE-ah say nay vAH-dah*
That (one) is a thief!	**Quello è un ladro!** *koo-AYl-loh EH oon lAH-droh*
He has snatched my bag!	**Mi ha scippato la borsa!** *mee ah sheep-pAH-toh lah bOHr-sah*

He has stolen _____.	**Mi ha rubato _____.** *mee ah roo-bAH-toh*
I have lost _____.	**Ho perduto _____.** *oh pehr-dOO-toh*
▨ my car	**la (mia) auto** *lah (mEE-ah) AH-oo-toh*
▨ my passport	**il (mio) passaporto** *eel (mEE-oh) pahs-sah-pOHr-toh*
▨ my purse	**la (mia) borsa** *lah (mEE-ah) bOHr-sah*
▨ my suitcase	**la (mia) valigia** *lah (mEE-ah) vah-lEE-jee-ah*
▨ my wallet	**il (mio) portafoglio** *eel (mEE-oh) pohr-tah-fOH-ly-ee-oh*
▨ my watch	**l'orologio (il mio orologio)** *loh-roh-lOH-jee-oh (eel mEE-oh oh-roh-lOH-jee-oh)*
This young man is annoying me.	**Questo giovanotto mi sta disturbando.** *koo-AYs-toh jee-oh-vah-nOHt-toh mee stah dee-stoor-bAHn-doh*

| He keeps following me. | **Sta continuando a seguirmi.** *stah kohn-tee-noo-AHn-doh ah say-goo-EEr-mee* |
| Stop that boy! | **Fermate quel ragazzo!** *fayr-mAH-teh koo-AYl ra-gAH-tsoh* |

TROUBLE

I haven't done anything.	**Non ho fatto niente.** *nohn oh fAHt-toh nee-AYn-teh*
It's a lie!	**È una bugia!** *EH oo-nah boo-jEE-ah*
It's not true.	**Non è vero.** *nohn EH vEH-roh*
I'm innocent.	**Sono innocente.** *sOH-noh een-noh-chEHn-teh*
I want a lawyer.	**Voglio un avvocato.** *vOH-ly-ee-oh oon ahv-voh-kAH-toh*
I want to go ____.	**Voglio andare ___.** *vOH-ly-ee-oh ahn-dAH-reh*
▦ to the American (British) (Australian) (Canadian) Consulate.	**al Consolato Americano (Inglese) (Australiano) (Canadese).** *ahl kohn-soh-lAH-toh ah-meh-ree-kAH-noh (een-glAY-seh) (ah-oo-strah-lee-ah-noh) (kah-nah-dAY-seh)*
▦ *to the police station.	**all'ufficio di polizia (al Commissariato)** *ahl-loof-fEE-chee-oh dee poh-lee-tsEE-ah (ahl kohm-mees-sah-ree-AH-toh)*
I need help, quick!	**Ho bisogno d'aiuto, subito!** *oh bee-sOH-ny-oh dah-ee-OO-toh sOO-bee-toh*

*NOTE: In small towns and villages without a local police force, ask to go to **la caserma dei carabinieri**.

Can you help me, please?	**Può aiutarmi, per favore?** *poo-OH ah-ee-oo-tAHr-mee pehr fah-vOH-reh*
Does anyone here speak English?	**Qui c'è qualcuno che parla inglese?** *koo-EE chEH koo-ahl-kOO-noh kay pAHr-lah een-glAY-seh*
I need an interpreter.	**Ho bisogno di un interprete.** *oh bee-sOH-ny-oh dee oon een-TEHR-preh-teh*

NUMBERS

You will use numbers the moment you land in Italy, whether it be to exchange money at the airport, purchase a bus ticket for a ride into town, or describe the length of your stay to a customs official. We list here first the cardinal numbers, then follow with ordinal numbers, fractions, and other useful numbers.

CARDINAL NUMBERS

0	**zero**	*tsEH-roh*
1	**uno**	*OO-noh*
2	**due**	*dOO-eh*
3	**tre**	*trEH*
4	**quattro**	*koo-AHt-troh*
5	**cinque**	*chEEn-koo-eh*
6	**sei**	*sEH-ee*
7	**sette**	*sEHt-teh*
8	**otto**	*OHt-toh*
9	**nove**	*nOH-veh*
10	**dieci**	*dee-EH-chee*
11	**undici**	*OOn-dee-chee*
12	**dodici**	*dOH-dee-chee*
13	**tredici**	*trEH-dee-chee*
14	**quattordici**	*koo-aht-tOHr-dee-chee*

15	**quindici**	*koo-EEn-dee-chee*
16	**sedici**	*sAY-dee-chee*
17	**diciassette**	*dee-chee-ahs-sEHt-teh*
18	**diciotto**	*dee-chee-OHt-toh*
19	**diciannove**	*dee-chee-ahn-nOH-veh*
20	**venti**	*vAYn-tee*
21	**ventuno**	*vayn-tOO-noh*
22	**ventidue**	*vayn-tee-dOO-eh*
23	**ventitrè**	*vayn-tee-trEH*
24	**ventiquattro**	*vayn-tee-koo-AHt-troh*
25	**venticinque**	*vayn-tee-chEEn-koo-eh*
26	**ventisei**	*vayn-tee-sEH-ee*
27	**ventisette**	*vayn-tee-sEHt-teh*
28	**ventotto**	*vayn-tOHt-toh*
29	**ventinove**	*vayn-tee-nOH-veh*
30	**trenta**	*trEHn-tah*
40	**quaranta**	*koo-ah-rAHn-tah*
50	**cinquanta**	*cheen-koo-AHn-tah*
60	**sessanta**	*sehs-sAHn-tah*
70	**settanta**	*seht-tAHn-tah*
80	**ottanta**	*oht-tAHn-tah*
90	**novanta**	*noh-vAHn-tah*
100	**cento**	*chEHn-toh*
101	**centouno**	*chEHn-toh OO-noh*
102	**centodue**	*chEHn-toh dOO-eh*
200	**duecento**	*doo-eh-chEHn-toh*
300	**trecento**	*treh-chEHn-toh*
400	**quattrocento**	*koo-aht-troh-chEHn-toh*
500	**cinquecento**	*cheen-koo-eh-chEHn-toh*
600	**seicento**	*seh-ee-chEHn-toh*
700	**settecento**	*seht-teh-chENn-toh*
800	**ottocento**	*oht-toh-chEHn-toh*

900	**novecento**	*noh-veh-chEHn-toh*
1.000	**mille**	*mEEl-leh*
1.001	**mille e uno**	*mEEl-leh eh OO-noh*
1.100	**mille e cento**	*mEEl-leh eh chEHn-toh*
1.200	**mille e duecento**	*mEEl-leh eh doo-eh-chEHn-toh*
1.350	**mille trecento cinquanta**	*mEE-leh treh-chEHn-toh cheen-koo-AHn-tah*
2.000	**duemila**	*dOO-eh mEE-lah*
5.000	**cinque mila**	*chEEn-koo-eh mEEl-lah*
10.000	**dieci mila**	*dee-EH-chee mEEl-lah*
100.000	**cento mila**	*ch-EHn-toh mEEl-lah*
1.000.000	**un milione**	*oon mee-lee-OH-neh*
2.000.000	**due milioni**	*dOO-eh mee-lee-OH-nee*
1991	**mille novecento novantuno**	*mEEl-leh noh-veh-chEHn-toh noh-vAHn-tOOn-noh*
1992	**mille novecento novanta due**	*mEEl-leh noh-veh-chEHn-toh noh-vAHn-tah dOO-eh*
2000	**due mila**	*dOO-eh mEEl-lah*

ORDINAL NUMBERS

first	**primo**	*prEE-moh*
second	**secondo**	*seh-kOHn-doh*
third	**terzo**	*tEHr-tsoh*
fourth	**quarto**	*koo-AHr-toh*
fifth	**quinto**	*koo-EEn-toh*
sixth	**sesto**	*sEHs-toh*
seventh	**settimo**	*sEHt-tee-moh*
eighth	**ottavo**	*oht-tAH-voh*
ninth	**nono**	*nOH-noh*
tenth	**decimo**	*dEH-chee-moh*
the last one	**l'ultimo**	*lOOl-tee-moh*

once	**una volta**	*oo-nah vOHl-tah*
twice	**due volte**	*dOO-eh vOHl-teh*
three times	**tre volte**	*trEH vOHl-teh*

QUANTITIES AND FRACTIONS

a bag of	**un sacchetto di**	*oon sahk-kAYt-toh dee*
a bottle of	**una bottiglia di**	*OO-nah boht-tEE-ly-ee-ah dee*
a box (can) of	**una scatola (lattina) di**	*OO-nah skAH-toh-lah (laht-tEE-nah) dee*
a dozen of	**una dozzina di**	*OO-nah doh-tsEE-nah dee*
a kilo of	**un chilo di**	*oon kEE-loh dee*
a liter of	**un litro di**	*oon lEE-troh dee*
a package of	**un pacchetto di**	*oon pahk-kAYt-toh dee*
a pair of	**un paio di**	*oon pAH-ee-oh dee*
a slice of	**una fetta di**	*OO-nah fAYt-tah dee*
a little of	**un po' di**	*oon pOH dee*
half of _____.	**la metà di _____.**	*lah meh-tAH dee*
▪ half of the money	**la metà dei soldi**	*lah meh-tAH day-ee sOHl-dee*
half a _____.	**mezzo**	*mEH-tsoh*
▪ half a kilo	**mezzo chilo**	*mEH-tsoh kEE-loh*
a fourth (quarter)	**un quarto**	*oon koo-AHr-toh*
a dozen	**una dozzina**	*OO-nah doh-tsEE-nah*
▪ a dozen oranges	**una dozzina d'arance**	*OO-nah doh-tsEE-nah dah-rAHn-cheh*
100 grams	**un etto**	*oon EHt-toh*
200 grams	**due etti**	*dOO-eh EHt-tee*
350 grams	**tre etti e mezzo**	*treh EHt-tee ay mEH-tsoh*
▪ a pair of shoes	**un paio de scarpe**	*oon pAH-ee-oh dee skAHr-peh*

WHEN YOU ARRIVE

PASSPORT AND CUSTOMS

Italian passport control is a very simple process. If the visitor's passport is in order (up to date), questions are hardly ever asked. In the event of difficulties, the following information will be useful.

My name is ___.	**Mi chiamo ___.**	*mee key-AH-moh*
I'm American (British) (Australian) (Canadian).	**Sono americano(a) (inglese) (australiano[a] (canadese).**	*sOH-noh ah-meh-ree kAH-noh(ah) (een-glAY-seh) (ah-oo-strah-lee-AH-noh[ah] (kah-nah-dAY-seh)*
My address is ___.	**Il mio indirizzo è ___.**	*eel mEE-oh een-dee-rEE-tsoh EH*
I'm staying at ___.	**Starò a ___.**	*stah-rOH ah*
Here is (are) ___.	**Ecco ___.**	*EHk-oh*
▦ my documents	**i (miei) documenti**	*ee (mee-EH-ee) doh-koo-mEHn-tee*
▦ my passport	**il (mio) passaporto**	*eel (mEE-oh) pahs-sah-pOHr-toh*
▦ my I.D. card	**la (mia) carta d'identità**	*lah (mEE-ah) kAHr-tah dee-dehn-tee-tAH*
I'm ___.	**Sono ___.**	*sOH-noh*
▦ on a business trip	**in viaggio d'affari**	*een vee-AH-jee-oh dahf-fAH-ree*
▦ on vacation	**in vacanza**	*een vah-kAHn-tsah*
▦ visiting relatives (friends)	**venuto(a) a trovare i parenti (gli amici)**	*vay-nOO-toh(ah) ah troh-vAH-reh ee pah-rEHn-tee (ly-ee ah-mEE-chee)*
▦ just passing through	**solo di passaggio**	*sOH-loh dee pahs-sAH-jee-oh*

I'll be staying here for ____.	**Resterò qui per ____.**	*ray-steh-rOH koo-EE pehr*
▨ a few days	**alcuni giorni**	*ahl-kOO-nee jee-OHr-nee*
▨ a few weeks	**alcune settimane**	*ahl-kOO-neh seht-tee-mAH-neh*
▨ a week	**una settimana**	*OO-nah seht-tee-mAH-nah*
▨ a month	**un mese**	*oon mAY-seh*
I'm traveling ____.	**Sto viaggiando ____.**	*stOH vee-ah-jee-AHn-doh*
▨ alone	**da solo(a)**	*dah sOH-loh(ah)*
▨ with my husband	**con mio marito**	*kohn mEE-oh mah-rEE-toh*
▨ with my wife	**con mia moglie**	*kohn mEE-ah mOH-ly-ee-eh*
▨ with my family	**con la mia famiglia**	*kohn lah mEE-ah fah-mEE-ly-ee-ah*
▨ with my friend	**con il mio amico (la mia amica)**	*kohn eel mEE-oh ah-mEE-koh (lah mEE-ah ah-mEE-kah)*

Customs (**la dogana**—*lah doh-gAH-nah*) in the major port-of-entry airports in Italy is divided into two sections: one, indicated by a red arrow, is for passengers with goods to declare (**merci da dichiarare**); another, marked with a green arrow, is for those with nothing to declare (**nulla da dichiarare**).

The following can be brought into Italy duty-free: 400 cigarettes and a quantity of cigars or pipe tobacco not exceeding 500 grams (1.1 lb), 2 bottles of wine, 1 bottle of hard liquor, 4.4 lbs of coffee, 6.6 lbs of sugar, and 2.2 lbs of cocoa. Generally, all items for personal use enter the country duty-free.

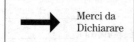

Merci da Dichiarare

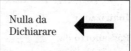

Nulla da Dichiarare

These are my bags.	**Queste sono le mie valigie.** *koo-AYs-teh sOH-noh leh mEE-eh vah-lEE-jee-eh*
I have nothing to declare.	**Non ho nulla da dichiarare.** *nohn oh nOOl-lah dah dee-key-ah-rAH-reh*
I only have _____.	**Ho solo _____.** *oh sOH-loh*
▪ a carton of cigarettes	**una stecca di sigarette** *OO-nah stAYk-kah dee see-gah-rAYt-teh*
▪ a bottle of whisky	**una bottiglia di whisky** *OO-nah boht-tEE-ly-ee-ah dee oo-EE-skey*
They're gifts.	**Sono regali.** *sOH-noh reh-gAH-lee*
They're for my personal use.	**Sono cose di uso personale.** *sOH-noh kOH-seh dee OO-soh pehr-soh-nAH-leh*
Do I have to pay duty?	**Devo pagare dogana?** *dAY-voh pah-gAH-reh doh-gAH-nah*
May I close the bag now?	**Posso chiudere la valigia adesso?** *pOHs-soh key-OO-deh-reh lah vah-lEE-jee-ah ah-dEHs-soh*

IDENTITY CARD

Upon entering the country (or on your flight into the country), you will be required to complete an identity card, usually with the following information.

Cognome: _____   Last name: _____

Nome: _____   First name: _____

Nazionalità: _____   Nationality: _____

Data di nascita: _____   Date of birth: _____

Professione: _____   Profession: _____

Indirizzo: _____   Address: _____

Passaporto da: _____   Passport from: _____

BAGGAGE AND PORTERS

Porters are scarce at European airports. You may be able to locate one, but you'll find it easier and faster to simply use the baggage carts provided at the baggage claim. You can usually wheel your bags right through customs out to the street.

Where can I find a baggage cart?	**Dove posso trovare un carrello portabagagli?** *dOH-veh pOHs-soh troh-vAH-reh oon kahr-rEHl-loh pohr-tah-bah-gAH-ly-ee*
I need a porter.	**Ho bisogno di un portabagagli.** *oh bee-sOH-ny-oh dee oon pohr-tah-bah-gAH-ly-ee*
Porter!	**Portabagagli! Facchino!** *pohr-tah-bah-gAH-ly-ee fahk-kEE-noh*
These are our (my) bags.	**Queste sono le nostre (mie) valigie.** *koo-AYs-teh sOH-noh leh nOH-streh (mEE-eh) van-lEE-jee-eh*
That big (little) one.	**Quella grande (piccola).** *koo-AYl-lah grAHn-deh (pEEk-koh-lah)*

These two black (green) ones.	**Queste due nere (verdi).** *koo-AYs-teh dOO-eh nAY-reh (vAYr-dee)*
Put them here (there).	**Le metta qui (lì).** *leh mAYt-tah koo-EE (lEE)*
Be careful with that one!	**Stia attento a quella lì!** *stEE-ah aht-tEHn-toh ah koo-AYl-lah lEE*
I'll carry this one myself.	**Questa la porto io.** *koo-AYs-tah lah pOHr-toh ee-oh*
I'm missing a suitcase.	**Mi manca una valigia.** *mee mAHn-kah OO-nah vah-lEE-jee-ah*
How much do I owe you?	**Quanto le devo?** *koo-AHn-toh leh dAY-voh*
Thank you (very much). This is for you.	**(Molte) grazie. Questo è per lei.** *(mOHl-teh) grAH-tsee-eh koo-AYs-toh EH pehr lEH-ee*
Where can I get a bus (taxi) to the city?	**Dove posso prendere l'autobus (il tassì) per andare in città?** *dOH-veh pOHs-soh prAYn-deh-reh lAH-oo-toh-boos (eel tahs-sEE) pehr ahn-dAH-reh een cheet-tAH*

Travel Tips Luggage is sometimes lost or arrives long after you do. To avoid problems, some people travel light and carry on everything. At the very least, take one complete change of clothing, basic grooming items, and any regular medication aboard with you. Because airlines will not replace valuable jewelry when paying for lost luggage, it should be carried on your person. Safer yet, select one set of basic, simple jewelry that can be worn everywhere— even in the shower—and wear it during your whole trip. Remember, carry-on bags must be small enough to fit in overhead bins or to slide under your seat.

BANKING AND MONEY MATTERS

Italy's money is based on the **lira** (*lEE-rah*). Although 100 **centesimi** make up 1 **lira**, these represent an infinitesimal amount and are not exchanged.

Banks in Italy are open five days a week (Monday through Friday) from 8:35 A.M. to 1:35 P.M. and from 3:00 to 4:00 P.M. They are closed all day Saturday and Sunday and on national holidays (see page 239). In some cities banks are open for one hour in the afternoon. Exchange offices in major airports and railroad stations keep longer hours. A passport is required to exchange cash and checks at a bank. Many hotels will exchange money for you but you will get a better exchange at a bank.

Italian money, the **lira**, is issued in the following denominations: notes—500, 1000, 2000, 5000, 10.000, 20.000, 50.000, and 100.000; coins—5, 10, 20, 50, 100, 200, and 500 lira.

No later than July 2002, the euro, the new European monetary currency, will replace all banknotes and national currencies of the countries that are members of the European Community. The euro will be divided into cents and will be issued in the following denominations: notes—5, 10, 20, 50, 100, 200, and 500; coins—1, 2, 5, 10, 20, 50 cent(s), 1 and 2 euro.

The ATMs in Italy are known as **bancomats**. They may be found in the large cities and in small towns. The machines are easy to operate. At the beginning of the transaction they prompt the user for the preferred language.

EXCHANGING MONEY

Where is the currency exchange (bank)?	**Dov'è l'ufficio di cambio (la banca)?** *doh-vEH loof-fEE-chee-oh dee kAHm-bee-oh (lah bAHn-kah)*
I wish to change _____.	**Desidero cambiare _____.** *day-sEE-deh-roh kahm-bee-AH-reh*
▪ money	**il denaro** *eel deh-nAH-roh*

▪ dollars (pounds)	**i dollari (le sterline)**	*ee-dOHl-lah-ree (le stehr-lEE-neh)*
▪ travelers' checks	**travelers' checks (assegni da viaggiatori)**	*(ahs-sAY-ny dah vee-ah-jee-ah-tOH-ree)*
May I cash a personal check?	**Posso cambiare un assegno personale?**	*pOHs-soh kahm-bee-AH-reh oon ahs-sAY-ny-ee-oh pehr-soh-nAH-leh*
What time do they open (close)?	**A che ora aprono (chiudono)?**	*ah kay OH-rah AH-proh-noh (key-OO-doh-noh)*
Where is the cashier's window?	**Dov'è lo sportello del cassiere?**	*doh-vEH loh spohr-tEHl-loh dayl kahs-see-AY-reh*

The current exchange rates are posted in banks that exchange money and are also published daily in the city newspapers. Since the rates fluctuate from day to day, it may be useful to convert the following lira amounts into their values in your own currency so that you can readily compare prices and determine values.

| | YOUR OWN | | YOUR OWN |
LIRE	CURRENCY	LIRE	CURRENCY
500		50,000	
1,000		75,000	
10,000		100,000	
25,000			

What's the current exchange rate for dollars (pounds)?	**Qual è il cambio corrente del dollaro (della sterlina)?** *koo-ahl-EH eel kAHm-bee-oh kohr-rEHn-teh dayl dOHl-lah-roh (dAYl-lah stehr-lEE-nah)*
What commission do you charge?	**Quale percentuale vi fate pagare?** *koo-AH-leh pehr-chehn-too-AH-leh vee fAH-teh pah-gAH-reh*
Where do I sign?	**Dove debbo firmare?** *dOH-veh dAYb-boh feer-mAH-reh*
I'd like the money ____.	**Vorrei i soldi ____.** *vohr-rEH-ee ee sOHl-dee*
▒ in large (small) bills	**in grosse (piccole) banconote** *een grOHs-seh (pEEk-oh-leh) bahn-koh-nOH-teh*
▒ in small change	**in spiccioli** *een spee-chee-oh-lee*
Give me two twenty (thousand)-lire bills.	**Mi dia due biglietti da ventimila lire.** *mee dEE-ah dOO-eh bee-ly-ee-AYt-tee dah vayn-tee mEE-lah lEE-reh*
▒ fifty thousand lire	**cinquanta mila lire** *cheen-koo-AHn-tah mEE-lah lEE-reh*
▒ one hundred thousand lire	**centomila lire** *chehn-toh-mEE-lah lEE-reh*
Do you accept credit cards?	**Si accettano carte di credito?** *see ah-chEHt-tah-noh kAHr-teh dee krEH-dee-toh*

BUSINESS BANKING TERMS

amount	**ammontare**	*ahm-mohn-tAH-reh*
bad check	**assegno scoperto**	*ahs-sAY-ny-oh skoh-pEHr-toh*
banker	**banchiere**	*bahn-key-EH-reh*
bill	**banconota, biglietto di banca**	*bahn-koh-nOH-tah bee-ly-AYt-toh dee bAHn-kah*
borrow (to)	**prendere a prestito**	*prAYn-deh-reh ah prEHs-tee-toh*
cashier	**cassiere**	*kahs-see-AY-reh*
capital	**capitale**	*kah-pee-tAH-leh*
cashier's office	**cassa**	*kAHs-sah*
checkbook	**libretto d'assegni**	*lee-brAYt-toh dahs-sEH-ny-ee*
endorse (to)	**firmare**	*feer-mAH-reh*
income	**reddito, entrata**	*rEHd-dee-toh ehn-trAH-tah*
interest rate	**tasso d'interesse**	*tAHs-soh deen-teh-rEHs-seh*
investment	**investimento**	*een-vehs-tee-mEHn-toh*
lend (to)	**prestare**	*preh-stAH-reh*
loss	**perdita**	*pEHr-dee-tah*
make change (to)	**cambiare la moneta (i soldi)**	*kahm-bee-AH-reh lah moh-nAY-tah (ee sOHl-dee)*
mortgage	**ipoteca**	*ee-poh-tEH-kah*

open an account (to)	**aprire un conto in banca** *ah-prEE-reh oon kOHn-toh een bAHn-kah*
premium	**l'interesse** *leen-teh-rEHs-seh*
profit	**guadagno, reddito, profitto** *goo-ah-dAH-ny-oh rEHd-dee-toh proh-fEEt-toh*
safe	**cassaforte** *kahs-sah-fOHr-teh*
secretary	**secretario(a)** *seh-kreh-tAH-ree-oh(ah)*
signature	**firma** *fEEr-mah*
window	**sportello** *spohr-tEHl-loh*

TIPPING

In many instances, a service charge is included in the price of the service rendered. The added-on service charge usually comes to about 15 to 20 percent, most times indicated on the bill. It is customary, however, to leave some small change in addition to the service included on the bill. This usually consists of 300 to 500 lire, or whatever small change you receive from paying the bill.

It is customary, particularly at the large, deluxe hotels, to leave a tip for the maid and to tip the bellhop, desk attendant, and doorman as well. If you take a tour, the guide will expect a tip, as will taxi drivers, theater ushers, and other service personnel. The following is a table of the most appropriate amounts. You are now required by law to obtain an official receipt when eating at restaurants.

SERVICE	TIP
Barber, hairdresser	15% of the total bill
Bathroom attendant	500–1,000 lire
Bellhop, porter	1,500 lira per bag
Cafes and bars	(at a table) 15% if service charge is not included in bill
	(standing at a counter or bar drinking expresso, cappuccino, etc.) 200 lire
	(standing at a counter or bar having alcoholic beverages, cocktails, desserts, pastries, sandwiches, etc.) 500 lire
Chambermaid	1,000 lire a day
Concierge	3,000 lire a day
Doorman (for calling a cab)	1,000 lire
Service station attendant	1,000 lire or more for extra service (cleaning windshield, giving directions)
Shoeshine	500–1,000 lire
Sightseeing guide and driver	2,000 lire minimum per person (for half-day tours)
	2,500 lire minimum per person (for full-day tours)
Taxi driver	10% of fare
Theater usher	1,000 lire (more for opera seats)
Waiter	12–15% included in bill + (optional)
	5–10% of check for good service
Waiter (room service)	1,000 lire

Travel Tips   Before departing for a foreign country, exchange about $50 into currency for telephone calls, taxis, or other expenses. Travelers' checks are safe but paying by credit card usually guarantees the best exchange rate.

AT THE HOTEL

If you are unfamiliar with the city to which you are going, you'll probably find it best to make a hotel reservation in advance from home. All major credit cards are honored in Italy. You'll also find that some terminals have reservation desks, at which you may be able to reserve a room. Lastly, if you are unable to locate a hotel once you arrive, go to the tourist information office; someone there will be able to speak English and will help you in locating a suitable hotel. The following is a listing of the major types of hotels you will encounter. By law, the official price of the room must be posted in the room (usually found on the inside of a closet door). The final bill, however, will also include the value-added tax (IVA).

ITALIAN HOTEL ASSOCIATIONS

Federalberghi, Via Toscana 1—00187 Roma
    Tel. 06 42741151
    Fax. 06 42871197

Asshotel, Via Farini 5—00185 Roma
    Tel. 06 4725
    Fax. 06 4746886

Federturismo, Via Pasteur 10—00144 Roma
    Tel. 06 5911758
    Fax. 06 5910390

YOUTH HOSTELS

AIG, Associazione Italiana Alberghi per la Gioventù
    (Italian Youth Hostels Association)
    Via Cavour 44—00184 Roma
    Tel. 06 4871152
    Fax. 06 4880492

CTS, Centro Turistico Studentesco (Tourist Student Center)
    Via Nazionale 66—00184 Roma
    Tel. 06 46791
    Fax. 06 4679207

CTG, Centro Turistico Giovanile (Youth Tourist Center)
  Via della Pigna 13/a—00100 Roma
  Tel. 06 6795077
  Fax. 06 6795078

TYPES OF LODGING

albergo or hotel	Hotels are classified in six categories: 5-Star Deluxe, 5-Star, 4-Star, 3-Star, 2-Star, and 1-Star. The extent of the services and luxuriousness of the furnishings will vary with the class.
motel	Situated near the autostrada, these are mostly new and getting better all the time.
locanda	These are lovely, small country inns.
pensione	Usually pretty casual, most of the time these are small residences similar to boardinghouses, in which you are customarily offered meals as well. **Pensione completa** refers to 3 meals a day, **mezza pensione** to 2 meals. Pensiones are also classed and vary in quality, but almost always are a good value. The term *pensione*, which describes a small hotel, is fading from everyday use in Italy. *Pensione* is now referred to as a 1-Star, 2-Star, or 3-Star hotel.
albergo diurno	These are daytime hotels; that is, they are open during the day to travelers seeking showers, bathrooms, and other facilities. They do not offer beds, and they usually close at night.

CHECKING IN • 33

GETTING TO YOUR HOTEL

I'd like to go to the ____ Hotel.	**Vorrei andare all'Hotel (all'Albergo) ____.** *vohr-rEH-ee-ahn-dAH-reh ahl-loh-tEHl (ahl-lahl-bEHr-goh)*
Is it near (far)?	**È vicino (lontano)?** *EH vee-chEE-noh (lohn-tAH-noh)*
Where can I get a taxi?	**Dove posso prendere un taxi?** *dOH-veh pOHs-soh prAYn-deh-reh oon tahs-sEE*
What buses go into town?	**Quali autobus vanno in città?** *koo-AH-lee AH-oo-toh-boos vAHn-noh een cheet-tAH*
Where is the bus stop?	**Dov'è la fermata dell'autobus?** *doh-vEH lah fehr-mAH-tah dayl-lAH-oo-toh-boos*
How much is the fare?	**Quant'è la corsa? (il biglietto?)** *koo-ahn-tEH lah kOHr-sah (eel bee-ly-ee-AYt-toh)*
Can I rent a car?	**Posso noleggiare una macchina?** *POHs-soh noh-lay-jee-AH-reh OO-nah mAH-key-nah?*

CHECKING IN

Most first-class or deluxe hotels will have personnel who speak English. If you are checking into a smaller hotel, you might find these phrases useful in getting what you want. A room for two persons with a double bed is called **una camera matrimoniale** (*oo-nah kAH-meh-rah mah-tree-moh-nee-AH-leh*) and a room with twin beds is **una camera con due letti** (*oo-nah kAH-meh-rah kohn dOO-eh lEHt-tee*).

I'd like a single (double) room for tonight.

Vorrei una camera singola (doppia) per stanotte. *vohr-rEH-ee OO-nah kAH-meh-rah sEEn-goh-lah (dOHp-pee-ah) pehr stah-nOHt-teh*

How much is the room _____?

Quant'è la camera _____? *koo-ahn-tEH lah kAH-meh-rah*

- with a shower

  con doccia *kohn dOH-chee-ah*

- with a private bath

  con bagno proprio (privato) *kohn bAH-ny-oh prOH-pree-oh (pree-vAH-toh)*

- with a balcony

  con terrazzino *kohn tehr-rah-tsEE-noh*

- facing the sea

  che dia sul mare *kay dEE-ah sool mAH-reh*

- facing (away from) the street

  che (non) dia sulla strada *kay (nohn) dEE-ah sOOl-lah strAH-dah*

- facing the courtyard

  che dia sul cortile *kay dEE-ah sOOl kohr-tEE-leh*

Does it have ____?	**Ha ____?** *ah*
▩ air-conditioning	**l'aria condizionata** *lAH-ree-ah kohn-dee-tsee-oh-nAH-tah*
▩ hot water	**l'acqua calda** *lAH-koo-ah kAHl-dah*
▩ television	**la televisione** *lah teh-leh-vee-see-OH-neh*

Can I get video
games?

Si possono avere videogiochi?
see pOHs-soh-noh ah-vAY-reh vee-deh-oh-jee-OH-key

Can I rent movies?

È possibile affittare dei film?
EH pohs-sEE-bee-leh ahf-feet-tAH-reh dAY-ee fEElm

Do you receive
satellite programs?

Ricevete i programmi via satellite?
ree-chay-vAY-teh ee proh-grAHm-mee VEE-ah sah-tehl-lee-teh

Do you have
cable TV?

Avete i programmi cable (via cavo)?
ah-vAY-teh ee proh-grAHm-mee kAH-bleh (vEE-ah kAH-voh)

Do you get CNN?

Ricevete le trasmissioni CNN?
ree-chay-vAY-teh leh trahs-mees-see-OH-nee CNN

Are there any
programs in
English?

Ci sono programmi in inglese?
chee sOH-noh proh-grAHm-mee een een-glAY-seh

Are there programs
that should be
blocked from
children?

**Ci sono programmi che dovrebbero
essere bloccati ai bambini?** *chee
sOH-noh proh-grAHm-mee kay doh-vrAYb-beh-roh EHs-seh-reh bloh-kAH-tee ah-ee bahm-bEE-nee*

At what time
are the adult
programs?

**A che ora ci sono i programmi/
spettacoli pornografici?** *ah kay
OH-rah chee sOH-noh ee proh-grAHm-mee/speht-tAH-koh-lee pohr-noh-grAH-fee-chee*

On what channels?	**Su quali canali?** *soo koo-AH-lee kah-nAH-lee*
On which channels do you have ____?	**Su quale canale ____?** *Soo koo-AH-leh kah-nAH-leh*
sports	**c'è lo sport** *chEH loh spOHrt*
cartoons	**ci sono i cartoni animati** *chee sOH-noh ee kahr-tOH-nee ah-nee-mAH-tee*
movies	**ci sono i film** *chee sOH-noh ee fEElm*
soap operas	**c'è soap opera** *chEH sOHp OH-peh-rah*
the news	**c'è il telegiornale** *chEH eel teh-leh-jee-ohr-nAH-leh*
the weather	**c'è il meteo/"Che tempo fa"** *chEH eel mEH-teh-oh/"kay tEHm-poh fAH"*
Is voice mail available in the hotel room?	**È possibile ricevere voice mail in camera?** *eh pohs-sEE-bee-leh ree-chAY-veh-reh voice mail een kAH-meh-rah*
Do you have automatic checkout?	**Si può pagare il conto automaticamente e andarsene?** *see poo-OH pah-gAH-reh eel kOHn-toh ah-oo-toh-mah-tee-kah-mEHn-teh ay ahn-dAHr-seh-neh*
I (don't) have a reservation.	**(Non) ho prenotazione.** *(nohn) oh preh-noh-tah-tsee-OH-neh*
Could you call another hotel to see if they have something?	**Potrebbe telefonare a un altro hotel per vedere se hanno qualcosa?** *poh-trAYb-beh teh-leh-foh-nAH-reh ah oon AHl-troh oh-tEHl pehr vay-dAY-reh say AHn-noh koo-ahl-kOH-sah*
May I see the room?	**Potrei vedere la camera?** *poh-trEH-ee veh-dAY-reh lah kAH-meh-rah*

I (don't) like it.	**(Non) mi piace.**	*(nohn) mee pee-AH-cheh*

Do you have something _____?

Ha qualche cosa _____? *ah koo-AHl-keh kOH-sah*

■ better **di meglio** *dee mEH-ly-ee-oh*

■ larger **più grande** *pee-OO grAHn-deh*

■ smaller **più piccolo** *pee-OO pEEk-koh-loh*

■ cheaper **meno costoso** *mAY-noh koh-stOH-soh*

■ quieter **più quieto (tranquillo)** *pee-OO quee-EH-toh (trahn-hoo-EEl-loh)*

What floor is it on? **A che piano è?** *ah kay pee-AH-noh EH*

Is there an elevator (lift)? **C'è l'ascensore?** *chEH lah-shehn-sOH-reh*

How much is the room _____? **Quanto si paga per una camera _____?** *koo-AHn-toh see pAH-gah pehr OO-nah kAH-meh-rah*

■ with the American plan (three meals a day) **con pensione completa** *kohn pehn-see-OH-neh kohm-plEH-tah*

■ with breakfast **con colazione** *kohn koh-lah-tsee-OH-neh*

■ with no meals **senza i pasti** *sEHn-tsah ee pAH-stee*

Is everything included? **È tutto compreso?** *EH tOOt-toh kohm-prAY-soh*

The room is very nice. I'll take it. **La camera è molto bella. La prendo.** *lah kAH-meh-rah EH mOHl-toh bEHl-lah lah prAYn-doh*

We'll be staying _____.	**Resteremo _____.** *rehs-teh-rAY-moh*
■ one night	**una notte** *OO-nah nOHt-teh*
■ a few nights	**alcune notti** *ahl-kOO-neh nOHt-tee*
■ one week	**una settimana** *OO-nah seht-tee-mAH-nah*

How much do you charge for children?	**Quanto fanno pagare per i bambini?** *koo-AHn-toh fAHn-noh pah-gAH-reh pehr ee bahm-bEE-nee*
Could you put another bed in the room?	**Si potrebbe avere un altro letto nella camera?** *see poh-trAYb-beh ah-vAY-reh oon AHl-troh lEHt-toh nAYl-lah kAH-meh-rah*
Is there a charge? How much?	**C'è da pagare? Quanto?** *chEH dah pah-gAH-reh koo-AHn-toh*

OTHER ACCOMMODATIONS

I'm looking for _____.	**Sto cercando _____.** *stOH chehr-kAHn-doh*
■ a boardinghouse	**una pensione** *OO-nah pehn-see-OH-neh*
■ a private house	**una casa privata (un villino)** *OO-nah kAH-sah pree-vAH-tah (oon veel-lEE-noh)*

I want to rent an apartment.	**Voglio affittare un appartamento.** *vOH-ly-ee-oh ahf-feet-tAH-reh oon ahp-pahr-tah-mEHn-toh*
I need a living room, bedroom, and kitchen.	**Ho bisogno di salotto, camera da letto, e cucina.** *oh bee-sOH-ny-oh dee sah-lOHt-toh, kAH-meh-rah dah lEHt-toh, ay koo chEE-nah*
Do you have a furnished room?	**Ha una camera ammobiliata?** *ah OO-nah kAH-meh-rah ahm-moh-bee-lee-AH-tah*

How much is the rent?	**Quant'è d'affitto?** *koo-ahn-teh dahf-fEEt-toh*
I'll be staying here for ____.	**Resterò qui per ____.** *rehs-teh-rOH koo-EE pehr*
▓ two weeks	**due settimane** *dOO-eh seht-tee-mAH-neh*
▓ one month	**un mese** *oon mAY-seh*
▓ the whole summer	**tutta l'estate** *tOOt-tah leh-stAH-teh*

I want a place ____.	**Voglio abitare ____.** *vOH-ly-ee-oh ah-bee-tAH-reh*
▓ that's centrally located	**al centro** *ahl chAYn-troh*
▓ near public transportation	**vicino ai servizi di trasporti pubblici** *vee-chEE-noh AH-ee sayr-vEE-tsee dee trah-spOHr-tee pOOb-blee-chee*
▓ in a safe neighborhood	**in un vicinato tranquillo e sicuro** *een oon vee-chee-nAH-toh trahn-koo-EEl-loh ay see-kOO-roh*
Is there a youth hostel around here?	**C'è un ostello per la gioventù qui vicino?** *chEH oon oh-stAYl-loh pehr lah jee-oh-vehn-tOO koo-EE vee-chEE-noh*

TRAVELERS WITH SPECIAL NEEDS

| Do you have facilities for the disabled? | **Ci sono servizi per disabili?** *chee sOH-noh sayr-vEE-tzee pehr dee-sAH-bee-lee* |
| Is there a special rate for the handicapped? | **Ci sono tariffe speciali per disabili?** *chee sOH-noh tah-rEEf-feh speh-chee-AH-lee pehr dee-sAH-bee-lee* |

Can you provide ____?	**È possibile avere ____?** *EH pohs-sEE-bee-leh ah-vAY-reh*
▓ a wheelchair	**una sedia a rotelle** *OO-nah seh-dee-ah ah roh-tEHl-leh*
▓ an assistant	**un assistente** *OOn ahs-see-stEHn-teh*
Is there room in the elevator for a wheelchair?	**C'è posto in ascensore per una sedia a rotelle?** *chEH pOHs-toh een ah-shayn-sOH-reh pehr OO-nah seh-dee-ah roh-tEHl-leh*
Do you allow seeing-eye dogs?	**È permesso avere un cane da guida?** *EH pehr-mAYs-soh ah-VAY-reh oon KAH-neh dah goo-EE-dah*
I (my father/mother) can't ____.	**Io non posso (mio padre/mia madre non può) ____.** *EE-oh nohn pOHs-soh (mEE-oh pAH-dreh/mEE-ah mAH-dreh nohn poo-OH)*
▓ climb/come down the stairs	**salire/scendere le scale** *sah-lEE-reh/shAYn-deh-reh leh skAH-leh*
▓ walk	**camminare** *kahm-mee-nAH-reh*
I have asthma (heart problems).	**Ho l'asma (problemi cardiaci).** *oh lAHs-mah (proh-blEH-mee kahr-dEE-ah-chee)*
I'm epileptic.	**Sono epilèttico.** *sOH-noh eh-pee-lEHt-tee-koh*
I'm diabetic.	**Sono diabetico.** *sOH-noh dee-ah-bEH-tee-koh*
I'm allergic to ____.	**Sono allergico ____.** *sOH-noh ahl-lEHr-jee-koh*
▓ dairy products	**ai latticini** *AH-ee laht-tee-chEE-nee*
▓ meat	**alla carne** *AHl-lah kAHr-neh*
▓ mold	**alla muffa** *AHl-lah mOOf-fah*

■ peanuts	**alle noccioline americane**	*AHl-leh noh-chee-oh-lEE-neh ah-meh-ree-kAH-neh*
■ pork	**alla carne di maiale**	*AHl-lah kAHr-neh dee mah-ee-AH-leh*
■ salt	**al sale**	*AHl sAH-leh*
■ shellfish	**ai crostacei**	*AH-ee kroh-stAH-cheh-ee*

I wanted it without ____.	**Lo volevo senza ____.**	*loh voh-lAY-voh sEHn-tsah*
■ alcohol	**alcol**	*AHl-cohl*
■ caffeine	**caffeina**	*kahf-feh-EE-nah*
■ meat	**carne**	*kAHr-neh*
■ sugar	**zucchero**	*tsOO-keh-roh*

I am a vegetarian.	**Sono vegetariano (a).**	*sOH-noh veh-jeh-tah-ree-AH-noh (nah)*

Do you have food ____?	**C'è cibo ____?**	*chEH chEE-boh*
■ low in calories	**con poche calorie**	*kohn pOH-keh kah-loh-rEE-eh*
■ low in cholesterol	**con poco colesterolo**	*kohn pOH-koh koh-leh-steh-rOH-loh*
■ low in fat	**con poco grasso**	*kohn pOH-koh grAHs-soh*

Do you have ____?	**C'è ____?**	*chEH*
■ an artificial sweetener	**qualche dolcificante artificiale**	*koo-AHl-keh dohl-chee-fee-kAHn-teh ahr-tee-fee-chee-AHl-eh*
■ saccharin	**della saccarina**	*dAYl-lah sahk-kah-rEE-nah*
■ Sweet 'n Low	**dello sweet e low**	*dAYl-loh soo-EEt ay lOH*

My father (mother) is elderly.	**Mio padre (mia madre) è vecchio(a).** *mEE-oh pAH-dreh (mEE-ah mAH-dreh) EH vEHk-key-oh(ah)*	

My parents are elderly.
I miei genitori sono anziani. *EE mee-EH-ee jeh-nee-tOH-ree sOH-noh AHn-tzee-AH-nee*

We need a ____.
Abbiamo bisogno di ____. *ahb-bee-AH-moh bee-sOH-ny-oh dee*

■ cane
un bastone *oon bah-stOH-neh*

■ crutch
una stambella *OO-nah stahm-bEHl-lah*

■ pair of crutches
un paio di stambelle *oon pAH-ee-oh dee stahm-bEHl-leh*

■ walker
un girello *oon jee-rEHl-loh*

Are there any ____?
Ci sono ____? *chee sOH-noh*

■ escalators
scale mobili *skAH-leh mOH-bee-lee*

■ ramps
rampe *rAHm-peh*

Are there any ____ we can contact in case of emergency?
Ci sono ____ che possiamo contattare in caso d'emergenza? *chee sOH-noh ____ kay pohs-see-AH-moh kohn-taht-tAH-reh een kAH-soh deh-mehr-jEHn-tzah*

■ agencies
agenzie *ah-jehn-tzEE-eh*

■ drugstores
farmacie *fahr-mah-chEE-eh*

■ emergency rooms
sale di pronto soccorso *sAH-leh dee prOHn-toh soh-k-kOHr-soh*

Is there a(n) ____ available?
C'è ____ disponibile? *chEH ____ dees-poh-nEE-bee-leh*

■ ambulance
un'ambulanza *oon-ahm-boo-lAHn-tzah*

■ car service
un servizio noleggio *oon sayr-vEE-tzee-oh noh-lAY-jee-oh*

■ taxi
un taxi *oon tahs-sEE*

Is there a doctor in the hotel?	**C'è un dottore nell'hotel?** *chEH oon doht-tOH-reh nayl-loh-tEHl*
How can we contact a doctor in case of emergency?	**Come possiamo contattare un medico in caso d'emergenza?** *KOH-meh pohs-see-AH-moh kohn-taht-tAH-reh oon mEH-dee-koh een kAH-soh deh-mehr-jEHn-tzah*
Are there doctors who make house calls?	**Ci sono dottori che vengono a visitare i pazienti in casa?** *chee sOH-noh doht-tOH-ree kay vEHn-goh-noh ah vee-see-tAH-reh ee pah-tzee-EHn-tee een kAH-sah*
Is there a visiting nurse service?	**C'è un servizio infermieri a domicilio?** *chEH oon sayr-vEE-tzee-oh een-fehr-mee-EH-ree ah doh-mee-chEE-lee-oh*
Is there oxygen available?	**C'è ossigeno disponibile?** *chEE ohs-sEE-jeh-noh dees-poh-nEE-bee-lee*
Do you have a toilet equipped for the handicapped?	**C'è un bagno equipaggiato per le persone disabili?** *chEH oon bAH-ny-oh ay-koo-ee-pah-jee-AH-toh pehr leh pehr-sOH-neh dee-sAH-bee-lee*
Is there a kneeling bus available?	**È disponibile un autobus che facilita la salita e la discesa per disabili?** *EH dees-poh-nEE-bee-leh oon ah-oo-toh-bOOs kay fah-chEE-lee-tah lah sah-lEE-tah ay lah dee-shAY-sah pehr dee-sAH-bee-lee*

ORDERING BREAKFAST

Larger hotels will offer breakfast. The Italian breakfast is a simple one—coffee and a sweet roll or brioche, sometimes **focaccia,** and jam or marmalade. At hotels that cater to

American or British tourists, you will also be able to order an English breakfast (juice, eggs, bacon, and toast). Larger hotels will have a dining room where you can eat breakfast, but the usual procedure is to have breakfast sent up to your room.

We'll have breakfast in the room.	**Faremo colazione in camera.** *fah-rAY-moh koh-lah-tsee-OH-neh een kAH-meh-rah*
Please send up ____.	**Per favore mandino ____.** *pehr fah-vOH-reh mAHn-dee-noh*
▓ one (two) coffee(s)	**un (due) caffè** *oon (dOO-eh) kahf-fEH*
▓ tea	**un tè** *oon tEH*
▓ hot chocolate	**una cioccolata calda** *OO-nah chee-oh-koh-lAH-tah kAHl-dah*
▓ a sweet roll (brioche)	**un berlingozzo (una brioche)** *oon behr-leen-gOH-tsoh (oon-ah brEE-osh)*
▓ fruit (juice)	**(un succo di) frutta** *(oon sOO-koh-dee) frOOt-tah*
I'll eat breakfast downstairs.	**Mangerò la colazione giù.** *mahn-jeh-rOH lah koh-lah-tsee-OH-neh jee-OO*
We'd both like ____.	**Noi due desideriamo ____.** *nOH-ee dOO-eh deh-see-deh-ree-AH-moh*
▓ bacon and eggs	**uova al tegamino con pancetta** *oo-OH-vah ahl teh-gah-mEE-noh kohn pahn-chAYt-tah*
▓ scrambled (fried, boiled) eggs	**uova al tegamino strapazzate (fritte, alla coque)** *oo-OH-vah ahl teh-gah-mEE-noh strah-pah-tsAH-teh (frEEt-teh ahl-lah kOHk)*
▓ toast	**pan tostato** *pAHn toh-stAH-toh*
▓ jam	**marmellata** *mahr-mehl-lAH-tah*

NOTE: See the food section (pages 114–149) for more phrases dealing with ordering meals.

HOTEL SERVICES

Where is _____?	**Dov'è _____?**	*doh-vEH*
the dining room	**la sala da pranzo**	*lah sAH-lah dah prAHn-tsoh*
the bathroom	**il bagno (la toilette)**	*eel bAH-ny-oh (lah too-ah lEHt)*
the elevator (lift)	**l'ascensore**	*lah-shehn-sOH-reh*
the phone	**il telefono**	*eel teh-lEH-foh-noh*

What is my room number?

Qual è il numero della mia camera? *koo-ah-lEH eel nOO-meh-roh dAYl-lah mEE-ah kAH-meh-rah*

May I please have my key?

Può darmi la chiave, per favore? *poo-OH dAHr-mee lah key-AH-veh pehr fah-vOH-reh*

I've lost my key.

Ho perduto la chiave. *oh pehr-dOO-toh lah key-AH-veh*

GETTING WHAT YOU NEED

I need _____.	**Ho bisogno di _____.**	*oh bee-sOH-ny-oh dee*
a bellhop	**un fattorino**	*oon faht-toh-rEE-noh*
a chambermaid	**una cameriera**	*OO-nah kah-meh-ree-EH-rah*

Please send _____ to my room.

Per piacere mi mandi _____ in camera. *pehr pee-ah-chAY-reh mee mAHn-dee _____ een kAH-meh-rah*

a towel	**un asciugamano**	*oon ah-shoo-gah-mAH-noh*
a bar of soap	**una saponetta**	*OO-nah sah-poh-nAYt-tah*

some hangers	**delle grucce (degli attaccapanni)** *dAYl-lay grOO-cheh (dAY-ly-ee aht-AHk-kah-pAHn-nee)*
a pillow	**un cuscino** *oon koo-shEE-noh*
a blanket	**una coperta** *OO-nah koh-pEHr-tah*
some ice cubes	**dei cubetti di ghiaccio** *dAY-ee koo-bAYt-tee dee ghee-AH-chee-oh*
some ice water	**dell'acqua ghiacciata** *dayl-lAH-koo-ah ghee-ah-chee-AH-tah*
a bottle of mineral water	**una bottiglia d'acqua minerale** *OO-nah boht-tEE-ly-ee-ah dAH-koo-ah mee-neh-rAH-leh*
an ashtray	**un portacenere** *oon pohr-tah-chAY-nay-reh*
toilet paper	**della carta igienica** *dAYl-lah kAHr-tah ee-jee-EH-nee-kah*
a reading lamp	**una lampada per la lettura** *OO-nah lAHm-pah-dah pehr lah leht-tOO-rah*
an electric adapter*	**un trasformatore elettrico** *oon trahs-fohr-mah-tOH-reh ay-lEHt-tree-koh*

*NOTE: If you bring electric appliances with you from the U.S. (electric shaver, for example), you may need to have an adapter so that the voltage corresponds with that in the hotel. Newer hotels have 110-volt systems and an adapter isn't necessary.

AT THE DOOR

Who is (was) it?	**Chi è (era)?** *key-EH (EH-rah)*
Just a minute.	**Un momento.** *oon moh-mEHn-toh*
Come in.	**Entri (venga).** *AYn-tree (vEHn-gah)*
Put it on the table.	**Lo metta sul tavolo.** *loh mAYt-tah sool tAH-voh-loh*

Please wake me tomorrow at ____.	**Per favore mi svegli domani alle ____.** *pehr fah-vOH-reh mee svAY-ly-ee doh-mAH-nee AHl-leh*

COMPLAINTS

There is no ____.	**Manca ____.** *mAHn-kah*
▓ running water	**l'acqua corrente** *lAH-koo-ah kohr-rEHn-teh*
▓ hot water	**l'acqua calda** *lAH-koo-ah kAHl-dah*
▓ electricity	**la luce elettrica** *lah lOO-cheh eh-lEHt-tree-kah*
The ____ doesn't work.	**____ non funziona.** *____ nohn foon-tsee-OH-nah*
▓ air-conditioning	**l'aria condizionata** *lAH-ree-ah kohn-dee-tsee-oh-nAH-tah*
▓ fan	**il ventilatore** *eel vehn-tee-lah-tOH-reh*
▓ faucet	**il rubinetto** *eel roo-bee-nAYt-toh*
▓ light	**la luce** *lah lOO-cheh*
▓ radio	**la radio** *lah rAH-dee-oh*
▓ electric socket	**la presa della corrente** *lah prAY-sa dehl-lah kohr-rEHn-teh*
▓ light switch	**l'interruttore** *leen-tehr-root-tOH-reh*
▓ television	**la televisione** *lah teh-leh-vee-see-OH-neh*
Can you fix it?	**Può farlo(la) riparare?** *poo-OH fAHr-loh(ah) ree-pah-rAH-reh*
The room is dirty.	**La camera è sporca.** *lah kAH-meh-rah EH spOHr-kah*
Can you clean it ____?	**Può farla pulire ____?** *poo-OH fAHr-lah poo-lEE-reh*
▓ now	**subito** *sOO-bee-toh*

as soon as possible	**il più presto possibile** *eel pee-OO prEH-stoh pohs-sEE-bee-leh*

AT THE DESK

Are there (any) _____ for me?	**Ci sono _____ per me?** *chee sOH-noh _____ payr mAY*
letters	**(delle) lettere** *(dAYl-leh) lAYt-teh-reh*
messages	**(dei) messaggi** *(dAY-ee) mehs-sAH-jee*
packages	**(dei) pacchi** *(dAY-ee) pAH-key*
postcards	**(delle) cartoline postali** *(dAYl-leh) kahr-toh-lEE-neh poh-stAH-lee*
Did anyone call for me?	**Mi ha cercato qualcuno?** *mee-AH chehr-kAH-toh koo-ahl-kOO-noh*
I'd like to leave this in your safe.	**Vorrei lasciare questo nella sua cassaforte.** *vohr-rEH-ee lah-shee-AH-reh koo-AYs-toh nAYl-lah sOO-ah kahs-sah-fOHr-teh*
Will you make this call for me?	**Può farmi questa telefonata?** *poo-OH fAHr-mee koo-AYs-tah teh-leh-foh-nAH-tah*

CHECKING OUT

I'd like the bill, please.	**Vorrei il conto per favore.** *vohr-rEH-ee eel kOHn-toh pehr fah-vOH-reh*
I'll be checking out today (tomorrow).	**Pagherò e partirò oggi (domani).** *pah-gheh-rOH ay pahr-tee-rOH OH-jee (doh-mAH-nee)*
Please send someone up for our baggage.	**Per favore mandi qualcuno a prendere le valigie.** *pehr fah-vOH-reh mAHn-dee koo-ahl-kOO-noh ah prAYn-deh-reh leh vah-lEE-jee-eh*

Travel Tips Packing for a trip abroad is an art. Porters may sometimes be hard to find, so never take more luggage than you can handle alone. Before closing your bag, mentally dress and groom yourself and take all your medications, as a checklist that nothing is forgotten.

GETTING AROUND TOWN

In smaller towns, you can walk to most places you want to visit, catching the flavor and color of the area at the same time. In the larger cities, you might want to get around using public transportation—another wonderful way to sample a country's way of life. For information on train or plane travel, see pages 65–73.

AUTOBUS	City buses running from 6 A.M. to midnight. In larger cities they provide the **servizio notturno** (*sayr-vEE-tzee-oh noht-tOOr-noh*), night runs.
TRAM (TRANVAI)	Trolley cars
FILOBUS	Trackless trolley (streetcar)
METROPOLITANA	Subway (underground)
AUTOCORRIERA	Bus services
AUTOPULLMAN	Orange is the color for city buses. Blue is the common color for **autopullman**
EUROWAYS	
EUROPABUS	
ALISCAFO	Hydrofoil
NAVE TRAGHETTO	Ferryboat
	Grandi Traghetti, Moby Lines, Navarma, Sardinia Ferries, and **Tirrenia** are some of the ferries that link Italy with its beautiful islands
VAPORETTO	Water buses
MOTOSCAFO	Slim, small, and fast boat
MOTONAVE	Two-tier boat
GONDOLA	Typical Venetian luxury form of transportation

THE SUBWAY (UNDERGROUND)

Getting around Rome is made easier because of its
metropolitana. You'll find maps posted in every station, as
well as in every train. The stops are clearly marked, and you
should have no problem reaching your destination. On the
street, the station entrances have a large **M** posted. Fares are
low, with one fare taking you through the entire system.
Milan has a subway that functions similarly.

Is there a subway (underground) in this city?	**C'è una metropolitana in questa città?** *chEH OO-nah meh-troh-poh-lee-tAH-nah een koo-AYs-tah cheet-tAH*
Do you have a map showing the stops?	**Ha una cartina che indica le fermate della metropolitana?** *ah OO-nah kahr-tEE-nah kay EEn-dee-kah lay fayr-mAH-teh dAYl-lah meh-troh-poh-lee-tAH-nah*
Where is the closest subway (underground) station?	**Dov'è la stazione più vicina della metropolitana?** *doh-vEH lah stah-tsee-OH-neh pee-OO vee-chEE-nah dAYl-lah meh-troh-poh-lee-tAH-nah*
How much is the fare?	**Quanto costa il biglietto?** *koo-AHn-toh kOHs-tah eel bee-ly-ee-AYt-toh*
Where can I buy a token (a ticket)?	**Dove posso comprare un gettone (un biglietto)?** *dOH-veh pOHs-soh kohm-prAH-reh oon jee-eht-tOH-neh (oon bee-ly-ee-AYt-toh)*
Which is the train that goes to ____?	**Qual è il treno che va a ____?** *koo-ah-lEH eel trEH-noh keh vah ah*
Does this train go to ____?	**Questo treno va a ____?** *koo-AYs-toh trEH-noh vAH ah*
How many more stops?	**Quante fermate ancora?** *koo-AHn-teh fehr-mAH-teh ahn-kOH-rah*

What's the next station?	**Qual è la prossima stazione?** *koo-ah-lEH lah prOHs-see-mah stah-tsee-OH-neh*
Where should I get off?	**Dove dovrei scendere?** *dOH-vay doh-vrEH-ee shAYn-deh-reh*
Do I have to change trains?	**Devo cambiare treno?** *dAY-voh kahm-bee-AH-reh trEH-noh*
Can you tell me when we get there?	**Può farmi sapere quando siamo arrivati(e)?** *poo-OH fAHr-mee sah-pAY-reh koo-AHn-doh see-AH-moh ahr-rEE-vah-tee(eh)*

THE BUS (STREETCAR, TRAM)

Oftentimes you can purchase a book of tickets, saving you the trouble of purchasing them each time you take the bus. Fares are charged by destination, and on less-traveled routes the driver also collects the fares.

Where is the bus stop (bus terminal)?	**Dov'è la fermata dell'autobus (il capolinea)?** *doh-vEH lah fehr-mAH-tah dayl-lAH-oo-toh-boos (eel kah-poh-lEE-neh-ah)*
Which bus (trolley) do I take to get to _____?	**Quale autobus (tram) devo prendere per andare a _____?** *koo-AH-leh AH-oo-toh-boos (trAH-m) dAY-voh prAYn-deh-reh pehr ahn-dAH-reh ah*
In which direction do I have to go?	**In quale direzione devo andare?** *een koo-AH-leh dee-reh-tsee-OH-neh dAY-voh ahn-dAH-reh*
How often do the buses run?	**Ogni quanto tempo passano gli autobus?** *OH-ny-ee koo-AHn-toh tEHm-poh pAHs-sah-noh ly-ee AH-oo-toh-boos*
Do you go to _____?	**Va a _____?** *vAH ah*

I want to go to _____.	**Voglio andare a _____.**	*vOH-ly-ee-oh ahn-dAH-reh ah*
Is it far from here?	**È lontano da qui?**	*EH lohn-tAH-noh dah koo-EE*
How many stops are there?	**Quante fermate ci sono**	*koo-AHn-teh fehr-mAH-teh chee sOH-noh*
Do I have to change buses?	**Devo cambiare autobus?**	*dAY-voh kahm-bee-AH-reh AH-oo-toh-boos*
How much is the fare?	**Quanto costa il biglietto?**	*koo-AHn-toh kOH-stah eel bee-ly-ee-AYt-toh*
Where do I get off?	**Dove devo scendere?**	*dOH-vay dAY-voh shAYn-deh-reh*
Can you tell me where to get off?	**Può dirmi dove devo scendere?**	*poo-OH dEEr-mee dOH-veh dAY-voh shAYn-deh-reh*

TAXIS

Taxis are metered, but it is still a good idea to ask the driver about how much it will cost to get to your destination. Most cabs add a supplement for travel after 10 P.M.

Is there a taxi stand near here?	**C'è un posteggio dei taxi qui vicino?**	*chEH oon poh-stAY-jee-oh dAY-ee tahs-sEE koo-EE vee-chEE-noh*
Please get me a taxi.	**Per favore mi chiami un taxi.**	*pehr fah-vOH-reh mee key-AH-mee oon tahs-sEE*
Taxi! Are you free?	**Taxi! È libero?**	*tahs-sEE EH lEE-beh-roh*

Take me (I want to go) _____.	**Mi porti (voglio andare) _____.** *mee pOHr-tee (vOH-ly-ee-oh ahn-dAH-reh)*
■ to the airport	**all'aeroporto** *ahl-lah-eh-roh-pOHr-toh*
■ to this address	**a questo indirizzo** *ah koo-AYs-toh een-dee-rEE-tsoh*
■ to the station	**alla stazione** *AHl-lah stah-tsee-OH-neh*
■ to _____ Street	**in via _____** *een vEE-ah*
Do you know where it is?	**Sa dove si trova?** *sah dOH-veh see trOH-vah*
How much is it to _____?.	**Qual è la tariffa per _____?** *koo-ah-lEH lah tah-rEEf-fah pehr*
Faster! I'm in a hurry.	**Più presto (veloce)! Ho fretta.** *pee-OO prEH-stoh (veh-lOH-cheh) oh frAYt-tah*
Please drive more slowly.	**Per cortesia guidi più piano.** *pehr kohr-tay-sEE-ah goo-EE-dee pee-OO pee-AH-noh*
Stop here at the corner.	**Si fermi qui all'angolo.** *see fAYr-mee koo-EE ahl-lAHn-goh-loh*
Stop at the next block.	**Si fermi alla prossima via.** *see fAYr-mee AHl-lah prOHs-see-mah vEE-ah*
Wait for me. I'll be right back.	**Mi aspetti. Torno subito.** *mee ah-spEHt-tee tOHr-noh sOO-bee-toh*
I think you are going the wrong way.	**Penso che lei stia andando nella direzione sbagliata.** *pEHn-soh kay lEH-ee stEE-ah ahn-dAHn-doh nAYl-lah dee-reh-tsee-OH-neh sbah-lyt-ee-AH-tah*

| How much do I owe you? | **Quanto le devo?** *koo-AHn-toh leh dAY-voh* |
| This is for you. | **Questo è per lei.** *koo-AYs-toh EH pehr lEH-ee* |

SIGHTSEEING AND TOURS

You'll want to visit a variety of sights—cathedrals, fountains and plazas, parks, and museums—so we'll give you here some phrases to help you locate English-language tours. In larger cities, you'll find facilities equipped for English-speaking tourists; in smaller towns, you may have to get along more on your own.

| Where is the Tourist Information Office? | **Dov'è l'Ente Locale (Nazionale) per il Turismo?** *doh-vEH lEHn-teh loh-kAH-leh (nah-tsee-oh-nAH-leh) pehr eel too-rEEs-moh* |
| Where can I buy an English guidebook? | **Dove posso comprare una guida turistica in inglese?** *dOH-veh pOHs-soh kohm-prAH-reh OO-nah goo-EE-dah too-rEEs-tee-kah een een-glAY-seh* |

I need an English-speaking guide.	**Ho bisogno di una guida che parli inglese.** *oh bee-sOH-ny-oh dee OO-nah goo-EE-dah kay pAHr-lee een-glAY-seh*
How much does he charge _____?	**Quanto si fa pagare _____?** *koo-AHn-toh see fah pah-gAH-reh*
■ per hour	**all'ora** *ahl-lOH-rah*
■ per day	**al giorno** *ahl jee-OHr-noh*
When does the tour begin?	**Quando inizia il tour (la gita)?** *koo-AHn-doh ee-nEE-tsee-ah eel tOOr (lah jEE-tah)*
How long is the tour?	**Quanto dura il tour (la gita)?** *koo-AHn-toh dOO-rah eel tOOr (lah jEE-tah)*
There are two (four, six) of us.	**Siamo in due (quattro, sei).** *see-AH-moh een-dOO-eh (koo-AHt-troh sEH-ee)*
We are here for one (two) day(s) only.	**Saremo qui un giorno (due giorni) soltanto.** *sah-rAY-moh koo-EE oon jee-OHr-noh (dOO-eh jee-OHr-nee) sohl-tAHn-toh*
Are there trips through the city?	**Si fanno (dei tour) delle gite turistiche della città?** *see fAHn-noh (dAY-ee tOOr) dAYl-leh jEE-teh too-rEE-stee-keh dAHl-lah cheet-tAH*
Where do they leave from?	**Da dove iniziano i tour (le gite)?** *dah dOH-veh ee-nEE-tsee-ah-noh ee tOOr (leh jEE-teh)*
We want to see _____.	**Vogliamo vedere _____.** *voh-ly-ee-AH-moh vay-dAY-reh*
■ the botanical garden	**il giardino botanico** *eel jee-ahr-dEE-noh boh-tAH-nee-koh*
■ the business center	**il centro commerciale** *eel chAYn-troh kohm-mehr-chee-AH-leh*
■ the castle	**il castello** *eel kahs-tEHl-loh*

- the cathedral **la cattedrale** *lah kaht-teh-drAH-leh*
- the church **la chiesa** *lah key-EH-sah*
- the concert hall **la sala dei concerti** *lah sAH-lah dAY-ee kohn-chEHr-tee*
- the downtown area **la zona del centro** *lah tsOH-nah dayl chAYn-troh*
- the fountains **le fontane** *leh fohn-tAH-neh*
- the library **la biblioteca** *lah bee-blee-oh-tEH-kah*
- the main park **il parco principale** *eel pAHr-koh preen-chee-pAH-leh*
- the main square **la piazza principale** *lah pee-AH-tsah preen-chee-pAH-leh*
- the market **il mercato** *eel mehr-kAH-toh*
- the mosque **la moschea** *lah moh-skEH-ah*
- the museum (of fine arts) **il museo (delle belle arti)** *eel moo-sEH-oh (dAYl-leh bEHl-leh AHr-tee)*
- a nightclub **un night club (locale notturno)** *oon nAH-eet klOOb (loh-kAH-leh noht-tOOr-noh)*
- the old part of town **la parte vecchia della città** *lah pAHr-teh vEHk-key-ah dAYl-la cheet-tAH*
- the opera **il teatro dell'opera** *eel teh-AH-troh dayl-lOH-peh-rah*
- the palace **il palazzo** *eel pah-lAH-tsoh*
- the stadium **lo stadio** *loh stAH-dee-oh*
- the synagogue **la sinagoga** *lah see-nah-gOH-gah*
- the university **l'università** *loo-nee-vehr-see-tAH*
- the zoo **il giardino zoologico (lo zoo)** *eel jee-ahr-dEE-no tsoh-oh-lOH-jee-koh (loh tsOH-oh)*

Is it all right to go in now? **Si può entrare adesso?** *see poo-OH ehn-trAH-reh ah-dEHs-soh*

Is it open (closed)?	**È aperto (chiuso)?**	*EH ah-pEHr-toh (key-OO-soh)*
At what time does it open (close)?	**A che ora aprono (chiudono)?**	*ah kay OH-rah AH-proh-noh (key-OO-doh-noh)*
What's the admission price?	**Quant'è l'entrata?**	*koo-ahn-tEH lehn-trAH-tah*
How much do children pay?	**Quanto pagano i bambini?**	*koo-AHn-toh pAH-gah-noh ee bahm-bEE-nee*
Can they go in free? Until what age?	**Possono entrare gratis? Fino a quale età?**	*pOHs-soh-noh ehn-trAH-reh grAH-tees fEE-noh ah koo-AH-leh eh-tAH*
Is it all right to take pictures?	**Si possono fare fotografie?**	*see pOHs-soh-noh fAH-reh foh-toh-grah-fEE-eh*
How much extra does it cost to take pictures?	**Quanto costa in più per fare delle fotografie?**	*koo-AHn-toh kOHs-tah een pee-OO pehr fAH-reh dAYl-leh foh-toh-grah-fEE-eh*
I do (not) use a flash attachment.	**Io (non) uso il flash.**	*EE-oh (nohn) OO-soh eel flEH-sh*

A SIGHTSEEING ITINERARY

Italy has long attracted foreigners with its natural beauty and its visible reminders of a continuous history, a history that reaches back through the ages to the heights of Roman and Greek civilizations and beyond. Its rugged mountains, rolling plains, clear lakes, blue seas, flowery gardens, picturesque castles, imposing palaces and villas, great cathedrals and churches, busy city squares, narrow, winding streets, and ancient ruins and excavations—all these give pleasure to both the eye and the mind. Italy remains one of the world's richest treasuries of Western history, art, and civilization.

While retaining a strong sense of the past, present-day Italy is a thoroughly modern country, offering the tourist a vast and efficient network of superhighways and public transportation systems as well as the most advanced facilities for everyday comfort.

Even today, the visitor to Italy would need a lifetime to know the country, since there are thousands of places and things to see, each with its own flavor and history. The following is only a limited itinerary of principal points of interest to help the traveler become acquainted with this fascinating and seductive land.

ROME

Rome is the heart of Italy. For unforgettable views of ancient Rome, its temples and monuments, see the Colosseum, the Roman Forum, the Capitol (**Campidoglio**), and the Pantheon, the most perfectly preserved ancient building. Visit St. Peter's, the Vatican Museums, and the Sistine Chapel. Stroll along the Via Veneto, renowned as the center of *la dolce vita* ("the sweet life") of film celebrities and the international jet set in the 1950s and 1960s. Descend the Spanish Steps to Via Condotti, Via del Babuino, Via Margutta (once an artists' quarter), and Piazza del Popolo. Smart boutiques, cafés, jewelry shops, and art galleries make this area very fashionable. Make a wish while tossing a coin in the famous Trevi Fountain. Piazza Navona, the old district of Trastevere, and the Sunday flea market at Porta Portese offer a glimpse of Roman daily life.

Near Rome, the gardens of Villa d'Este, with their water cascades and fountains, and the ruins of the Roman emperor Hadrian's Villa, both in Tivoli, are a must.

FLORENCE

Florence is the seat of the Italian Renaissance. Visit the Cathedral of Santa Maria del Fiore and the Academia Museum to see Michelangelo's renowned *David*. Stroll through the Piazza della Signoria to the Uffizi, one of the world's most famous art museums. Cross the Ponte Vecchio, glancing in the gold- and silversmiths' shops lined up along the sides of the bridge, and from there walk to the Pitti Palace and through the Boboli Gardens. Ride to Piazzale Michelangelo for a bird's-eye view of the city with which such illustrious names as Dante, Michelangelo, Leonardo da Vinci, Giotto, Machiavelli, and Galileo are associated. Be sure to take a side trip to nearby Pisa to see the Leaning Tower and the Baptistry with its echo.

MILAN

Italy's business and financial capital, Milan is also a historical city. Visit the Duomo, the dazzling Gothic cathedral with its hundred pinnacles; La Scala, the world-famous opera house; the Castello Sforzesco; and the Church of Santa Maria delle Grazie, to see Leonardo da Vinci's *Last Supper* in the refectory of the adjoining Dominican monastery. The shops in Via Montenapoleone are among the most elegant in Europe.

MILAN TO VENICE

The route from Milan to Venice passes through the Po Valley, Italy's richest agricultural region. Stop off at Lake Garda, which can probably be best viewed from the lovely little town of Sirmione near the southern end of the lake. On the way to Venice, stop in Verona to see "the house of Juliet," the Roman Arena (where operas are performed in the summer), and the well-preserved historical center of the city, especially Piazza dei Signori and Piazza delle Erbe (the old market square).

VENICE

With its lagoons, canals, and palaces built on water, Venice inevitably enchants the visitor. Visit St. Mark's Square (Piazza San Marco) to see St. Mark's Church, its freestanding bell tower (Campanile), and the Palace of the Doges. Take a stroll through the narrow streets to the Rialto Bridge, which arches over the Grand Canal. A boat trip to the picturesque island towns of Murano and Burano, famous centers of glass and lace making, will prove fascinating.

VENICE TO RAVENNA, SAN MARINO, AND ASSISI

Ravenna, on the coast south of Venice, is most famous for the magnificent mosaics in the Churches of San Vitale and Sant' Apollinare Nuovo and in the Mausoleum of Galla Placidia. A visit to the tomb of Dante, the father of Italian literature, will be interesting.

San Marino is an independent republic perched on a rocky pinnacle not far south of Ravenna. Tourists are attracted by its castles and picturesque old houses. This is an excellent place to buy stamps, coins, medieval armor, and gold jewelry.

The route from San Marino to Assisi passes through the Apennines, the rugged mountain chain that is called the backbone of Italy since it runs north-south down the Italian peninsula.

The town of Assisi is a very important pilgrimage center and tourist attraction. The old town is well preserved, with its medieval houses and narrow streets. Visit the magnificent Basilica of San Francesco, which contains celebrated frescoes by Giotto and Cimabue.

ROME TO NAPLES

On the way to Naples, stop in Cassino to visit the Abbey of Montecassino, destroyed in World War II and rebuilt as a monument to faith, the arts, and culture.

Italy's third largest city, Naples is the gateway to the largely unspoiled beauty of southern Italy. Visit the Cathedral of San Gennaro (the city's patron saint), the steep, narrow-staired streets of the old quarter (Spaccanapoli), and the opera house of San Carlo. In the vicinity of Naples, discover the excavated Roman cities of Pompeii and Herculaneum in the shadow of Mt. Vesuvius. Take a ride on the breathtaking serpentine Amalfi Drive, or go out to the island of Capri.

SICILY

From Naples there are direct airplane and boat connections to Palermo, Sicily. The island of Sicily is fascinating for its landscapes and the relics of its long, complex history. Visit the ancient Greek temples at Agrigento and Siracusa, reminders of the Greek foundations of Sicilian culture.

SARDINIA

And on to Sardinia! You can get there from Genoa, Civitavecchia, Rome, Naples, Palermo, and Trapani. This picturesque island is ready to be discovered. Relax on the sand beaches of modern **Costa Smeralda.** Return to the Bronze and Iron Ages while standing and admiring the numerous and massive prehistoric towers called **nuraghi.** Visit the pleasant metropolis of Cagliari and the partially submerged town of Nora. Listen to the sounds and voices of the inhabitants of Nuoro speaking a dialect very similar to Latin. And find the small treasures of old and modern times scattered throughout the island!

RELIGIOUS SERVICES

In addition to viewing the churches and cathedrals throughout Italy, you may wish to attend services.

Catholic Churches: Torso and upper arms must be covered. Shorts and skirts must extend below the knee. Churches open early in the morning, close at 12 noon for about two hours, and then reopen till evening. More important cathedrals and basilicas are usually open all day.

National Catholic Churches:
In Rome: *(American)* St. Susanna—Via XX Settembre, 14
    Tel. 06-4751510
    (Canadian) Santi Martiri Canadesi—Via G.B. De Rossi, 46
    Tel. 06-857448

In Florence: Santa Maria del Fiore (Duomo)—Saturdays at 5 P.M.
    Piazza del Duomo
    Tel. 055-29 45 14
    Church of Hospital St. John of God—Sundays and holidays at 10 A.M.
    Borgo Ognissanti, 16

Non-Catholic Churches
In Rome: Anglican Church of All Saints
Via del Babuino, 153
Tel. 06-6794357

Baptist Church
Viale Jonio, 203
Tel. 06-8814838

International Protestant
Via Chiovenda, 57
Tel. 06-745400

Methodist
Via Firenze, 38
Tel. 06-4743695

In Florence: American Episcopal Church, St. James
Via B. Rucellai, 9
Tel. 055-294417

Church of England
Via del Bollo, 5
Tel. 02-8056215

In Milan: Anglican Church of All Saints
Via Solferino, 12
Tel. 02-6552258

Christ Church
Via del Bollo, 5
Tel. 02-8056215

Synagogues
In Ancona: Via Manfredo Fanti 2/Bis, 60121 – Tel. (071) 202638
Bologna: Via Gombruti 9, 40123 – (051) 232066
Florence: Via Farini 4, 50121 – (055) 245252
Genoa: Via Bertora 6, 16122 – (010) 8391513
Leghorn: Piazza Benamozegh 1, 57100 – (0586) 896290

Milan:	Via Sally Mayer 2, 20146 – (02) 4830280
Naples:	Via Capella Vecchia 31, 80121 – (081) 7643480
Padua:	Via S Martino E Solferino 9, 35122 – (049) 875110
Pisa:	Via Palestro 24, 56100 – (050) 542580
Rome:	Lungre Cenci (Tempio), 00186 – (06) 6840061
Turin:	Via S. Pio V 12, 10125 – (011) 6692387
Trieste:	Via S. Francesco 19, 3413 – (040) 371446
Venice:	Campo Ghetto Nuovo 2899, 30121 – (041) 715012
Verona:	Via Portici 3, 37121 – (045) 8007112

Mosques

In Albenga (SV):	Moschea Arrahma – P.S. Francesco, 38, 17031 – Tel. (0182) 556056
Brescia:	Moschea di Brescia – VC Moro 7/N, 25122 – Tel. (030) 3752502
Modena:	Moschea Centro Islamico – Via Delle Suore 213, 4110 – Tel. (059) 450820
Naples:	La Moschea di Marasco Olga – Via Orazio, 82, 80122 – Tel. (081) 662195
Padua:	Moschea di Padova – Via S. Biagio, 88, 35121 – Tel. (049) 8759805/2460
Rome:	Centro Islamico—Via della Moschea 85 – Tel. (06) 8082258
Segrate (Milan):	Moschea Alrahaman – Centro Islamico di Milano – Via Cassanese, 1, 20090 – Tel. (02) 26921533
Turin:	Moschea di Torino – Via Barretti Giuseppe, 31, 10125 – Tel. (011) 655465

Is there a _____ near here?	**C'è qui vicino una _____?** *chEH koo-EE vee-chEE-noh OO-nah*
■ Catholic church	**chiesa cattolica** *key-EH-sah kaht-tOH-lee-kah*
■ Protestant church	**chiesa protestante** *key-EH-sah proh-teh-stAHn-teh*
■ synagogue	**sinagoga** *see-nah-gOH-gah*
■ mosque	**moschea** *moh-skEH-ah*

PLANNING A TRIP

During your stay you may want to plan some excursions into the country or to other Italian cities. Visitors to Italy can move around the country by airplane, train, bus, boat, and car (see Driving a Car). For air travel within Italy, look for signs to the domestic terminal (sometimes separate from the international terminal).

AIR SERVICE

Alitalia	The Italian national airline offers domestic and international flights.
Air One, Azzurra Air, Federico II Airways, Minerva Airlines	The national domestic airlines linking major cities.
Alisarda	Flights to the island of Sardinia.
When is there a flight to _____?	**Quando c'è un volo per _____?** *koo-AHn-doh chEH oon vOH-loh pehr*
I would like _____.	**Vorrei _____.** *vohr-rEH-ee*
■ a round-trip (one-way) ticket _____.	**un biglietto di andata e ritorno (di andata)** *oon bee-ly-ee-AYt-toh dee ahn-dAH-tah ay ree-tOHr-noh (dee ahn-dAH-tah)*
■ in tourist class	**in classe turistica** *een klAHs-seh too-rEE-stee-kah*
■ in first class	**in prima classe** *een prEE-mah klAHs-seh*

Can I use this ticket for frequent flyer miles?	**Posso usare questo biglietto per il club "Mille miglia," frequent flyer miles** *pOHs-soh oo-sAH-reh koo-AYs-toh bee-ly-AYt-toh pehr eel kloob mEEl-leh mEE-ly-ee-ah frequent flyer miles*
I would like a seat _____.	**Vorrei un posto _____.** *vohr-rEH-ee OOn pOH-stoh*
■ in the (non) smoking section	**tra i (non)fumatori** *trAH ee (nohn)foo-mah-tOH-ree*
■ next to the window	**accanto al finestrino** *ah-kAHn-toh ahl fee-neh-strEE-noh*
■ on the aisle	**vicino al corridoio** *vee-chEE-noh ahl kohr-ree-dOH-ee-oh*
What is the fare?	**Qual è il prezzo del biglietto?** *koo-ah-lEH eel prEH-tsoh dAYl bee-ly-ee-EHt-toh*
Are meals served?	**Sono inclusi i pasti?** *sOH-noh een-klOO-see ee pAH-stee*
When does the plane leave (arrive)?	**A che ora parte (arriva) l'aereo?** *ah kay OH-rah pAHr-teh (ahr-ree-vAH) lah-EH-reh-oh*
When must I be at the airport?	**Quando dovrò trovarmi all'aeroporto?** *koo-AHn-doh doh-vrOH troh-vAHr-mee ahl-lah-eh-roh-pOHr-toh*
What is my flight number?	**Qual è il (mio) numero di volo?** *koo-AH-lEH eel (mEE-oh) nOO-meh-roh dee vOH-loh*
What gate do we leave from?	**Qual è la nostra porta d'uscita?** *koo-ah-lEH lah nOH-strah pOHr-tah doo-shEE-tah*

I want to confirm (cancel) my reservation for flight ____.	**Desidero confermare (cancellare) la mia prenotazione per il volo** ____. *day-sEE-deh-roh kohn-fayr-mAH-reh (kahn-chehl-lAH-reh) lah mEE-ah preh-noh-tah-tsee-OH-neh pehr eel vOH-loh*
I'd like to check my bags.	**Vorrei consegnare le valigie.** *vohr-rEH-ee kohn-say-ny-AH-reh leh vah-lEE-jee-eh*
I have only carry-on baggage.	**Ho soltanto bagagli a mano.** *oh sohl-tAHn-toh bah-gAH-ly-ee ah MAH-noh*
Please pass my film (camera) through by hand.*	**Per piacere mi passi il rollino (la macchina fotografica) a mano.** *pehr pee-ah-chAY-reh mee pAHs-see eel rohl-lEE-noh (lah mAH-kee-nah foh-toh-grAH-fee-koh) ah MAH-noh*

*NOTE: Some high-speed film can be damaged by airport security X rays. It is best to pack film in your suitcase, protected in a lead insulated bag. If you have film in your camera or carry-on baggage, avoid problems and ask the guard to pass it through by hand instead. If the guard refuses, bow to his wishes.

TRAIN SERVICE

The major train lines are fast and comfortable, although all service slows a bit during the tourist season. Trains have two classes—first and second—with first class being the advisable one to choose. People often disregard the signs distinguishing the classes; thus you are apt to find second-class passengers sitting in first-class seats. Just politely ask the person to move.

You can purchase the train tickets at authorized travel agencies, at station ticket windows, and at self-service machines, which are located in the major train terminals only.

An additional supplement is charged when buying tickets for Eurocity, Intercity, Eurostar Italia, and trains requiring advance bookings. Before boarding, passengers must validate their ticket(s) with the special yellow stamping machines (**le obliteratrici di colore giallo**) located along the station platforms. (There is a small surcharge if tickets are stamped on the train.) When traveling on Espressi, Intercity, Intercity Notte, Eurocity, and Euronight trains, there is no surcharge if stamping machines are inoperable or missing at the boarding terminals or when the ticket is upgraded from second to first class for lack of seats. Eurostar Italia offers home delivery. For a minimum charge of about U.S. $2, you may purchase rail tickets for long- and medium-distance trips over the telephone and have them delivered to your address within 24 hours before departure. At present, this service is available in the following cities: Ancona (tel. 071.42250), Bologna (tel. 051.249876), Florence (tel. 055.4528087), Genoa (tel. 010.2461823), Milan (tel. 02.66981464), Naples (tel. 081.283737), Palermo (tel. 091.6169566), Reggio Calabria (tel. 0965.23640), Rome (tel. 06.486594), Trieste (tel. 040.4528087), Venice (tel.2750492), and Verona (tel. 045.8008179).

Call the **FS** (Italian Railway Network) at **1478-88088** for information on service, time schedules, and ticket prices all over Italy every day from 7:00 A.M. to 9:00 P.M. During the night, an automated answering machine will provide time schedule information only. You can contact the internet site at *http://www.fs-on-line.com*

The Intercity-Eurostar trains and those trains displaying the seal for people in need of special assistance are equipped with special toilets and offer boarding and disembarking assistance.

For additional information, physically challenged travelers may call Intercity-Eurostar in all major cities:

Bologna:	**051-6303132**
Cogliari:	**070-663256**
Florence:	**055-2352275**
Milan:	**02-67070958**
Naples:	**081-5672990**
Palermo:	**091-6161806**
Rome:	**06-4881726**
Turin:	**011-66900447**
Venice:	**041-785570**

Discounts are available for

Seniors

- **Carta d'Argento/Silver Card** (for travelers over 60, with up to a 40% discount)
- **Carta Rail Europ Senior—RES Card** (for travelers over 60, with up to a 30% discount)

Youths

- **Carta Verde/Green Card** (for travelers between 12 and 26, with a 20% discount)
- **Tessera Inter Rail/Inter Rail Card** (valid for up to 22 days or a month in second class for travelers up to 26 years old, with up to a 50% discount)
- **Euro Domino Junior** (for second class only and for travelers up to 26 years old. Discount given at time of purchase)

Travelers with special needs

- **Carta Blu/Blue Card** (valid for five years and issued to handicapped people who present a valid medical certificate. The price of the ticket includes an escort and a 20% discount)

Group discounts

- 20% for groups of 6 to 24 paying travelers
- 30% for groups of 25 to 50 paying travelers

Other discounts

- **Biglietto Chilometrico/Kilometric Ticket** (valid for up to 3,000 kilometers and a maximum of 20 trips in either first or second class)
- **Carta Amico Treno/The Friendly Train Card** (with a 20 to 50% discount)
- **Carta Club Eurostar** (30% discount on first-class tickets)
- **Carta Famiglia/Minigruppi/Family Card/Small Groups** (for up to five people, with a 30% discount)
- **Carta Prima/First Card** (30% discount, if you travel in first class)
- **Euro Domino** (valid for one month. It allows the traveler to select 3, 5, or 10 days to travel in first or second class on the railroads of participating countries)

- **Inter Rail 26+** (valid for up to 22 days of second-class travel)
- **FS/RIT (Rail Inclusive Tours)**

Refunds for unused train tickets can be received within a year from the date of purchase. Unused tickets must be stamped "unused" by an official of the European Rail Roads. Administration fees and a 15% cancellation charge are added. Rates are subject to change without notice and refunds for tickets purchased in Europe cannot be obtained in the United States.

The following is a brief description of the varieties of Italian trains.

R	**Rapido**	High-speed luxury train between major cities (supplementary fare required)
E	**Espresso**	Express train
DD	**Direttissimo**	Fast train, stopping only at main stations between large cities
R	**Regionale**	Regional train (better known as the **diretto**)
I	**Interregionale**	Local train, making all stops (also called **accelerato**)
Il	**Pendolino**	The "Leaning Train" is Italy's fastest train.
EC	**Eurocity**	High-speed international luxury day trains
ES	**Eurostar**	
EN	**Euronight**	International overnight trains with sleeping cars and berths (**cuccette**, *koo-chEHt-teh*)
IC	**Intercity** **Intercity** **Notte**	Domestic express trains within Italy. First-class cars are air-conditioned. Payment of a supplementary fare may be waived for holders of BTLC or Eurailpasses. Reservations are advisable.

Important symbols:

R̄	Reservation required.
R	Reservation optional (with charge if you want to reserve a seat).
Ⓡ	Reservation required (without charge) for passengers traveling in first class; reservation optional (with charge) for passengers traveling in second class.
Handicap symbol	Train with facilities for disabled.

Where is the train station?	**Dov'è la stazione ferroviaria?** *doh-vEH lah stah-tsee-OH-neh fehr-roh-vee-AH-ree-ah*
When does the train leave (arrive) for (from) _____?	**Quando parte (arriva) il treno per (da) _____?** *koo-AHn-doh pAHr-teh (ahr-rEE-vah) eel trEH-noh pehr (dah)*
Does this train stop at _____?	**Questo treno si ferma a _____?** *koo-AYs-toh trEH-noh see fAYr-mah ah*

BUYING A TICKET

I would like _____.	**Vorrei _____.** *vohr-rEH-ee*
▪ a first- (second-) class ticket for _____.	**un biglietto di prima (seconda) classe per _____.** *oon bee-ly-ee-AYt-toh dee prEE-mah (say-kOHn-dah) klAHs-seh pehr*
▪ a half-price ticket	**un biglietto a tariffa ridotta** *oon bee-ly-ee-AYt-toh ah tah-rEEf-fah ree-dOHt-tah*
▪ a one-way (round-trip) ticket	**un biglietto di andata (andata e ritorno)** *oon bee-ly-ee-AYt-toh dee ahn-dAH-tah (ahn-dAH-tah ay ree-tOHr-noh)*
▪ with supplement for the rapid train	**con supplemento rapido** *kohn soop-pleh-mEHn-toh rAH-pee-doh*
▪ with reserved seat	**con prenotazione** *kohn prey-noh-tAH-tzee-oh-neh*

Are there discounts for _____?	**Ci sono sconti per _____?** *chee sOH-no skOHn-tee pehr*
▪ seniors	**anziani** *ahn-tzee-AH-nee*
▪ youths	**giovani** *jee-OH-vah-nee*
▪ groups	**gruppi** *grOOp-pee*
▪ travelers with special needs	**disabili** *dee-sAH-bee-lee*
How can I obtain a refund?	**Come posso ottenere il rimborso?** *kOH-meh pOHs-soh oht-ten-nAY-reh eel reem-bOHr-soh*
Are there special passes?	**Ci sono sconti speciali?** *chee sOH-noh skOHn-tee speh-chee-AH-lee*
▪ weekly	**settimanali** *seht-tee-mah-nAH-lee*
▪ monthly	**mensili** *mehn-sEE-lee*
▪ for groups	**per gruppi** *pehr grOOp-pee*
▪ for tourists	**per turisti** *pehr too-rEEs-tee*
Is the train late?	**Il treno è in ritardo?** *eel trEH-noh EH een ree-tAHr-doh*
How long does it stop?	**Quanto tempo si ferma?** *koo-AHn-toh tEHm-poh see fAYr-mah*

ON THE TRAIN

Is there time to get a bite?	**C'è tempo per comprare un boccone?** *chEH tEHm-poh pehr kohm-prAH-reh oon boh-kOH-neh*
Is there a dining car (a sleeping car)?	**C'è un vagone ristorante (un vagone letto)?** *chEH oon vah-gOH-neh ree-stoh-rAHn-teh (oon vah-gOH-neh lEHt-toh)*
Is this an express (local) train?	**È questo un treno rapido (locale)?** *EH koo-AYs-toh oon trEH-noh rAH-pee-doh (loh-kAH-leh)*

Do I have to change trains?	**Debbo cambiar treno?** *dAYb-boh kahm-bee-AHr trEH-noh*
Is this seat taken?	**È occupato questo posto?** *EH oh-koo-pAH-toh koo-AYs-toh pOH-stoh*
Excuse me, but you are in my seat.	**Mi scusi ma lei ha occupato il mio posto.** *mee skOO-see mah lEH-ee ah oh-koo-pAH-toh eel mEE-oh pOHs-toh*
Where is the train station?	**Dov'è la stazione ferroviaria?** *doh-vEH lah stah-tsee-OH-neh fehr-roh-vee-AH-ree-ah*

SHIPBOARD TRAVEL

If you want to visit some of the islands (Capri, Sicily, Sardinia), you'll have to arrange to take a boat there.

| Where is the port (dock)? | **Dov'è il porto (molo)?** *doh-vEH eel pOHr-toh (mOH-loh)* |

When does the next boat leave for ____?	**Quando parte il prossimo battello per ____?** *koo-AHn-doh pAHr-teh eel prOHs-see-moh baht-tEHl-loh pehr*
How long does the crossing take?	**Quanto dura la traversata?** *koo-AHn-toh dOO-rah lah trah-vehr-sAH-tah*
Do we stop at any other ports?	**Ci fermiamo in qualche altro porto?** *chee fayr-mee-AH-moh een koo-AHl-keh AHl-troh pOHr-toh*
How long will we remain in port?	**Quanto tempo resteremo in porto?** *koo-AHn-toh tEHm-poh reh-stay-rEH-moh een pOHr-toh*
When do we land?	**Quando sbarcheremo?** *koo-AHn-do sbahr-keh-rAY-moh*
At what time do we have to go back on board?	**A che ora ritorniamo a bordo?** *ah kay OH-rah-ree-tohr-nee-AH-moh ah bOHr-doh*

Travel Tips Most airlines allow passengers to select a seat location and the type of meal preferred at the time reservations are made. Especially on overseas flights, good choices mean the difference between a pleasant or a miserable trip. To get some sleep, choose a window seat well away from the galley (kitchen area). If you like to walk around, request an aisle seat. To watch the movie, avoid the row facing the bulkhead. If you don't smoke, ask to be placed well away from the smokers. The reservations agent will know the aircraft being used and can help you pick the best location. Among the meal options are vegetarian, kosher, and low-fat menus. If you have other special dietary needs, ask the reservations agent if those can be met. Be sure to confirm your seat assignment and meal choice when you confirm your flight.

DRIVING A CAR

To drive in Italy you will be best off with an International Driving Permit (equivalent to a regular driver's license), best obtained before you leave home. You will need the car's registration documents with the **bollo** *(bOHl-loh)*, the annual circulation charge, and a hazard triangle. Insurance is compulsory.

Motorways are indicated by the letter "A" followed by a number written in white on a green background. Tolls are paid in cash or with Viacard or Viacard Telepass cards (an electronic pass system that makes automatic payment possible without stopping at the toll booths).

The road signs with the symbol of a wrench have buttons for emergency calls in case of breakdowns and those with a red cross symbol are for first aid.

Buckling up is mandatory for the driver and all passengers. The use of portable telephones is prohibited if they need to be held by hand when driving.

Service areas along the motorways are always open and provide gasoline, restrooms, restaurants, shopping areas, bars, banks, and information offices. Gasoline is called **benzina** *(behn-tsEE-nah)*. Unleaded gas is **benzina senza piombo** *(behn-tsEE-nah sEHn-tsah pee-Ohm-boh)* and diesel fuel is **gasolio** *(gah-sOH-lee-oh)*.

The Italian police **(Polizia Stradale, Carabinieri,** and **Vigili)** *(poh-lee-tsEE-ah strah-dAH-leh, kah-rah-bee-nee-EH-ree, vEE-jee-lee)* can stop at will any car on the road for spot checks and for traffic offenses. Tickets are paid on the spot. The traffic moves on the right, and passing is on the left. The speed limit—90–140 kilometers per hour or 56–87 miles per hour—depends upon engine capacity.

The roads in Italy are classified as **Autostrade** *(ah-oo-toh-strAH-deh)* with "pay tolls" (motorways or expressways); **S.S., Strade Statali** *(strAH-deh stah-tAH-lee)*, state roads; **S.P., Strade Provinciali** *(strAH-deh proh-veen-chee-AH-lee)*, provincial roads; **S.C., Strade Comunali** *(strAH-deh koh-moo-nAH-lee)*, village roads.

For road emergency, dial 116.
For police and ambulance, dial 113.
The Head Office of ACI, Automobile Club of Italy, is Via
Marsala 8—00185 Roma
Tel. 06 49981
Fax. 06 49982469

CAR RENTALS

Rentals can be arranged before departure for Italy through
a travel agent or upon arrival in Italy at a rental office in the
major airports or in or near the railroad station in a larger city
or town. Some automobile rental companies are nationwide or
worldwide organizations (like Avis and Hertz), enabling you
to pick up and drop off a rented car at local offices throughout
Italy.

To rent an automobile, you must be at least 21 years old
and have an International Driving Permit, obtainable before
departure or in Italy at the nearest office of the Automobile
Club of Italy.

Where can I rent _____?	**Dove posso noleggiare _____?** *dOH-veh pOHs-soh noh-leh-jee-AH-reh*
▪ a car	**una macchina** *OO-nah mAHk-kee-nah*
▪ a motorcycle	**una motocicletta** *OO-nah moh-toh-chEE-klAYt-tah*
▪ a motor scooter	**una vespa (una lambretta)** *OO-nah vEH-spah (OO-nah lahm-brAYt-tah)*
▪ a moped	**un motorino** *oon moh-toh-rEE-noh*
▪ a bicycle	**una bicicletta** *OO-nah bee-chee-klAYt-tah*
I want (I'd like) _____.	**Voglio (Vorrei) _____.** *vOH-ly-ee-oh (vohr-rEH-ee)*

a small car	**una macchina piccola** *OO-nah mAHk-kee-nah pEE-koh-lah*
a large car	**una macchina grande** *OO-nah mAHk-kee-nah grAHn-deh*
a sports car	**una macchina sportiva** *OO-nah mAHk-kee-nah spohr-tEE-vah*
I prefer automatic transmission.	**Preferisco il cambio automatico.** *preh-feh-rEE-skoh eel kAHm-bee-oh ah-oo-toh-mAH-tee-koh*
How much does it cost _____?	**Quanto costa _____?** *koo-AHn-toh kOH-stah*
per day	**al giorno** *ahl jee-OHr-noh*
per week	**alla settimana** *AHl-lah seht-tee-mAH-nah*
per kilometer	**per chilometro** *pehr key-lOH-meh-troh*
for unlimited mileage	**a chilometraggio illimitato** *ah key-loh-meh-trAH-jee-oh eel-lee-mee-tAH-toh*
How much is the (complete) insurance?	**Quant'è l'assicurazione (completa)?** *koo-ahn-tEH lahs-see-koo-rah-tsee-OH-neh (kohm-plEH-tah)*
Is gas included?	**È inclusa la benzina?** *EH een-klOO-sah lah behn-tsEE-nah*
Do you accept credit cards?	**Accetta(no) carte di credito?** *ah-chEHt-tah(noh) kAHr-teh dee krEH-dee-toh*
Here's my (international) driver's license.	**Ecco la mia patente (internazionale) di guida.** *EHk-koh lah mEE-ah pah-tEHn-teh (een-tehr-nah-tsEE-oh-nAH-leh) dee goo-EE-dah*

Do I have to leave a deposit?	**Devo lasciare un acconto (un deposito)?** *dAY-voh lah-shee-AH-reh oon ahk-kOHn-toh (oon day-pOH-see-toh)*
Is there a drop-off charge?	**C'è un supplemento per la consegna dell'auto?** *chEH oon soop-pleh-mEHn-toh pehr lah kohn-sEH-ny-ee-ah dayl-lAH-oo-toh*
I want to rent the car here and leave it in Turin.	**Desidero noleggiare l'auto qui e consegnarla a Torino.** *day-sEE-deh-roh noh-lay-jee-AH-reh lAH-oo-toh koo-EE ay kohn-say-ny-ee-AHr-lah ah toh-rEE-noh*
What kind of gasoline does it take?	**Che tipo di carburante usa?** *kay tEE-poh dee kahr-boo-rAHn-teh OO-sah*

PARKING

Parallel parking is prohibited in the centers of many Italian cities and towns, especially where the street is so narrow that parked cars would obstruct traffic. Moreover, the historical center **(centro storico)** of a city or town may sometimes be entirely or partly closed to automobile traffic (as, for example, in Rome and Verona).

In larger cities and towns, automobiles should be left in an attended parking place **(posteggio)** or in a garage **(autorimessa)**. When an automobile is left in an attended outdoor parking place—often a square **(piazza)** or widening of the street **(largo)**—the driver must pay the attendant **(posteggiatore)** on leaving the vehicle (sometimes also leaving the keys) and tip him on reclaiming it.

ON THE ROAD

Excuse me. Can you tell me _____?	**Mi scusi. Può dirmi _____?** *mee skOO-see poo-OH dEEr-mee*
■ which way is it to _____	**qual'è la via per _____** *koo-ah-lEH lah vEE-ah pehr*
■ how I get to _____	**come potrei raggiungere _____** *kOH-meh poh-trEH-ee rah-jee-OOn-jeh-reh*
I think we're lost.	**Penso che ci siamo perduti(e).** *pEHn-soh kay chee see-AH-moh pehr-dOO-tee(eh)*
Is this the road (way) to _____?	**È questa la strada (via) per _____?** *EH koo-AYs-tah lah strAH-dah (vEE-ah) pehr*
Where does this road go?	**Dove porta questa strada?** *dOH-veh pOHr-tah koo-AYs-tah strAH-dah*
How far is it from here to the next town?	**Quanto dista da qui la prossima città?** *koo-AHn-toh dEE-stah dah koo-EE lah prOHs-see-mah cheet-tAH*
How far away is _____?	**Quanto dista _____?** *koo-AHn-toh dEE-stah*
Do you have a road map?	**Ha una cartina stradale?** *AH OO-nah kahr-tEE-nah strah-dAH-leh*
Can you show it to me on the map?	**Può indicarmelo sulla cartina?** *poo-OH een-dee-kAHr-meh-loh sOOl-lah kahr-tEE-nah*
Is it a good road?	**È buona la strada?** *EH boo-OH-nah lah strAH-dah*

Guarded railroad crossing

Yield

Stop

Right of way

Dangerous intersection ahead

Gasoline (petrol) ahead

Parking

No vehicles allowed

Dangerous curve

Pedestrian crossing

Oncoming traffic has right of way

No bicycles allowed

No parking allowed

No entry

No left turn

No U-turn

No passing

Border crossing

Traffic signal ahead

Speed limit

Traffic circle (roundabout)
ahead

Minimum speed limit

All traffic turns left

End of no passing zone

One-way street

Detour

Danger ahead

Entrance to expressway

Expressway ends

Is this the shortest way?	**È questa la via più corta?** *EH koo-AYs-tah lah vEE-ah pee-OO kOHr-tah*
Are there any detours?	**Ci sono deviazioni?** *chee sOH-noh day-vee-ah-tsee-OH-nee*
Do I go straight?	**Posso proseguire diritto?** *pOHs-soh proh-seh-goo-EE-reh dee-rEEt-toh*
Turn to the right (to the left).	**Giri a destra (a sinistra).** *jEE-ree ah dEH-strah (ah see-nEE-strah)*

AT THE SERVICE STATION

Gasoline is sold by the liter in Europe, and for the traveler accustomed to gallons, it may seem confusing, especially if you want to calculate your mileage per gallon (kilometer per liter). Here are some tips on making those conversions.

LIQUID MEASURES (APPROXIMATE)					
Liters	US Gallons	Imperial Gallons	Liters	US Gallons	Imperial Gallons
10	$2\frac{3}{4}$	$2\frac{1}{4}$	50	$13\frac{1}{4}$	11
20	$5\frac{1}{4}$	$4\frac{1}{2}$	60	$15\frac{3}{4}$	13
30	8	$6\frac{1}{2}$	70	$19\frac{1}{8}$	$15\frac{1}{2}$
40	$10\frac{1}{2}$	$8\frac{3}{4}$	80	21	$17\frac{1}{2}$

DISTANCE MEASURES (APPROXIMATE)			
Kilometers	Miles	Kilometers	Miles
1	0.62	50	31
5	3	60	$37\frac{1}{4}$
10	$6\frac{1}{4}$	70	$43\frac{1}{2}$
20	$12\frac{1}{2}$	80	$49\frac{1}{2}$
30	$18\frac{1}{2}$	90	$55\frac{3}{4}$
40	$24\frac{3}{4}$	100	62

Where is there a gas (petrol) station?	**Dov'è una stazione di servizio?** *doh-vEH OO-nah stah-tsee-OH-neh dee sayr-vEE-tsee-oh*
Give me 15 (25) liters.	**Mi dia quindici (venticinque) litri.** *mee dEE-ah koo-EEn-dee-chee (vayn-tee-chEEn-koo-eh) lEE-tree*
Fill'er up with _____.	**Faccia il pieno di _____ .** *fAH-chee-ah eel pee-AY-noh dee*
▪ diesel	**diesel** *dEE-eh-sehl*
▪ regular (standard)	**normale** *nohr-mAH-leh*
▪ super (premium)	**super** *sOO-pehr*
Please check _____.	**Per favore mi controlli _____.** *pehr fah-vOH-reh mee kohn-trOHl-lee*
▪ the antifreeze	**l'acqua** *lAH-koo-ah*
▪ the battery	**la batteria** *lah baht-teh-rEE-ah*
▪ the carburetor	**il carburatore** *eel kahr-boo-rah-tOH-reh*
▪ the oil	**l'olio** *lOH-lee-oh*
▪ the spark plugs	**le candele** *leh kahn-dAY-leh*
▪ the tires	**i pneumatici (le gomme)** *ee pneh-oo-mAH-tee-chee (leh gOHm-meh)*
▪ the tire pressure	**la pressione delle gomme** *lah prehs-see-OH-neh dAYl-leh gOHm-meh*
Change the oil (please).	**Mi cambi l'olio (per favore).** *mee kAHm-bee lOH-lee-oh (pehr fah-vOH-reh)*
Lubricate the car (please).	**Mi lubrifichi la macchina (per favore).** *mee loo-brEE-fee-key lah mAHk-kee-nah (pehr fah-vOH-reh)*

Charge the battery.	**Mi carichi la batteria.** *mee kAH-ree-key lah baht-teh-rEE-ah*
Change this tire.	**Mi cambi questa ruota.** *mee kAHm-bee koo-AYs-tah roo-OH-tah*
Wash the car.	**Mi faccia il lavaggio alla macchina.** *mee fAH-chee-ah eel lah-vAH-jee-oh AHl-lah mAHk-kee-nah*
Where are the restrooms?	**Dove sono i gabinetti?** *dOH-veh sOH-noh ee gah-bee-nAYt-tee*

ACCIDENTS AND REPAIRS

My car has broken down.	**Mi si è guastata la macchina.** *mee see-EH goo-ah-stAH-tah lah mAHk-kee-nah*
It overheats.	**Si surriscalda.** *see soor-ree-skAHl-dah*
It doesn't start.	**Non si avvia.** *nohn see ahv-vEE-ah*

TIRE PRESSURES			
LBS. PER SQ. IN.	KG. PER CM.	LBS. PER SQ. IN.	KG. PER CM.
17	1.2	30	2.1
18	1.3	31	2.2
20	1.4	33	2.3
21	1.5	34	2.4
23	1.6	36	2.5
24	1.7	37	2.6
26	1.8	38	2.7
27	1.9	40	2.8
28	2.0		

I have a flat tire.	**Ho una gomma bucata.** *oh OO-nah gOHm-mah boo-kAH-tah*
The radiator is leaking.	**Il radiatore perde acqua.** *eel rah-dee-ah-tOH-reh pEHr-deh AH-koo-ah*
The battery is dead.	**La batteria è scarica.** *lah baht-teh-rEE-ah EH skAH-ree-kah*
The keys are locked inside the car.	**Le chiavi sono rimaste chiuse in macchina.** *leh key-AH-vee sOH-noh ree-mAH-steh key-OO-seh een mAHk-kee-nah*
Is there a garage near here?	**C'è un'autorimessa qui vicino?** *chEH oon-ah-oo-toh-ree-mEHs-sah koo-EE vee-chEE-noh*
I need a mechanic (tow truck).	**Ho bisogno di un meccanico (carroattrezzi).** *oh bee-sOH-ny-oh dee oon mehk-kAH-nee-koh (kAHr-roh-aht-trAY-tsee)*
Can you give me a push?	**Può darmi una spinta?** *poo-OH dAHr-mee OO-nah spEEn-tah*
I don't have any tools.	**Non ho gli attrezzi.** *nohn-OH ly-ee aht-trAY-tsee*
Can you lend me ____?	**Può prestarmi ____?** *poo-OH preh-stAHr-mee*
▦ a flashlight	**una lampadina tascabile** *OO-nah lahm-pah-dEE-nah tah-skAH-bee-leh*
▦ a hammer	**un martello** *oon mahr-tEHl-loh*
▦ a jack	**un cricco** *oon krEEk-koh*
▦ a monkey wrench	**una chiave inglese** *OO-nah key-AH-veh een-glAY-seh*
▦ pliers	**delle pinze** *dAYl-leh pEEn-tseh*

■ a screwdriver **un cacciavite** *oon kah-chee-ah-vEE-teh*

I need _____. **Ho bisogno di _____.** *oh bee-sOH-ny-oh dee*

■ a bulb **una lampadina** *OO-nah lahm-pah-dEE-nah*

■ a filter **un filtro** *oon fEEl-troh*

■ a fuse **un fusibile** *oon foo-sEE-bee-leh*

Can you fix the car? **Può ripararmi la macchina?** *poo-OH ree-pah-rAHr-mee lah mAHk-kee-nah*

Can you repair it temporarily? **Può farmi una riparazione provvisoria?** *poo-OH fAHr-mee OO-nah ree-pah-rah-tsee-OH-neh prohv-vee-sOH-ree-ah*

Do you have the part? **Ha il pezzo di recambio?** *ah eel pEH-tsoh dee ree-kAHm-bee-oh*

I think there's something wrong with _____. **Penso che ci sia un guasto _____.** *pEHn-soh kay chee sEE-ah oon goo-AH-stoh*

■ the adjustable driver's seat **al sedile di guida regolabile** *ahl say-dEE-leh dee goo-EE-dah reh-goh-lAH-bee-leh*

■ the antilock brake system (ABS) **al l'antibloccaggio Abs** *ahl lahn-tee-blohk-kAH-jee-oh ah-bee-EHs-seh*

■ the automatic transmission **al cambio automatico a controllo elettronico** *ahl kAHm-bee-oh ah-oo-toh-mAH-tee-koh ah kohn-trOHl-loh eh-leht-trOH-nee-koh*

■ the climate control and dust/ pollen filtration system **al climatizzatore con filtro antipolline e antipolvere** *ahl klee-mah-tee-tsAH-toh-reh kohn fEEl-troh ahn-tee-pOHl-lee-neh ay ahn-tee-pOHl-veh-ray*

▒ the compact disc changer	**al lettore multiplo di compact disk** *ahl leht-tOH-reh mOOl-tee-ploh dee compact disc*	
▒ the defogger/ defroster	**al lo sbrinatore** *ahl loh sbree-nah-tOH-reh*	
▒ the directional signal	**alla freccia** *AHl-lah frAY-chee-ah*	
▒ the door handle	**alla maniglia della porta** *AHl-lah mah-nEE-ly-ee-ah dAYl-la pOHr-tah*	
▒ the electrical system	**all'impianto elettrico** *ahl-leem-pee-AHn-toh eh-lEHt-tree-koh*	
▒ the fan	**alla ventola** *AHl-lah vEHn-toh-lah*	
▒ the fan belt	**alla cinghia del ventilatore** *AHl-lah chEEn-ghee-ah dayl vehn-tee-lah-tOH-reh*	
▒ the fog lights	**al fendinebbia** *ahl fEHn-dee-nAYb-bee-ah*	
▒ the forward and backward seat adjustment	**allo schienale (sedile) ribaltabile** *AHl-loh skee-eh-nAH-leh (say-dEE-leh) ree-bahl-tAH-bee-leh*	
▒ the front airbags	**alle airbag frontali** *AHl-leh airbag frohn-tAH-lee*	
▒ the fuel pump	**alla pompa della benzina** *AHl-lah pOHm-pah dAHl-lah behn-tsEE-nah*	
▒ the gear shift	**al cambio** *ahl kAHm-bee-oh*	
▒ the headlights	**agli abbaglianti** *AH-ly-ee ahb-bah-ly-ee-AHn-tee*	
▒ the head restraint	**al poggiatesta** *ahl poh-jee-ah-tEHs-tah*	
▒ the heated sideview power mirrors	**ai retrovisori riscaldabili e regolabili elettricamente** *ah-ee reh-troh-vee-sOH-ree ree-skahl-dAH-bee-lee ay reh-goh-lAH-bee-lee ay-lEHt-tree-kah-mEHn-teh*	
▒ the horn	**al clacson** *ahl klAH-ksohn*	

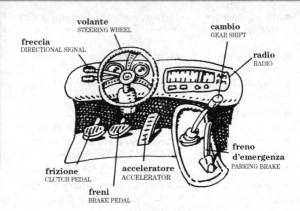

volante STEERING WHEEL
freccia DIRECTIONAL SIGNAL
cambio GEAR SHIFT
radio RADIO
freno d'emergenza PARKING BRAKE
frizione CLUTCH PEDAL
acceleratore ACCELERATOR
freni BRAKE PEDAL

the ignition	**all'accensione** *ahl-lah-chehn-see-OH-neh*
the lap-shoulder safety belts	**alle cinture di sicurezza a tre punti di ancoraggio** *AHl-leh cheen-tOO-reh dee see-koo-rEH-tzah ah tray pOOn-tee dee ahn-koh-rAH-jee-oh*
the locking system with remote	**alla chiusura centralizzata con telecomando** *AHl-lah key-oo-sOO-rah chayn-trah-lee-tsAH-tah kohn tay-leh-koh-mAHn-doh*
transmitter navigational system	**al sistema di navigazione satellitare** *ahl see-stEH-mah dee nah-vee-gah-tsee-OH-neh sah-tehl-lee-tAH-reh*
the power windows	**agli alzacristalli elettrici** *AH-ly-ee AHl-tsah-kree-stAHl-lee ay-lEHt-tree-chee*
the radio	**alla radio** *AHl-lah rAH-dee-oh*
the starter	**al motorino d'avviamento** *ahl moh-toh-rEE-noh dahv-vee-ah-mEHn-toh*

■	the steering wheel	**al volante** *ahl voh-lAHn-teh*
■	the steering wheel power adjustment	**al servosterzo elettrico** *ahl sehr-vo-stEHr-zoh eh-lEHt-tree-koh*
■	the taillight	**al fanalino posteriore** *ahl fah-nah-lEE-noh poh-steh-ree-OH-reh*
■	the theft protection system	**all'antifurto** *ahl-lahn-tee-fOOr-toh*
■	the transmission	**alla trasmissione** *AHl-lah trah-smees-see-OH-neh*
■	the water pump	**alla pompa dell'acqua** *AHl-lah pOHm-pah dayl-AH-koo-ah*
■	the windshield (windscreen) wiper	**al tergicristallo** *ahl tehr-jee-kree-stAHl-loh*

	Can you take a look at (check out) _____?	**Può dare un'occhiata (una controllata) _____?** *poo-OH dAH-reh oo-noh-key-AH-tah (OO-nah kohn-trohl-lAH-tah)*
■	the brakes	**ai freni** *ah-ee frAY-nee*
■	the bumper	**al paraurti** *ahl pah-rah-OOr-tee*
■	the exhaust system	**al tubo di scappamento** *ahl tOO-boh dee skahp-pah-mEHn-toh*
■	the fender	**al parafango** *ahl pah-rah-fAHn-goh*
■	the gas tank	**al serbatoio (della benzina)** *ahl sehr-bah-tOH-ee-oh dAYl-lah behn-tsEE-nah*
■	the hood	**al cofano** *ahl kOH-fah-noh*
■	the trunk (boot)	**al portabagagli** *ahl pohr-tah-bah-gAH-ly-ee*

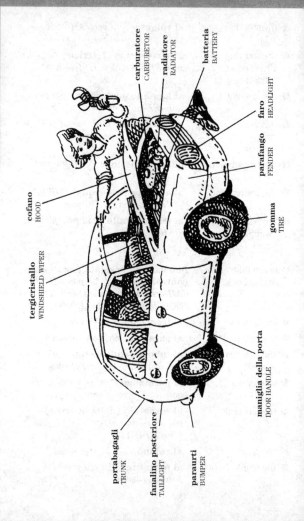

carburatore CARBURETOR

radiatore RADIATOR

batteria BATTERY

faro HEADLIGHT

parafango FENDER

cofano HOOD

gomma TIRE

tergicristallo WINDSHIELD WIPER

maniglia della porta DOOR HANDLE

portabagagli TRUNK

fanalino posteriore TAILLIGHT

paraurti BUMPER

What's the matter?	**Che cosa c'è che non va?** *kay kOH-sah chEH kay nohn vAH*
Is it possible to (can you) fix it today?	**È possibile (può) aggiustarlo oggi?** *EH pohs-sEE-bee-leh (poo-OH) ah-jee-oo-stAHr-loh OH-jee*
How long will it take?	**Quanto tempo ci vorrà?** *koo-AHn-toh tEHm-poh chee vohr-rAH*
How much do I owe you?	**Quanto le devo?** *koo-AHn-toh leh dAY-voh*

ENTERTAINMENTS AND DIVERSIONS

MOVIES, THEATER, CONCERTS, OPERA, BALLET

Open-air festivals, ballets, and concerts echo the sound of music from majestic amphitheaters through old cities and squares where fountains and monuments are part of the enchanting stage called Italy. The Arena of Verona, the Baths of Caracalla in Rome, and the Theater of Taormina in Sicily enchant visitors. The summer **Festival dei Due Mondi** (in Umbria), the **Festival Roma Europa** in the Eternal City, and the **Festival della Canzone Napoletana** (Festival of Neapolitan Songs) in Naples are a few of the performances worth watching in the nightly view.

In Italy, foreign-language films shown in commercial theaters are dubbed rather than subtitled. Cinema houses are classified first run (**prima visione**), second run (**seconda visione**), and so on. All films are interrupted by an intermission (**intervallo**), during which refreshments are sold. No smoking is allowed by law. Not all cinemas are open at a given time in the summer, as each closes for a period (usually a month).

Most theater presentations are performed by repertory companies, some of which go on tour to smaller towns. Musical comedies are rare in Italy. In recent years, cabaret theater has become popular. Theaters are closed in the summer.

The opera season varies from place to place; however, most of the major opera houses offer out-of-season events (concerts, ballets).

Theater and opera tickets are easily purchased at the box office.

Ushers in cinemas, theaters, and opera houses expect to be tipped (see pages 29–30). You also must buy a program; you will not be given one.

Let's go to the _____.	**Andiamo al _____.** *ahn-dee-AH-moh ahl*
movies (cinema)	**cinema** *chEE-neh-mah*
theater	**teatro** *teh-AH-troh*
What are they showing today?	**Che spettacoli ci sono oggi?** *kay speht-tAH-koh-lee chee sOH-noh OH-jee*
Is it a _____?	**È _____?** *EH*
mystery	**un giallo** *oon jee-AHl-loh*
comedy	**una commedia** *OO-nah kohm-mEH-dee-ah*
drama	**un dramma** *oon drAHm-mah*
musical	**un'operetta** *oo-noh-peh-rAYt-tah*
romance	**un romanzo** *oon roh-mAHn-tsoh*
Western	**un western** *oon oo-EH-stehrn*
war film	**un film di guerra** *oon fEElm dee goo-EHr-ra*
science fiction film	**un film di fantascienza** *oon fEElm dee fahn-tah-shee-EHn-tsah*
Is it in English?	**È parlato in inglese?** *EH pahr-lAH-toh een een-glAY-seh*
Has it been dubbed?	**È stato doppiato?** *EH stAH-toh dohp-pee-AH-toh*
Where is the box office?	**Dov'è il botteghino?** *doh-vEH eel boht-tay-ghEE-noh*
What time does the (first) show begin?	**A che ora comincia lo (il primo) spettacolo?** *ah kay OH-rah koh-mEEn-chee-ah loh (eel prEE-moh) speht-tAH-koh-loh*
What time does the (last) show end?	**A che ora finisce lo (l'ultimo) spettacolo?** *ah kay OH-rah fee-nEE-sheh loh (lOOl-tee-moh) speht-tAH-koh-loh*

I want a seat near the middle (front, rear).	**Desidero un posto al centro (davanti, dietro).** *day-sEE-deh-roh oon pOHs-toh ahl chAYn-troh (dah-vAHn-tee dee-EH-troh)*
Can I check my coat?	**Posso consegnare (lasciare) il mio cappotto?** *pOHs-soh kohn-seh-ny-ee-AH-reh (lah-shee-AH-reh) eel mEE-oh kahp-pOHt-toh*

BUYING A TICKET

I need _____ tickets for tonight (tomorrow night).	**Mi occorrono _____ biglietti per stasera (domani sera).** *mee oh-kOHr-roh-noh _____ bee-ly-ee-AYt-tee pehr stah-sAY-rah (doh-mAH-nee sAY-rah)*
■ two orchestra seats	**due poltrone d'orchestra** *doo-eh pohl-trOH-neh dohr-kEHs-trah*
■ two box seats	**due poltrone nei palchi** *doo-eh pohl-trOH-neh nAY-ee pAHl-kee*
■ two mezzanine seats	**due poltrone** *doo-eh pohl-trOH-neh*
■ two gallery seats	**due posti in galleria** *doo-eh pOHs-tee een gahl-leh-rEE-ah*

MORE ABOUT MUSIC

How much are the front-row seats?	**Qual è il prezzo dei posti di prima fila?** *koo-ah-lEH eel prEH-tsoh dAY-ee pOH-stee dee prEE-mah fEE-lah*
What are the least expensive seats?	**Quali sono i posti meno costosi?** *koo-AH-lee sOH-noh ee pOH-stee mAY-noh koh-stOH-see*
Are there any seats for tonight's performance?	**Ci sono posti per lo spettacolo di stasera?** *chee sOH-noh pOH-stee pehr loh speht-tAH-koh-loh dee stah-sAY-rah*

We would like to attend _____.	**Vorremmo assistere ad _____.** *vohr-rEHm-moh ahs-sEE-steh-reh ahd*
■ a ballet	**un balletto** *oon bahl-lAYt-toh*
■ a concert	**un concerto** *oon kohn-chEHr-toh*
■ an opera	**un'opera** *oo-nOH-peh-rah*
What are they playing (singing)?	**Che cosa recitano (cantano)?** *kay kOH-sah rEH-chee-tah-noh (kAHn-tah-noh)*
Who is the conductor?	**Chi è il direttore d'orchestra?** *key-EH eel dee-reht-tOH-reh dohr-kEH-strah*
I prefer _____.	**Preferisco _____.** *preh-feh-rEE-skoh*
■ classical music	**la musica classica** *lah mOO-see-kah clAHs-see-kah*
■ popular music	**la musica popolare** *lah mOO-see-kah poh-poh-lAH-reh*
■ folk dance	**la danza folcloristica** *lah dAHn-tsah fohl-kloh-rEE-stee-kah*
■ ballet	**il balletto** *eel bahl-lAYt-toh*

When does the season begin (end)?	**Quando cominicia (finisce) la stagione (lirica)?** *koo-AHn-doh koh-mEEn-chee-ah (fee-nEE-sheh) lah stah-jee-OH-neh (lEE-ree-kah)*
Should I get the tickets in advance?	**Debbo comprare i biglietti in anticipo?** *dAYb-boh kohm-prAH-reh ee bee-ly-ee-AYt-tee een ahn-tEE-chee-poh*
Do I have to dress formally?	**È prescritto l'abito da sera?** *EH preh-skrEEt-toh lAH-bee-toh dah sAY-rah*
May I buy a program?	**Posso comprare il programma di sala?** *pOHs-soh kohm-prAH-reh eel proh-grAHm-mah dee sAH-lah*
What opera (ballet) are they performing?	**Quale opera (balletto) danno?** *koo-AH-leh OH-peh-rah (bahl-lAYt-toh) dAHn-noh*
Who's singing (tenor, soprano, baritone, contralto)?	**Chi sta cantando (il tenore, il soprano, il baritono, il contralto)?** *key stah kahn-tAHn-doh (eel teh-nOH-reh, eel soh-prAH-noh eel bah-rEE-toh-noh, eel kohn-trAHl-toh)*

NIGHTCLUBS, DANCING

Let's go to a night-club.	**Andiamo al night club.** *ahn-dee-AH-moh ahl nAH-eet klOOb*
Is a reservation necessary?	**È necessaria la prenotazione?** *EH neh-chehs-sAH-ree-ah lah preh-noh-tah-tsee-OH-neh*
We haven't got a reservation.	**Non abbiamo la prenotazione.** *nohn ahb-bee-AH-moh lah preh-noh-tah-tsee-OH-neh*

Is there a good discotheque here?	**C'è una buona discoteca qui?** *chEH OO-nah boo-OH-nah dee-skoh-tEH-kah koo-EE*
Is there dancing at the hotel?	**Si balla in albergo (all'hotel)?** *see bAHl-lah een ahl-bEHr-goh (ahl-loh-tEHl)*
We'd like a table near the dance floor.	**Vorremmo un tavolo vicino alla pista (di ballo).** *vohr-rEHm-moh oon tAH-voh-loh vee-chEE-noh AHl-lah pEE-stah (dee bAHl-loh)*
Is there a minimum (cover charge)?	**C'è un prezzo minimo (per il tavolo)?** *chEH oon prEH-tsoh mEE-nee-moh (pehr eel tAH-voh-loh)*
Where is the checkroom?	**Dov'è il guardaroba?** *doh-vEH eel goo-ahr-dah-rOH-bah*
At what time does the floor show go on?	**A che ora comincia lo spettacolo (di varietà)?** *ah kay OH-rah koh-mEEn-chee-ah loh speht-tAH-koh-loh (dee vah-ree-eh-tAH)*

QUIET RELAXATION

Italians have been world champions of bridge, and you'll find playing bridge or any other card game an excellent way to meet people and learn the language.

Where can I get a deck of cards?	**Dove posso trovare un mazzo di carte?** *dOH-veh pOHs-soh troh-vAH-reh oon mAH-tsoh dee kAHr-teh*
Let's play a game!	**Facciamoci una partita!** *fah-chee-AH-moh-chee OO-nah pahr-tEE-tah*

I would like to play ____.	**Vorrei giocare ____.**	*vohr-rEH-ee jee-oh-kAH-reh*
cards	**a carte**	*ah kAHr-teh*
bridge	**a bridge**	*ah bree-dge*
blackjack	**a sette e mezzo**	*ah sEHt-teh ay mEH-tsoh*
poker	**a poker**	*ah pOH-kehr*

I've won (lost). **Ho vinto (perduto).** *oh vEEn-toh (pehr-dOO-toh)*

I win (lose). **Vinco (perdo) io.** *vEEn-koh (pehr-doh) EE-oh*

BOARD GAMES

Do you want to play ____?	**Vuole giocare ____?**	*voo-OH-leh jee-oh-kAH-reh*
checkers (draughts)	**a dama**	*ah dAH-mah*
chess	**a scacchi**	*ah skAHk-key*
dominoes	**a domino**	*ah dOH-mee-noh*

We need ____.	**Abbiamo bisogno ____.**	*ahb-bee-AH-moh bee-sOH-ny-oh*
a board	**di una scacchiera**	*dee OO-nah skahk-key-EH-rah*
dice	**dei dadi**	*dAY-ee dAH-dee*
the pieces	**dei pezzi**	*dAY-ee pEH-tsee*

Check. **Scacco.** *skAHk-koh*

Checkmate. **Scaccomatto.** *skahk-koh-mAHt-toh*

SPORTS AND LEISURE ACTIVITIES

Soccer is the national sport. The national team, **gli Azzurri** *(ly-ee ah-tzOOr-ree)*, electrifies soccer fans worldwide. The games begin at the end of August and end in May. The soccer season culminates with the **Coppa Italia** *(kOHp-pah ee-tAH-lee-ah)*. The main stadiums are: Rome, **Stadio Olimpico**; Milan, **Stadio San Siro**; Turin, **Stadio delle Alpi**; Genoa, **Stadio Marassi**; Naples, **Stadio San Paolo**; and Bari, **Stadio Sant'Elia**.

Bicycling is also very popular. **Il Giro d'Italia** *(eel jEE-roh dee-tAH-lee-ah)* or Tour of Italy is a very prestigious cycling race that attracts competitors from all over the world.

Skiing. The Italian ski resorts are some of the best in Europe. Italy offers prime winter and summer skiing centers. Several, such as Cervinia, Cortina d'Ampezzo, Courmayer, and Sestriere are well known internationally. The Dolomites offer the best equipped ski resorts. Smaller ski centers are in the Apennines and in Sicily. For information on package ski holidays, contact the **Federazione Arrampicata Sportiva Italiana** *(feh-deh-rah-tzee-OH-neh ahr-rahm-pee-kAH-tah spohr-tEE-vah ee-tah-lee-AH-nah)*, the Italian Sport Climbing Federation.

Golf, fishing, flying and hang gliding, horseback riding, scuba diving and spear fishing, tennis, walking, water skiing and yachting, etc. are accessible throughout Italy. Swimming pools are very expensive in Italy but water parks provide pools, slides, games, and wave machines. You may want to contact the **Aeroclub d'Italia** *(ah-EH-roh-kloob dee-tAH-lee-ah)* for hang gliding and flying courses; the **Federazione Italiana di Canoa e Kayak** *(feh-deh-rah-tzee-OH-neh ee-tah-lee-AH-nah dee kah-nOH-ah ay kah-ee-AHk)* for canoeing and kayaking; the **Federazione Italiana di Vela** *(feh-deh-rah-tzee-OH-neh ee-tah-lee-AH-nah dee vAY-lah)* for sailing; the **Federazione Italiana di Sport Equestre** *(feh-deh-rah-tzee-OH-neh ee-tah-lee-AH-nah de spOHrt eh-koo-EHs-treh)* for riding lessons, trips, and outings; the **Federazione Italiana di Attività Subacque** *(feh-deh-rah-tzee-OH-neh ee-tah-lee-AH-nah dee aht-tee-vee-tAH soob-AHk-oo-eh)* for underwater diving courses; the **Club Alpino Italiano (CAI)** *(klEHb ahl-pEE-noh ee-tah-lee-AH-noh)* for trekking and climbing; the **Italian Birds Protection League** for nature walks and bird watching; and the **World Wide Fund for Nature (WWF)** for walking and trekking.

SPECTATOR SPORTS

I'd like to watch a soccer game.	**Vorrei vedere una partita di calcio.** *vohr-rEH-ee veh-dAY-reh OO-nah pahr-tEE-tah dee kAHl-chee-oh*
Where's the stadium?	**Dov'è lo stadio?** *doh-vEH loh stAH-dee-oh*
At what time does the match begin?	**A che ora comincia la partita?** *ah kay OH-rah koh-mEEn-chee-ah lah pahr-tEE-tah?*
What teams are playing?	**Quali squadre giocano?** *koo-AH-lee skoo-AH-dreh jee-OH-kah-noh*
What is the score?	**Qual è il punteggio?** *koo-ah-lEH eel poon-tAY-jee-oh*
Go!	**Forza!** *fOHr-tsah*
Is there a racetrack here?	**C'è un ippodromo qui?** *chEH oon eep-pOH-droh-moh koo-EE*
Is there a track and field stadium (sports arena) in this city?	**C'è uno stadio con piste e campo sportivo in questa città?** *chEH OO-noh stAH-dee-oh kohn pEEs-teh ay kAHm-poh spohr-tEE-voh een koo-AY-stah cheet-tAH*
What are the main events today (tomorrow)?	**Quali sono gli spettacoli principali di oggi (domani)?** *koo-AH-lee sOH-noh ly-ee speht-tAH-koh-lee preen-chee-pAH-lee dee OH-jee (doh-mAH-nee)*

Do you think I can get a ticket?	**Pensa che è possibile avere un biglietto?** *pEHn-sah kay-EH pohs-sEE-bee-leh ah-vAY-reh oon bee-ly-ee-AYt-toh*
How much is a ticket?	**Quanto costa un biglietto?** *koo-AHn-toh kOHs-tah oon bee-ly-ee-AYt-toh*

SPORTS VOCABULARY

I like to _____.	**Mi piace _____.** *mee pee-AH-cheh*
■ do aerobics	**fare esercizi aerobici** *fAH-reh eh-sehr-chEE-tzee ah-eh-rOH-bee-chee*
■ play baseball	**giocare a pallabase (baseball)** *jee-oh-kAH-reh ah pAHl-lah-bah-seh (baseball)*
■ play basketball	**giocare a pallacanestro** *jee-oh-kAH-reh ah pAHl-lah-kah-nAY-stroh*
■ go bicycling	**andare in bicicletta** *ahn-dAH-reh een bee-chee-klAYt-tah*
■ go boating	**andare in barca** *ahn-dAH-reh een bAHr-kah*
■ do bodybuilding	**fare i pesi (bodybuilding)** *fAH-reh ee pAY-see (bodybuilding)*
■ go canoeing	**andare in canoa** *ahn-dAH-reh een kah-nOH-ah*
■ go diving	**fare immersioni** *fAH-reh eem-mehr-see-OH-nee*
■ fish	**pescare** *pay-skAH-reh*
■ play golf	**giocare a golf** *jee-oh-kAH-reh ah gOHlf*
■ play hockey	**giocare ad hockey** *jee-oh-kAH-reh ahd OH-key*
■ go horseback riding	**andare a cavallo** *ahn-dAH-reh ah kah-vAHl-loh*
■ go hunting	**andare a caccia** *ahn-dAH-reh ah kAH-chee-ah*

- ice-skate **pattinare su ghiaccio** *paht-tee-nAH-reh soo ghee-AH-chee-oh*
- go mountain climbing **fare alpinismo** *fAH-reh ahl-pee-nEEs-moh*
- roller-skate **pattinare** *paht-tee-nAH-reh*
- go sailing **andare in barca** *ahn-dAH-reh een bAHr-kah*
- scuba dive **fare il nuoto subacqueo** *fAH-reh eel noo-OH-toh soob-AH-koo-eh-oh*
- ski **sciare** *shee-AH-reh*
- surf **surf** *sOOrf*
- swim **nuotare** *noo-oh-tAH-reh*
- play tennis **giocare a tennis** *jee-oh-kAH-reh ah tEHn-nees*
- play volleyball **giocare a palla a volo** *jee-oh-kAH-reh ah pAHl-lah ah vOH-loh*

PLAYING FIELDS

Shall we go to the _____. **Andiamo _____?** *ahn-dee-AH-moh*

- beach **alla spiaggia/al mare** *ahl-lah spee-AH-jee-ah/ahl mAH-reh*
- court **in cortile** *een kohr-tEE-leh*
- tennis court **sul campo da tennis** *sool kAHm-poh dah tEHn-nees*
- field **al campo sportivo** *ahl kAHm-poh spohr-tEE-voh*
- golf course **al campo di golf** *ahl kAHm-poh dee gOHlf*
- gymnasium **in palestra** *een pah-lEH-strah*
- mountain **in montagna** *een mohn-tAH-ny-ee-ah*
- ocean **in oceano** *een oh-chEH-ah-noh*

■ park	**al parco (ai giardini pubblici)** *ahl pAHr-koh (ah-ee jee-ahr-dEE-nee pOOb-blee-chee)*
■ path	**sul sentiero (viottolo)** *sool sehn-tee-EH-roh (vee-OHt-toh-loh)*
■ pool	**in piscina** *een pee-shEE-nah*
■ rink	**in pista** *een pEE-stah*
■ sea	**al mare** *ahl mAH-reh*
■ stadium	**allo stadio** *AHl-loh stAH-dee-oh*
■ track	**in pista** *een pEE-stah*

SPORTS EQUIPMENT

I need _____.	**Ho bisogno di _____.** *oh bee-sOH-ny-oh dee*
■ a ball	**una palla** *OO-nah pAHl-lah*
■ a bat	**una mazza** *OO-nah mAHt-zah*
■ a bicycle	**una bicicletta** *OO-nah bee-chee-clAYt-tah*
■ a boat	**una barca** *OO-nah bAHr-kah*
■ boxing gloves	**guantoni da boxe** *goo-ahn-tOH-nee dah boxe*
■ a canoe	**una canoa** *OO-nah kah-nOH-ah*
■ a diving suit	**una tuta da sub** *OO-nah tOO-tah dah soob*
■ a fishing rod	**una canna da pesca** *OO-nah kAHn-nah dah pAY-skah*
■ golf clubs	**mazze da golf** *mAHt-zeh dah gOHlf*
■ a hockey stick	**un bastone da hockey** *oon bah-stOH-neh dah OH-key*
■ ice skates	**pattini per il ghiaccio** *pAHt-tee-nee pehr eel ghee-AH-chee-oh*
■ jogging shoes	**scarpette da corsa (per jogging)** *skahr-pAYt-teh dah kOHr-sah (pehr jogging)*

■ a jogging suit	**una tuta da ginnastica (da jogging)** *OO-nah tOO-tah dah jeen-nAH-stee-kah (dah jogging)*
■ a net	**una rete** *OO-nah rAY-teh*
■ a puck	**un disco di gomma per hockey** *oon dEE-skoh dee gOHm-mah pehr OH-key*
■ a racket	**una racchetta** *OO-nah rahk-kAYt-tah*
■ rollerblades	**pattini-roller blades** *pAHt-tee-nee-rOHl-lehr blAY-deh*
■ a sailboard	**una tavola a vela (un windsurf)** *OO-nah tAH-voh-lah ah vAY-lah (oon wEEn-soorf)*
■ scuba gear	**un equipaggiamento per il nuoto subacqueo** *oon eh-koo-ee-pah-jee-ah-mEHn-toh pehr eel noo-OH-toh soob-AH-koo-eh-oh*
■ a skateboard	**un monopattino** *oon moh-noh-pAHt-tee-noh*
■ skis	**sci** *shee*
■ a surfboard	**una tavola da surf** *OO-nah tAH-voh-lah dah sOOrf*
■ weights	**pesi** *pAY-see*
■ a wet suit	**una muta da sub (per immersioni)** *OO-nah mOO-tah dah sOOb (pehr eem-mehr-see-OH-nee)*

ACTIVE SPORTS

Do you play tennis?	**Gioca a tennis?** *jee-OH-kah ah tEHn-nees*
I (don't) play very well.	**(Non) gioco molto bene.** *(nohn) jee-OH-koh mOHl-toh bEH-neh*

Do you play singles (doubles)?	**Gioca il singolo (in doppio)?** *jee-OH-kah eel sEEn-goh-loh (een dOHp-pee-oh)*
Do you know where there is a court?	**Sa dove c'è un campo da tennis?** *sAH doh-veh-chEH oon kAHm-poh dah tEHn-nees*
Is it a private club? I'm not a member.	**È un club privato? Io non sono socio.** *EH oon clEHb pree-vAH-toh EE-oh nohn sOH-noh sOH-chee-oh*
How much do they charge per hour?	**Quanto si paga all'ora?** *koo-AHn-toh see pAH-gah ahl-lOH-rah*
Can I rent a racquet?	**Posso affittare una racchetta?** *pOHs-soh ahf-feet-tAH-reh OO-nah rahk-kAYt-tah*
Do you sell balls for a hard (soft) surface?	**Vendono palle per fondo duro (morbido)?** *vAYn-doh-noh pAHl-leh pehr fOHn-doh dOO-roh (mOHr-bee-doh)*
Let's rally first to warm up.	**Prima scambiamo qualche battuta per riscaldarci.** *prEE-mah skahm-bee-AH-moh koo-AHl-keh baht-tOO-tah pehr rees-kahl-dAHr-chee*
I serve (you serve) first.	**Io servo (lei serve) per primo.** *EE-oh sEHr-voh (lEH-ee sEHr-veh) pehr prEE-moh*
You play very well.	**Lei gioca molto bene.** *lEH-ee jee-OH-kah mOHl-toh bEH-neh*
Let's play another set.	**Giochiamo un altro set.** *jee-oh-key-AH-moh oon AHl-troh seht*

Do you know where there is a handball (squash) court?*	**Sa dov'è un campo cintato per giocare a palla a muro (squash)?** *sah doh-vEH oon kAHm-poh cheen-tAH-toh pehr jee-oh-kAH-reh ah pAHl-lah ah mOO-roh (squash)*
Are there racquetball courts?*	**Ci sono campi per giocare a palla a muro con la racchetta?** *chee sOH-noh kAHm-pee pehr jee-oh-kAH-reh ah pAHl-lah ah mOO-roh kohn lah rah-kAYt-tah*
Where is a safe place to run (to jog)?	**Dov'è un posto buono dove si può correre (fare del footing)?** *doh-vEH oon pOHs-toh boo-OH-noh dOH-veh see poo-OH kOHr-reh-reh (fAH-reh dayl fOO-teeng)*
Where is there a health club?	**Dove si può trovare un centro fitness?** *dOH-veh see poo-OH troh-vAH-reh oon chAYn-tro feet-nEHs*
Where can I play bocci?	**Dove posso giocare alle bocce?** *dOH-veh pOHs-soh jee-oh-kAH-reh AHl-leh bOH-cheh*
Where can I rent a ____?	**Dove posso noleggiare ____?** *dOH-veh pOHs-soh noh-lay-jee-AH-reh*
■ bicycle	**una bicicletta** *OO-nah bee-chee-klAYt-tah*
■ mountain bike	**un rampichíno (una mountain bike)** *oon rahm-pee-kEE-noh (OO-nah mAH-oon-tahn bAH-eek)*
■ racing bike	**una bicicletta da corsa** *OO-nah bee-chee-klAYt-tah dah kOHr-sah*
■ touring bike	**una bicicletta da passeggio** *OO-nah bee-chee-klAYt-tah dah pahs-sAY-jee-oh*

Where can I rent ___?	**Dove posso affittare ___?** *dOH-veh pOHs-soh ahf-feet-tAH-reh*
■ (inline) skates	**i roller blade** or **pattini a rotelle (in linea)** *ee rOHl-lehr blAY-deh* or *pAHt-tee-nee ah roh-tEHl-leh (een lEE-neh-ah)*
■ skateboards	**monopattini** *moh-noh-pAHt-tee-nee*

*NOTE: These are not popular sports in Italy, so you will have great difficulty locating facilities.

AT THE BEACH/POOL

Is there a beach nearby?	**C'è una spiaggia qui vicino?** *chEH OO-nah spee-AH-jee-ah koo-ee vee-chEE-noh*
Let's go to the beach (to the pool).	**Andiamo alla spiaggia (in piscina).** *ahn-dee-AH-moh AHl-lah spee-AH-jee-ah (een pee-shEE-nah)*
Which bus will take us to the beach?	**Quale autobus ci porterà alla spiaggia?** *koo-AH-leh AH-oo-toh-boos chee pohr-teh-rAH AHl-lah spee-AH-jee-ah*
Is there an indoor (outdoor) pool in the hotel?	**C'è una piscina coperta (scoperta) nell'hotel?** *chEH OO-nah pee-shEE-nah koh-pEHr-tah (skoh-pEHr-tah) nayl-loh-tEHl*
I (don't) know how to swim well.	**(Non) so nuotare bene.** *(nohn) soh noo-oh-tAH-reh bEH-neh*
Is it safe to swim here?	**Si può nuotare qui senza pericolo?** *see poo-OH noo-oh-tAH-reh koo-EE sEHn-tsah peh-rEE-koh-loh*
Are there big waves?	**Ci sono onde alte?** *chee sOH-noh OHn-deh AHl-teh*

Are there sharks?	**Ci sono pescecani?**	*chee sOH-noh pay-sheh-kAH-nee*
Is it dangerous for children?	**È pericoloso per i bambini?**	*EH peh-ree-koh-lOH-soh pehr ee bahm-bEE-nee*
Is there a lifeguard?	**C'è un bagnino?**	*chEH oon bah-ny-EE-noh*
Help! I'm drowning!	**Aiuto! Affogo!**	*ah-ee-OO-toh! Ahf-fOH-goh*
Where can I get _____?	**Dove posso trovare _____?**	*dOH-vey pOHs-soh troh-vAH-reh*
■ an air mattress	**un materassino pneumatico**	*oon mah-teh-rahs-sEE-noh pneh-oo-mAH-tee-koh*
■ a bathing suit	**un costume da bagno**	*oon koh-stOO-meh dah bAH-ny-oh*
■ a beach ball	**un pallone per la spiaggia**	*oon pahl-lOH-neh pehr lah spee-AH-jee-ah*
■ a beach chair	**una sedia per la spiaggia**	*OO-nah sEH-dee-ah pehr lah spee-AH-jee-ah*
■ a beach towel	**una tovaglia da spiaggia**	*OO-nah toh-vAH-ly-ee-ah dah spee-AH-jee-ah*
■ diving equipment	**un equipaggiamento subacqueo**	*oon ay-koo-ee-pah-jee-ah-mEHn-toh soob-AH-koo-eh-oh*
■ sunglasses	**degli occhiali da sole**	*dAY-ly-ee oh-key-AH-lee dah sOH-leh*
■ suntan lotion	**una lozione per l'abbronzatura**	*OO-nah loh-tsee-OH-neh pehr lahb-brohn-tsah-tOO-rah*
■ water skis	**degli sci acquatici**	*dAY-ly-ee shEE ah-koo-AH-tee-chee*

ON THE SLOPES

Which ski area do you recommend?	**Quali campi di sci consiglia?** *koo-AH-lee kAHm-pee dee shee kohn-sEE-ly-ee-ah*
I am a novice (intermediate, expert) skier.	**Sono uno sciatore (una sciatrice) (principiante, dilettante, esperto(a)).** *sOH-noh OO-noh shee-ah-tOH-reh (OO-nah shee-ah-trEE-ceh) (preen-chee-pee-AHn-teh dee-leht-tAHn-teh ehs-pEHr-toh(ah))*
What kind of lifts are there?	**Come sono le sciovie?** *kOH-meh sOH-noh leh shee-oh-vEE-eh*
How much does the lift cost?	**Quant'è il biglietto per la sciovia?** *koo-ahn-tEH eel bee-ly-ee-AYt-toh pehr lah shee-oh-vEE-ah*
Do they give lessons?	**Danno lezioni?** *dAHn-noh leh-tsee-OH-nee*

Is there enough snow this time of the year?	**C'è abbastanza neve in questo periodo dell'anno?** *chEH ahb-bah-stAHn-tsah nAY-veh een koo-AYs-toh peh-rEE-oh-doh dayl-lAHn-noh*
Is there any cross-country skiing?	**C'è anche lo sci do fondo?** *chEH AHn-keh loh shee dee fOHn-doh*
How do I get there?	**Come ci si va?** *kOH-meh chee see vAH*
Can I rent _____ there?	**Posso affittare _____ sul posto?** *pOHs-soh ahf-feet-tAH-reh _____ sOOl pOH-stoh*
■ equipment	**l'attrezzatura** *laht-treh-tsah-tOO-rah*
■ poles	**le racchette da sci** *leh rah-kAYt-teh dah shEE*
■ skis	**gli sci** *ly-ee shEE*
■ ski boots	**gli scarponi da sci** *ly-ee skahr-pOH-nee dah shEE*

ON THE LINKS

Is there a golf course here?	**C'è un campo di golf (qui)?** *chEH oon kAHm-poh dee gOHlf (koo-EE)*
Can one rent clubs?	**Si possono affittare le mazze?** *see pOHs-soh-noh ahf-feet-tAH-reh leh mAH-tseh*

CAMPING

Is there a camping area near here?	**C'è un campeggio qui vicino?** *chEH oon kahm-pAY-jee-oh koo-EE vee-chEE-noh*
Do we pick our own site?	**Possiamo scegliere il posto che ci piace?** *pohs-see-AH-moh shay-ly-ee-EH-reh eel pOHs-toh kay chee pee-AH-cheh*

We only have a tent.	**Noi abbiamo solo una tenta.** *nOH-ee ahb-bee-AH-moh sOH-loh OO-nah tEHn-tah*
Where is it on this map?	**Dov'è su questa cartina?** *doh-vEH soo koo-AY-stah kahr-tEE-nah*
Can we park our trailer (caravan)?	**Possiamo posteggiare la nostra roulotte?** *pohs-see-AH-moh poh-steh-jee-AH-reh lah nOH-strah roo-lOH-te*
Can we camp for one night only?	**Possiamo accamparci per una notte solamente?** *pohs-see-AH-moh ahk-kahm-pAHr-chee pehr OO-nah nOHt-teh soh-lah-mEHn-teh*
Is (are) there ____?	**C'è (ci sono) ____?** *cheh (chee sOH-noh)*
■ drinking water	**acqua potabile** *AH-koo-ah poh-tAH-bee-leh*
■ showers	**docce?** *dOH-cheh*
■ grills	**caminetti** *kah-mee-nAYt-tee*
■ picnic tables	**tavoli per il pic-nic** *tAH-voh-lee pehr eel peek-nEEk*
■ electricity	**l'elettricità** *leh-leh-tree-chee-tAH*
■ a grocery store	**un negozio di generi alimentari** *oon nay-gOH-tsee-oh dee jEH-neh-ree ah-lee-mehn-tAH-ree*
■ a children's playground	**un posto dove far giocare i bambini** *oon pOH-stoh dOH-veh fahr jee-oh-kAH-reh ee bahm-bEE-nee*
■ flush toilets	**gabinetti** *gah-bee-nAYt-tee*
How much do they charge per person (per car)?	**Quanto si paga a persona (per macchina)?** *koo-AHn-toh see pAH-gah ah pehr-sOH-nah (pehr mAHk-key-nah)*

| We intend to stay ____ days (weeks). | **Pensiamo di stare ____ giorni (settimane).** *pehn-see-AH-moh dee stAH-reh ____ jee-OHr-nee (seht-tee-mAH-neh)* |

IN THE COUNTRYSIDE

Are there tours to the countryside?	**Si organizzano gite in campagna?** *see ohr-gah-nEE-tsah-noh jEE-teh een kahm-pAH-ny-ah*
What a beautiful landscape!	**Che bel panorama!** *kay bEHl pah-noh-rAH-mah*
Look at ____.	**Osserva (guarda) ____.** *ohs-sAYr-vah (goo-AHr-dah)*

- the barn **la stalla** *lah stAHl-lah*
- the birds **gli uccelli** *ly-ee oo-chEHl-lee*
- the bridge **il ponte** *eel pOHn-teh*
- the castle **il castello** *eel kah-stEHl-loh*
- the cottages (small houses) **i villini** *ee veel-lEE-nee*
- the farm **la fattoria** *lah faht-toh-rEE-ah*
- the fields **i campi** *ee kAHm-pee*
- the flowers **i fiori** *ee fee-OH-ree*
- the forest **il bosco** *eel bOH-skoh*
- the hill **la collina** *lah kohl-lEE-nah*
- the lake **il lago** *eel lAH-goh*
- the mountains **le montagne** *leh mohn-tAH-ny-eh*
- the plants **le piante** *leh pee-AHn-teh*
- the pond **lo stagno** *loh stAH-ny-oh*
- the river **il fiume** *eel fee-OO-meh*
- the sea **il mare** *eel mAH-reh*

■ the stream   **il ruscello**   *eel roo-shEHl-loh*

■ the trees   **gli alberi**   *ly-ee AHl-beh-ree*

■ the valley   **la valle**   *lah vAHl-leh*

■ the village   **il paese (il villaggio)**   *eel pah-AY-seh (eel veel-lAH-jee-oh)*

■ the waterfall   **la cascata**   *lah kah-skAH-tah*

Where does this
path lead to?   **Dove porta questo sentiero?**
                    dOH-veh pOHr-tah koo-AYs-toh sehn-tee-EH-roh

What kind of a   **Che pianta è questa?**   *kay pee-*
tree is this?   *AHn-tah EH koo-AYs-tah*

These gardens   **Questi giardini sono belli.**
are beautiful.   *koo-AYs-tee jee-ahr-dEE-nee sOH-noh bEHl-lee*

Travel Tips   Touring on a budget? Then it pays to do your homework. Look for hotels or bed-and-breakfast places that include a morning meal in the price of a room. Often the breakfast is hearty enough to allow a light lunch. Carry nutrition bars from home in your tote bag for snacking when only expensive airport or restaurant food is available. Use public transportation whenever possible. Rail and air passes are sold for Europe and other regions but often can only be purchased in the U.S. before departure. If you must rent a car and have booked one from home, double-check local prices. Sometimes better deals can be arranged on the spot. When you first arrive in a country, check with a visitors' bureau. Agents there will explain discount cards or money-saving packets offered by local governments or merchants. The discount plans often cover transportation, food, lodging, museums, concerts, and other entertainment.

FOOD AND DRINK

How wonderful it is when a tourist can not only appreciate the sights and sounds of a country, but also enjoy its wonderful flavors. The food of Italy is world famous, and justifiably so. To savor the great range of culinary delights, you must first understand the differences among places that serve food and drink as well as the customs of the country. Always ask for **un posto dove si mangia bene**, a place where you can eat well.

Bar or Snack Bar	Ice cream, coffee, pastries, and drinks are served. This is also a favorite place for a quick breakfast consisting of a hot, foamy **cappuccino** and a **mottino**, or a **maritozzo**, a **cornetto**, a **tramezzino**, or other pastry.
Trattoria or Osteria	Small, family-operated inn serving simple but delicious local dishes prepared while you wait.
Tavola Calda	Small, self-service cafeteria with simple, hot dishes that you choose from a hot table. In some places local specialties and dishes from other countries are prepared.
Rosticceria	Generally a take-out place for grilled meats.
Pizzeria	Small, family-operated pizza parlor. Local pizza specialties and other simple dishes are served. In some places they are called **pizzeria-rosticceria**, where you can sit and enjoy a nice meal.
Panineria	A sandwich bar, where a quick meal can be served.
Autogrill	A self-service cafeteria or snack area on the **autostrade** (motorway, turnpike) with bar, restaurant, tourist market, souvenirs, telephones, and bedrooms.

Ristorante	Elegant place classified by stars (some restaurants are rated according to their decor, others by the quality of their cuisine). *Often closed on Mondays.*

Most tourists will have their breakfast in the hotel, so much of the information that follows applies to lunch and dinner. Breakfast, **la prima colazione**, for an Italian consists of **caffelatte** (coffee with milk) and a **croissant**, **panini** (rolls) with butter **(burro)** and jam or marmalade **(marmellata)** or cheese **(formaggio)**. If your hotel doesn't serve breakfast, or you prefer to go out, you'll find a suitable Italian breakfast at a caffé or bar.

LUNCH—IL PRANZO

Lunch is served from about noon or 12:30 to 3 P.M. (Usually siesta time is after **il pranzo**.) A regular **pranzo** includes:

antipasto	*ahn-tee-pAH-stoh*	appetizer
primo	*prEE-moh*	pasta or soup **(minestra in brodo)**
secondo	*say-kOHn-doh*	a meat or fish dish with vegetable, wine, and water
formaggi	*fohr-mAH-jee*	cheese course
dolci	*dOHl-chee*	sweet dessert
frutta	*frOOT-ta*	fruit
caffé	*kahf-fEH*	coffee

DINNER—LA CENA

Dinner follows the same general arrangement as lunch. It is served from around 7 P.M. to 10 P.M. In Northern Italy, dinner is served earlier than in Southern Italy.

THE MENU

Many restaurants offer a special plate of the day **(il piatto del giorno)** or have a tourist menu at a set price **(il menù turistico a prezzo fisso)**. These are usually very good values. You should also watch for the specialty of the chef or of the restaurant **(la specialità del cuoco o del ristorante)**. Often the local wine is included in the price of a meal **(vino incluso)**.

The bill may or may not include a service charge **(servizio)**, which is usually 12 to 15 percent of the bill. Other items that may appear on the bill are the tip **(mancia)**, bread and cover charge **(pane e coperto)**, and a surcharge **(supplemento)**. Even if the service and tip are included, you should leave some remaining change; it is a token of your appreciation for good service and excellent food.

EATING OUT

Do you know a good restaurant?	**Scusi, conosce un buon ristorante?** *skOO-see koh-nOH-sheh oon boo-OHn ree-stoh-rAHn-teh*
Is it very expensive (dressy)?	**È molto costoso (elegante)?** *eh mOHl-toh koh-stOH-soh (eh-leh-gAHn-teh)*
Do you know a restaurant that serves typical dishes?	**Conosce un ristorante tipico (del luogo)?** *koh-nOH-sheh oon res-toh-rAHn-teh tEE-pee-koh (dAYl loo-OH-goh)*
Waiter!	**Cameriere!** *kah-meh-ree-EH-reh*
A table for two, please.	**Un tavolo per due, per favore.** *oon tAH-voh-loh pehr dOO-eh pehr fah-vOH-reh*
■ in the corner	**all'angolo** *ahl-lAHn-goh-loh*
■ near the window	**vicino alla finestra** *vee-chee-noh AHl-lah fee-nEHs-trah*
■ on the terrace	**sul terrazzo** *sOOl tehr-rAH-tsoh*

I'd like to make a reservation ____.	**Vorrei fare una prenotazione** ____. *vohr-rEH-ee fAH-reh oon-ah preh-noh-tah-tsee-OH-neh*
■ for tonight	**per stasera** *pehr stah-sAY-rah*
■ for tomorrow evening	**per domani sera** *pehr doh-mAH-nee sAY-rah*
■ for two (four) persons	**per due (quattro) persone** *pehr dOO-eh (koo-AHt-troh) pehr-SOH-neh*
■ at 8 P.M.	**per le venti** *pehr leh vAYn-tee*
■ at 8:30 P.M.	**per le venti e trenta** *pehr leh vAYn-tee ay trEHn-tah*
We'd like to have lunch (dinner) now.	**Vorremmo pranzare adesso.** *vohr-rAYm-moh prahn-tsAH-reh ah-dEHs-soh*
The menu, please.	**Il menù, per piacere.** *eel may-nOO pehr pee-ah-chAY-reh*
I'd like the set menu.	**Vorrei il menù turistico. (Il menù a prezzo fisso.)** *vohr-rEH-ee eel meh-nOO too-rEEs-tee-koh (eel meh-nOO ah prEH-tsoh fEEs-soh)*
What's today's special?	**Qual è il piatto del giorno?** *koo-ah-lEH eel pee-AHt-toh dayl jee-OHr-noh*
What do you recommend?	**Che cosa mi consiglia lei?** *kay kOH-sah mee kohn-sEE-ly-ee-ah lEH-ee*
What's the house specialty?	**Qual è la specialità della casa?** *koo-ah-lEH lah speh-chee-ah-lee-tAH dAYl-lah kAH-sah*
Do you serve children's portions?	**Si servono porzioni per bambini?** *see sEHr-voh-noh pohr-tsee-OH-nee pehr bahm-bEE-nee*

I'm (not) very hungry.	**(Non) ho molta fame.** *(nohn) oh mOHl-tah fAH-meh*
Are the portions small (large)?	**Le porzioni sono piccole (grandi)?** *leh pohr-tsee-OH-nee sOH-noh pEE-koh-leh (grAHn-dee)*
To begin with, please bring us _____.	**Per cominciare, ci porti _____.** *pehr koh-meen-chee-AH-reh chee pOHr-tee*
◼ an aperitif	**un aperitivo** *oon ah-peh-ree-tEE-voh*
◼ a cocktail	**un cocktail** *oon kOHk-tayl*
◼ some white (red) wine	**del vino bianco (rosso)** *dayl vEE-noh bee-AHn-koh (rOHs-soh)*
◼ some water	**dell'acqua** *dayl-LAH-koo-ah*
◼ a bottle of mineral water, carbonated (noncarbonated)	**una bottiglia d'acqua minerale gassata (naturale)** *OO-nah boht-tEE-ly-ee-ah dAH-koo-ah mee-neh-rAH-leh gahs-sAH-tah (nah-too-rAH-leh)*
◼ a beer	**una birra** *OO-nah bEEr-rah*
I'd like to order now.	**Vorrei ordinare adesso** *vohr-rEH-ee ohr-dee-nAH-reh ah-dEHs-soh*
I'd like _____.	**Vorrei _____.** *vohr-rEH-ee*

(See the listings that follow for individual dishes, and also the regional specialties noted on pages 136–145.)

Do you have a house wine?	**Hanno il vino della casa?** *AHn-noh eel VEE-noh dAYl-lah kAH-sah*
Is it dry (mellow, sweet)?	**È vino secco (amabile, dolce)?** *EH vEE-noh sAY-koh (ah-mAH-bee-leh dOHl-cheh)*

Please also bring us ____.	**Per piacere ci porti anche ____.** *pehr pee-ah-chAY-reh chee pOHr-tee AHn-keh*
■ a roll	**un panino** *oon pah-nEE-noh*
■ bread	**il pane** *eel pAH-neh*
■ bread and butter	**pane e burro** *pAH-neh ay bOOr-roh*
Waiter, we need ____.	**Cameriere(a), abbiamo bisogno di ____.** *kah-meh-ree-EH-reh(ah) ahb-bee-AH-moh bee-sOH-ny-oh dee*
■ a knife	**un coltello** *oon kohl-tEHl-loh*
■ a fork	**una forchetta** *OO-nah fohr-kAYt-tah*
■ a spoon	**un cucchiaio** *oon koo-key-AH-ee-oh*
■ a teaspoon	**un cucchiaino** *oon koo-key-ah-EE-noh*
■ a soup spoon	**un cucchiaio per la minestra (il brodo)** *oon koo-key-AH-ee-oh pehr lah mee-nEHs-trah (eel brOH-doh)*
■ a glass	**un bicchiere** *oon bee-key-EH-reh*
■ a cup	**una tazza** *OO-nah tAH-tsah*
■ a saucer	**un piattino** *oon pee-aht-tEE-noh*
■ a plate	**un piatto** *oon pee-AHt-toh*
■ a napkin	**un tovagliolo** *oon toh-vah-ly-ee-ee-OH-loh*

APPETIZERS (STARTERS)

Antipasti mostly consist of raw salads, cooked chilled vegetables dressed with a vinaigrette, and massive varieties of sausages and salamis. Some key terms are:

acciughe	*ah-chee-OH-gheh*	anchovies
antipasto misto	*ahn-tee-pAHs-toh mEEs-toh*	assorted appetizers
carciofi	*kahr-chee-OH-fee*	artichoke

mortadella	*mohr-tah-dEHl-lah*	cold sausage, similar to bologna
prosciutto crudo	*proh-shee-OOt-toh krOO-doh*	dry-cured spiced ham
tartufi	*tahr-tOO-fee*	truffles (white)

SOUPS

Soups can be either thick or thin, and thus are given different names. **Brodi** are generally broths, while **zuppe** are thick and hearty.

brodo di manzo	*brOH-doh dee mAHn-tsoh*	broth, generally meat-based
brodo di pollo	*brOH-doh dee pOHl-loh*	chicken broth
brodo magro di vegetali	*brOH-doh mAH-groh dee veh-jeh-tAH-lee*	vegetable broth
crema di ____	*krEH-mah dee*	creamed ____ soup
buridda	*boo-rEEd-dah*	fish stew
cacciucco	*kah-chee-OO-koh*	seafood chowder
minestra in brodo	*mee-nEHs-trah een brOH-doh*	pasta in broth
minestrone	*mee-nehs-trOH-neh*	thick vegetable soup
zuppa di ____	*tsOOp-pah dee*	thick soup

PASTA OR RICE COURSE

A pasta course normally precedes your entree, so it is usually a small serving offered in a special presentation. Since the varieties of pasta are almost endless, you'll find them offered on menus as **agnellotti, cappelletti, fettuccine, lasagne, tagliatelle, tortellini,** and many more. It will be sauced, perhaps with a cream and cheese mixture or with a tomato sauce. It may also be stuffed or baked, or served in a soup.

In parts of northern Italy, rice is often substituted for pasta. These dishes are generally less well known, but are no less tasty. Generally you'll find it on a menu as a plain rice dish (**riso**) or as a **risotto**, a creamy rice mixture often combined with cheese, fruit, vegetables, or meat.

A few other "pasta" dishes you will find on some menus are **polenta** (*poh-lEHn-tah*)—a cornmeal mush often sliced and served with sausages or chicken—and **gnocchi** (*ny-OH-key*)—dumplings made from potatoes and often mixed with spinach, cheese, or cornmeal. Egg dishes are also often offered for this course. A **frittata** (*free-tAH-tah*) is an omelet, often filled with vegetables.

ENTREES (MEAT AND FISH DISHES)

The "main course" of an Italian meal is usually somewhat plain, either a sautéed or grilled meat or a baked fish or chicken. Along the coast and in Sicily and Sardinia, you'll find unusual and exciting varieties of seafood.

acciughe	*ah-chee-OO-gheh*	anchovies
anguille	*ahn-goo-EEl-leh*	eel
aragosta	*ah-rah-gOHs-tah*	lobster (spiny)
aringa	*ah-rEEn-gah*	herring
■ **affumicata**	*ahf-foo-mee-kAH-tah*	smoked
baccalà	*bah-kah-lAH*	dried salt cod
branzino (nasello)	*brahn-tsEE-noh (nah-sEHl-loh)*	bass (hake)

calamari (seppie)	*kah-lah-mAH-ree (sAYp-pee-eh)*	squid
cozze	*kOH-tseh*	mussels
gamberetti	*gAHm-beh-rAY-tee*	prawns
granchi	*grAHn-key*	crabs
lumache	*loo-mAH-keh*	snails
merluzzo	*mayr-lOOt-tsoh*	cod
ostriche	*OHs-tree-keh*	oysters
polipo	*pOH-lee-poh*	octopus
salmone	*sahl-mOH-neh*	salmon
sardine	*sahr-dEE-neh*	sardines
scampi	*skAHm-pee*	shrimps
sogliola	*sOH-ly-ee-oh-lah*	flounder (sole)
trota	*trOH-tah*	trout
tonno	*tOHn-noh*	tuna
vongole	*vOHn-goh-leh*	clams
trance di pesce alla griglia	*trAHn-cheh dee pAY-sheh AHl-lah grEE-ly-ee-ah*	grilled fish steaks
fritto misto di pesce	*frEEt-toh mEEs-toh dee pAY-sheh*	mixed fried fish

Meat dishes are often sauced or served with some type of gravy. Here are some basic terms you'll encounter on Italian menus.

agnello (abbacchio)	*ah-ny-EHl-loh (ahb-bAH-key-oh)*	lamb
capretto	*kah-prAHy-toh*	goat

EATING OUT • 123

maiale	*mah-ee-AH-leh*	pork
manzo	*mAHn-tsoh*	beef
montone	*mohn-tOH-neh*	mutton
vitello	*vee-tEHl-loh*	veal

And some common cuts of meat, plus other terms you'll find on a menu:

affettati	*ahf-fayt-tAH-tee*	cold cuts
costate	*kohs-tAH-teh*	chops
animelle	*ah-nee-mEHl-leh*	sweetbreads
cervello	*chehr-vEHl-loh*	brains
fegato	*fAY-gah-toh*	liver
bistecca	*bees-tAY-kah*	steak
lingua	*lEEn-goo-ah*	tongue
pancetta	*pahn-chAYt-tah*	bacon
polpette	*pohl-pAYt-teh*	meatballs
prosciutto cotto	*proh-shee-OOt-toh kOHt-toh*	ham (cooked)
rognoni	*roh-ny-OH-nee*	kidneys

And some terms for fowl and game:

anitra	*AH-nee-trah*	duck
beccaccia	*bay-kAH-chee-ah*	woodcock
cappone	*kahp-pOH-neh*	capon
carne di cervo	*kAHr-neh dee chEHr-voh*	venison
coniglio	*koh-nEE-ly-ee-oh*	rabbit
fagiano	*fah-jee-AH-noh*	pheasant

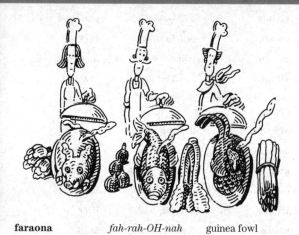

faraona	*fah-rah-OH-nah*	guinea fowl
lepre	*lEH-preh*	hare
oca	*OH-kah*	goose
pernice	*pehr-nEE-cheh*	partridge
piccioncino	*pEE-chee-ohn-chEE-noh*	squab (pigeon)
pollo	*pOHl-loh*	chicken
porcellino di latte	*pohr-chehl-lEE-noh dee lAHz-teh*	suckling pig
quaglia	*koo-AH-ly-ee-ah*	quail
tacchino	*tah-kEY-noh*	turkey

I like it _____. **Mi piace _____.** *mee pee-AH-cheh*

■ baked **al forno** *ahl fOHr-noh*

■ boiled **bollito** *bohl-lEE-toh*

■ braised **brasato al forno** *brah-sAH-toh ahl fOHr-noh*

■ breaded	**impanato**	*eem-pah-nAH-toh*
■ broiled (grilled)	**alla griglia**	*AHl-lah grEE-ly-ee-ah*
■ browned	**rosolato**	*roh-soh-lAH-toh*
■ chopped	**tritato**	*tree-tAH-toh*
■ fried	**fritto**	*frEEt-toh*
■ in its natural juices	**nei suoi succhi naturali**	*nAY-ee soo-OH-ee sOO-key nah-too-rAH-lee*
■ mashed	**passato (puré)**	*pahs-sAH-toh (poo-rAY)*
■ poached	**bollito**	*bohl-lEE-toh*
■ pureed	**passato (puré)**	*pahs-sAH-toh (poo-rAY)*
■ roasted	**arrosto**	*ahr-rOHs-toh*
■ with sauce	**in salsa**	*een sAHl-sah*
■ sautéed	**soffritto**	*sohf-frEEt-toh*
■ steamed	**al vapore**	*ahl vah-pOH-reh*
■ stewed	**stufato**	*stoo-fAH-toh*
■ wrapped in aluminum foil	**in cartoccio**	*een kahr-tOH-chee-oh*

I prefer my eggs ____.	**Preferisco le uova ____.**	*preh-feh-rEEs-koh leh oo-OH-vah*
■ fried	**al tegame (fritte)**	*ahl teh-gAH-meh (frEEt-teh)*
■ hard-boiled	**sode**	*sOH-deh*
■ medium-boiled	**mollette**	*mohl-lEH-teh*
■ poached	**affogate (in camicia)**	*ahf-foh-gAH-teh (een kah-mEE-chee-ah)*
■ scrambled	**strapazzate**	*strah-pah-tzAH-teh*
■ soft-boiled	**alla coque (al guscio)**	*AHl-lah kOHk (ahl gOO-shee-oh)*

I'd like an omelet.	**Vorrei una frittata.**	*vohr-rEH-ee OO-nah freet-tAH-tah.*

I like the meat ___.	**La carne mi piace ___.** *lah kAHr-neh mee pee-AH-cheh*
☐ well done	**ben cotta** *bEHn kOHt-tah*
☐ medium	**cotta a puntino** *kOHt-tah ah poon-tEE-noh*
☐ rare	**al sangue** *ahl sAHn-goo-eh*
☐ tender	**tenera** *tEH-neh-rah*

VEGETABLES

Italians love vegetables, so you will find many types, prepared in a variety of ways.

asparagi	*ahs-pAH-rah-jee*	asparagus
carciofi	*kahr-chee-OH-fee*	artichoke
carote	*kah-rOH-teh*	carrots
cavoli	*kAH-voh-lee*	cabbage
cavolfiori	*kah-vohl-fee-OH-ree*	cauliflower
ceci	*chay-chee*	chickpeas
cetriolo	*cheh-tree-OO-loh*	cucumber
fagioli	*fah-jee-oh-lEE*	beans (dried)
fagiolini	*fah-jee-oh-lEE-nee*	green beans
fave	*fAH-veh*	broad beans
finocchi	*fee-nOH-key*	fennel
funghi	*fOOn-ghee*	mushrooms
granturco	*grahn-tOO-rkoh*	corn (maize)
lattuga	*laht-tOO-gah*	lettuce
lenticchie	*len-tEE-key-eh*	lentils

EATING OUT • 127

melanzana	*meh-lahn-tsAH-nah*	eggplant (aubergine)
patate	*pah-tAH-teh*	potatoes
■ **patatine fritte**	*pah-tah-tEE-neh frEEt-teh*	French fries (chips)
peperoni	*peh-peh-rOH-nee*	pepper
piselli	*pee-sEHl-lee*	peas
pomodoro	*poh-moh-dOH-roh*	tomato
porcini	*pohr-chEE-nee*	wild mushroom, similar to cèpes
sedano	*sAY-dah-noh*	celery
spinaci	*spee-nAH-chee*	spinach
zucchini	*tsoo-KEY-nee*	green squash (courgettes)

SEASONINGS

Although Italians season their food well, personal preferences sometimes intercede. Here's how to ask for what you want.

I'd like ____.	**Vorrei ____.**	*vohr-rEH-ee*
■ butter	**burro**	*bOOr-roh*
■ horseradish	**rafano**	*rAH-fah-noh*
■ ketchup	**ketchup**	*keh-chOHp*
■ margarine	**margarina**	*mahr-gah-rEE-nah*
■ mayonnaise	**maionese**	*mah-ee-oh-nAY-seh*
■ mustard	**senape, mostarda**	*sEH-nah-peh moh-stAHr-dah*
■ olive oil	**olio d'oliva**	*OH-lee-oh doh-lEE-vah*

■ pepper (black)	**pepe (nero)**	*pAY-peh (nAY-roh)*
■ pepper (red)	**pepe (rosso)**	*pAY-peh (rOHs-soh)*
■ salt	**sale**	*sAH-leh*
■ sugar	**zucchero**	*tsOO-keh-roh*
■ saccharin	**saccarina, dolcificante**	*sah-kah-rEE-nah dohl-chee-fee-kAHn-teh*
■ vinegar	**aceto**	*ah-chAY-toh*

CHEESE

Every region has its own cheese or cheeses, which vary in shape, taste, and aging. As a dish, cheese is served at the beginning of a meal or before fruit and dessert. Wine is its best companion.

Many traditional dishes such as **la pastasciutta** *(lah pAH-stah-ah-shee-OOt-tah)*, **la trippa** *(lah trEEp-pah)*, **il minestrone** *(eel mee-nehs-trOH-neh)*, **i ravioli** *(ee rah-vee-OH-lee)*, **i risotti** *(ee ree-sOHt-tee)*, **i maccheroni** *(ee mahk-keh-rOH-nee)*, and some vegetable dishes owe their good taste and nutritional value to the grated cheese that is added when serving. The people from the Po River Valley region wouldn't even think about enjoying a dish of maccheroni, minestrone, ravioli, or risotto without adding grated cheese such as **grana** *(grAH-nah)*, **pecorino** *(peh-koh-rEE-noh)*, or sharp **provolone** *(proh-voh-lOH-neh)*.

The discovery of the use of fresh cheeses in recipes is partly attributed to Southern Italians. They love **mozzarella in carrozza** *(moh-tza-rEHl-lah een kah-rOH-tzah)*, **crostini di provatura** *(kroh-stEE-nee dee proh-vah-tOO-rah)*, **supplì "al telefono"** *(soop-lEE ahl teh-lEH-foh-noh)*, and **pizza**.

There are many, many varieties of Italian cheeses, and if you order a cheese course you will have the opportunity to try some that are never exported. Rather than give you the names of all the types, we offer a few useful words you can use in discussing your choices with the waiter.

Is the cheese _____?	È il formaggio _____?	eh eel fohr-mAH-jee-oh
■ mild	**dolce**	dOHl-cheh
■ sharp	**piccante**	pee-kAHn-teh
■ hard	**duro**	dOO-roh
■ soft	**molle**	mOHl-leh

FRUITS AND NUTS

Since the Italian meal is a filling one, often Italians will conclude their meal with a piece of fruit. Here are the names of some.

What kind of fruit do you have?	**Che frutta c'è?**	kay frOOt-tah chEH
albicocca	ahl-bee-kOH-kah	apricot
ananasso	ah-nah-nAHs-soh	pineapple
anguria	ahn-gOO-ree-ah	watermelon
arancia	ah-rAHn-chee-ah	orange
castagne	kahs-tAH-ny-eh	chestnuts
cedro	chAY-droh	lime
ciliege	chee-lee-EH-jee-eh	cherries
datteri	dAHt-teh-ree	dates
fichi	fEE-key	figs
fragole	frAH-goh-leh	strawberries
lampone	lahm-pOH-neh	raspberry
limone	lee-mOH-neh	lemon
mandarini	mahn-dah-rEE-nee	tangerines
mandorle	mAHn-dohr-leh	almonds
mela	mAY-lah	apple

more	mOH-reh	mulberries
noci	nOH-chee	nuts
nocciole	noh-chee-OH-leh	hazelnuts (filberts)
melone	meh-lOH-neh	melon
pera	pAY-rah	pear
pesca	pAYs-kah	peach
pompelmo	pohm-pEHl-moh	grapefruit
prugne	prOO-ny-eh	plum
uva	OO-vah	grape

DESSERT—SWEETS

Many restaurants do not serve elaborate desserts, since Italians don't generally eat pastries after a meal. We list below a few things you are likely to find on a menu. In particular, Italian ice cream is something not to be missed. Since it is not beaten with air, it is very rich and creamy.

torta	tOHr-tah	cake
dolci	dOHl-chee	sweets
macedonia di frutta	mah-cheh-dOH-nee-ah dee frOOt-tah	fresh fruit salad
mousse al cioccolato	mOOs ahl chee-oh-koh-lAH-toh	chocolate mousse
crema inglese	krEH-mah een-glAY-seh	custard
crostata	kroh-stAH-tah	pie
budino	boo-dEE-noh	pudding
■ di pane	dee pAH-neh	bread
■ di crema	dee krEH-mah	cream
■ di riso	dee rEE-soh	rice

crema di caramello	*crEH-mah dee kah-rah-mEHl-loh*	caramel custard
gelato	*jeh-lAH-toh*	ice cream
■ **al cioccolato**	*ahl chee-oh-koh-lAH-toh*	chocolate
■ **alla vaniglia**	*AHl-lah vah-nEE-ly-ee-ah*	vanilla
■ **alla fragola**	*AHl-lah frAH-goh-lah*	strawberry
■ **di caffè (con panna)**	*dee kahf-fEH (kOHn pAHn-nah)*	coffee (with whipped cream)

SPECIAL CIRCUMSTANCES

Many travelers have special dietary requirements, so here are a few phrases that might help you get what you need or avoid what does you wrong.

I am on a diet.	**Sono a dieta.** *sOH-noh ah dee-EH-tah*
I'm a vegetarian.	**Sono vegetariano(a).** *SOH-noh veh-jeh-tah-ree-AH-noh(nah)*
I can't eat anything made with _____.	**Non posso mangiare niente con _____.** *nohn pOHs-soh mahn-jee-AH-reh nee-EHn-teh kohn*
I can't have any _____.	**Non posso avere _____.** *Nohn pOHs-soh ah-vAY-reh*
■ alcohol	**sostanze alcoliche** *soh-stAHn-tzeh ahl-kOH-lee-keh*
■ dairy products	**latticini** *laht-tee-chEE-nee*
■ saturated fats	**grassi animali** *grAHs-see ah-nee-mAH-lee*
■ seafood	**frutti di mare** *frOOt-tee dee mAH-reh*

I'm on a _____ diet.	**Faccio una dieta _____.** *fAH-chee-oh OO-nah dee-EH-tah*
■ diabetic	**per diabetici** *pehr dee-ah-bEH-tee-chee*
■ low-fat	**a basso contenuto di grassi** *ah bAHs-soh kohn-teh-nOO-toh dee grAHs-see*
■ low-sodium	**a basso contenuto di sale** *ah bAHs-soh kohn-teh-nOO-toh dee sAH-leh*
■ restricted	**stretta** *strAYt-tah*
■ simple	**semplice** *sAYm-plee-cheh*
I'm looking for a dish _____.	**Cerco un piatto _____.** *chAYr-koh oon pee-AHt-toh*
■ high in fiber	**ricco di fibra** *rEEk-koh dee fEE-brah*
■ low in cholesterol	**a basso contenuto di colesterolo** *ah bAHs-soh kohn-teh-nOO-toh dee koh-leh-steh-rOH-loh*
■ low in fat	**a basso contenuto di grassi** *ah bAHs-soh kohn-teh-nOO-toh dee grAHs-see*
■ low in sodium	**a basso contenuto di sale** *ah bAHs-soh kohn-teh-nOO-toh dee sAH-leh*
■ nondairy	**senza prodotti lattici** *sEHn-tsah proh-dOHt-tee lAHt-tee-chee*
■ salt-free	**senza sale** *sEHn-tsah sAH-leh*
■ sugar-free	**senza zucchero** *sEHn-tsah tsOO-keh-roh*
■ without artificial coloring	**senza coloranti artificiali** *sEHn-tsah koh-loh-rAHn-tee ahr-tee-fee-chee-AHl-ee*
■ without preservatives	**senza preservativi** *sEHn-tsah pray-sayr-vah-tEE-vee*

I don't want anything fried (salted).	**Non posso mangiare cose fritte (salate).** *nohn pOHs-soh mahn-jee-AH-reh kOH-seh frEEt-teh (sah-lAH-teh)*
Is this very spicy?	**Questo è molto piccante?** *koo-AY-stoh eh mOHl-toh pee-kAHn-teh*
Do you have any dishes without meat?	**Hanno piatti (cibi) senza carne?** *AHn-noh pee-AHt-tee (chEE-bee) sEHn-tsah kAHr-neh*

CULINARY PROBLEMS

It's _____.	**È _____.** *EH*
■ bitter	**acre** *AH-kreh*
■ burned	**bruciato(a)** *broo-chee-AH-toh(ah)*
■ cold	**freddo(a)** *frAYd-doh(ah)*
■ overcooked	**troppo cotto(a)** *trOHp-poh kOHt-toh(ah)*
■ spoiled	**guasto(a)** *goo-AHs-toh(ah)*
■ too rare	**non è cotto(a) abbastanza** *nohn eh kOHt-toh(ah) ahb-bah-stAHn-tzah*
■ too salty	**troppo salato(a)** *trOHp-poh sah-lAH-toh(ah)*
■ too spicy	**troppo piccante** *trOHp-poh pee-kAHn-teh*
■ too sweet	**troppo dolce** *trOHp-poh dOHl-che*
■ tough	**duro(a)** *dOO-roh(ah)*
It doesn't smell good.	**Non ha un odore gradevole.** *nohn ah oon oh-DOh-reh grah-dAY-voh-leh*
It smells bad.	**Ha un odore sgradevole.** *ah oon oh-DOh-reh sgrah-dEH-voh-leh*

BEVERAGES

See pages 145–149 for information on Italian wines. As for other beverages, we give you the following phrases to help you ask for exactly what you wish.

Waiter, please bring me _____.	**Cameriere(a), per piacere mi porti _____.**	*kah-meh-ree-EH-reh(ah) pehr pee-ah-chAY-reh mee pOHr-tee*
coffee (regular or American)	**caffè**	*kahf-fEH*
■ with milk	**caffelatte**	*kahf-fEH-lAHt-teh*
■ with sugar	**con zucchero**	*kohn tsOO-keh-roh*
■ without sugar	**senza zucchero**	*sEHn-tsah tsOO-keh-roh*
■ with saccharin	**con saccarina**	*kohn sah-kah-rEE-nah*
■ with cream	**con panna**	*kohn pAHn-nah*
Italian coffee	**espresso**	*ehs-prEHs-soh*
■ with anisette	**corretto all' anisetta**	*kohr-rEHt-toh ahl-lah-nee-sAYt-tah*
iced (coffee)	**freddo**	*frAYd-doh*
tea	**tè**	*tEH*
■ with milk	**con latte**	*kohn lAHt-teh*
■ with lemon	**con limone**	*kohn lee-mOH-neh*
■ with sugar	**con zucchero**	*kohn tsOO-keh-roh*
■ iced	**con ghiaccio**	*kohn ghee-AH-chee-oh*
water	**acqua**	*AH-koo-ah*
■ cold	**fredda**	*frAYd-dah*
■ iced	**con ghiaccio**	*kohn ghee-AH-chee-oh*

■ mineral	**minerale**	*mee-neh-rAH-leh*
■ (carbonated)	**gassata**	*gahs-sAH-tah*
■ (non-carbonated)	**naturale**	*nah-too-rAH-leh*
a glass of ____.	**un bicchiere di ____.**	*oon bee-key-EH-reh dee*
■ milk (cold)	**latte (fresco)**	*lAHt-teh (frAY-skoh)*
■ malted milk	**latte con malto**	*lAHt-teh kOHn mAHl-toh*
■ milk shake	**frullato di latte**	*frool-lAH-toh dee lAHt-teh*
■ orangeade	**aranciata**	*ah-rahn-chee-AH-tah*
■ punch	**punch**	*pOHn-ch*
■ soda	**bibita analcolica (soda)**	*bEE-bee-tah ah-nahl-kOH-lee-kah*
■ (fruit) juice	**succo di (frutta)**	*sOO-koh dee (frOOt-tah)*
■ lemonade	**limonata**	*lee-moh-nAH-tah*

SETTLING UP

The bill normally includes a surcharge for service. Tips are never included in the bill and customers leave from 10 to 15 percent of the bill in appreciation of courteous service, only 10 percent if the service wasn't that good.

The check, please.	**Il conto, per favore.**	*eel kOHn-toh pehr fah-vOH-reh*
Separate checks.	**Conti separati.**	*kOHn-tee seh-pah-rAH-tee*
Is the service included?	**È incluso il servizio?**	*EH een-klOO-soh eel sehr-vEE-tsee-oh*

I haven't ordered this.	**Non ho ordinato questo.**	*nohn oh ohr-dee-nAH-toh koo-AY-stoh*
I don't think the bill is right.	**Non penso che il conto sia corretto.**	*nohn pEHn-soh kay eel kOHn-toh sEE-ah kor-rEHt-toh*
We're in a hurry.	**Abbiamo fretta.**	*ahb-bee-AH-moh frAYt-tah*
This is for you.	**Questo è per lei.**	*koo-AYs-toh EH pehr lEH-ee*

REGIONAL ITALIAN SPECIALTIES

We can give only a limited example of the extensive and varied cuisines of Italy. In whatever part of the country you are, ask for the local specialties and regional dishes.

There is no "Italian" cuisine; Italy is divided into regions, and each region has a cuisine based on its resources. Regions that border on the sea are often strong in seafood, while mountainous regions have wonderful meat dishes. Likewise, Italy can be divided somewhat gastronomically north and south, with favorites such as polenta and rice more to the north, while southern regions concentrate on pasta. Likewise, the lusher portions of Italy (mostly in the north) have a cuisine rich with meats and game, whereas the southern regions are poorer and consequently use more vegetables and fish in their dishes. The delicate pasta of the north is enriched with eggs, whereas in the south it is firmer and often factory-made.

There is another thing to note about Italian food, especially in contrast with French food. Italian food is basically from the home—that is, every good cook knows how to make a sauce at home, and the food you get in restaurants is founded on good home cooking. Just as every home has its favorite version of a sauce or soup, so Italian restaurants will differ greatly in their preparations of well-known Italian dishes, such as minestrone.

The following is a list of Italy's regions, along with some of the specialties you are likely to find there.

- VALLE D'AOSTA (Aosta) This northernmost area of Italy is actually French-speaking, but the food is quite coarse, with a lot of game, dark breads, and thick soups. Most famous is the **chamois**, a high mountain goat that is cooked in red wine and spiked with **grappa** (a dry, colorless brandy). **Motzetta** is the name for chamois when it is cured and sliced, served on bread. The sausages are also good here, mostly hard salami types. The **costoletta di vitello con fontina** is a veal chop stuffed with fontina cheese, coated with bread crumbs, and sautéed. Potatoes are usually served with these heavy game and meat dishes. The honey from this region is quite good, as is the butter.

- PIEMONTE (Torino) Turin is the center of this northern region of Italy. The area borders on Switzerland, so one of its famous dishes is **fonduta**, an Italian version of fondue, made with melted fontina cheese lightened with egg yolks and milk, and graced with slivers of white truffles. It is served like a soup, often poured over polenta. Also from this region is **bagna cauda**, a dipping sauce of oil and butter flavored with anchovies and sprinkled with white truffles. The mountain streams flow with trout, which these Italians prepare very simply—broiled or sautéed, sometimes with a touch of sage. **Riso alla piemontese** is stubby Italian rice with white truffles, topped with a meat sauce. For the pasta in this area, you'll most often be served **agnolotti**, small studded pillows. The **gnocchi** here are made with fontina cheese, and the polenta is often topped with melted fontina. For a sweet taste, the people in this region are fond of **gianduiotti**, chocolate drops from Turin.

- LOMBARDIA (Milano) This is a region very rich in good food. The inventiveness of Milanese cooks has made the cuisine famous throughout the world. It is also the region that produces the best-known cheeses, such as Bel Paese, Robiola, Gorgonzola (white), Mascarpone, and Stracchino. Some specialties you're likely to see on a menu are: **ossibuchi** (a veal shank braised in an herbed white wine and tomato sauce), **costoletta alla milanese** (a crisp-fried, breaded veal chop), **polenta** (a cornmeal mush, eaten as an accompaniment to stews and liver, or by itself with cheese or a sauce), **risotto** (a hearty rice dish in which rice is simmered in broth, often with butter, Parmesan cheese, and saffron), **riso con la luganega** (rice cooked with chopped Monza sausage and cheese), **busecca** (stewed tripe, served on French bread and covered with cheese), minestrone with rice, **lesso misto** (often called **bollito misto**, a boiled mixed meats dish in a rich broth), **stufato** (a tender and succulent beef stew), and **panettone** (a buttery yeast cake studded with raisins and candied fruits, usually enjoyed around Christmastime).

● TRENTINO ALTO ADIGE (Bolzano) This area of northern Italy borders on Austria and Switzerland, so don't be surprised to see sauerkraut (**crauti**) or Tirolean noodles. It is a German-speaking area, very mountainous with valleys where rye, corn, and wheat grow. They have what is called the Elephant Platter, an enormous quantity of food including at least 6 types of meats and 12 kinds of vegetables. There are also trout from the streams and much smoked pork. The **nockerln** are similar to gnocchi, offered as an accompaniment to meat dishes. There are also endless varieties of strudel, most of them involving fruits or cream wrapped in a paper-thin crust and sprinkled with chopped nuts.

● VENETO (Venezia, Padova, Verona) Early traders brought many unusual spices and seasonings to Venice, so the food from this area is very colorful. Saffron colors the polenta, while ginger and cloves accent the sweets. Seafood is prominent, with eels a favorite, either fried or marinated. Sardines, mullet, mussels, cuttlefish, and salted cod (**baccalà**) are the foundations for soups (**brodeto**). **Fegato alla veneziana** is a famous dish—thin slices of calf's liver lightly sautéed with onions and butter. Rice plays a prominent role, in **risi e bisi** (rice with peas), in **risotto nero** (rice with octopus), and in multiple other varieties. **Scampi** (shrimp) are served in a myriad of ways, sometimes fried, other times in a dish with rice, or in a soup. This is also an area for sweets, including **fritole di Venezia**, little fritters flavored with cinnamon, raisins, pignoli, and lemon peel. **Focaccia pasquale veneziana** is the traditional Easter cake in the shape of a dove, filled with eggs and sprinkled with kirsch and grappa.

● FRIULI-VENEZIA GIULIA (Trieste) This is not a rich area, so the food of the region reflects that, with an emphasis on poultry rather than meat, soups based on vegetables, and all of it served with a lot of bread. The prosciutto from San Daniele, however, is world famous. The **lujarnis** is their long and thin sausage, usually grilled. **Brovada** is a vegetable dish based on turnips. **Broeto** is a fish chowder, a variation of **brodetto**. In Trieste, the foods reflect some Austrian influences, with **liptauer** (a spreadable mixture of cheese and spices) made from gorgonzola and mascarpone instead. Trieste also has its own versions of calf's liver, flavored with cloves and lemon juice, and its own **risi e bisi**, more of a pea-and-rice puree served over pasta.

● LIGURIA (Genoa) This is a small region, dominated by the city of Genoa, but its foods are vast and varied. There is a lot of seafood, but not as much as you might expect from this seacoast region. From this area come some very famous Italian specialties, including **pesto**, that fragrant puree of basil leaves, olive oil, Parmesan cheese, and pignoli nuts. **Ravioli** is also from here, filled with minced meat and herbs. The minestrone is thick and creamy, varying as much among Ligurian cooks as it does throughout Italy. Also from this region are fish soups that are simply flavored with fennel and/or other herbs. The **focaccia** is a flatbread similar to a pizza without the topping. **Torta pasqualina** is their Easter cake made with many layers of puff pastry, filled with artichoke hearts, hard-cooked eggs, and cheese. For a sweet, **pandolce** is a yeast cake punctuated with grapes, raisins, and pignolis.

● EMILIA-ROMAGNA (Bologna, Ravenna) This region of
northern Italy extends across the country following the
ancient Emilian way. The fertile farmland produces a
lot of wheat for pasta, but the sausages from this region
are also famous, as is its prosciutto from Parma.
Zampone di Mantova is a very large sausage of chopped
seasoned meats and pork skin that is simmered, then
sliced and served with lentils and onions. **Cotechina**,
from Modena, is another sausage, simmered in wine and
served with a thick sauce. From Bologna comes
mortadella, a smooth, heavily spiced sausage that has
traveled around the world as "bologna," and **tortellini**,
circles of pasta that are stuffed with meat and cheese,
then folded into rings and served with a sauce.
Tortellini mantovani are bite-sized pastas stuffed with
pureed pumpkin. When a pasta is served **alla
bolognese**, expect a meat sauce thick with tomatoes.

This region stretches to the Adriatic, and along the
coast you'll find much seafood, particularly turbot
(**rombo**), tuna (**tonno**), mackerel (**sgombero**), mullet
(**barboni, triglie di scoglio**), angler fish (**rospo**), eel
(**anguilla**), octopus (**seppia**), squid (**calamaro,
totano**), spiny lobster (**agagosta**), crayfish
(**gambero**), and scallops (**cappa santa**). For desserts,
this area has to offer the **mandorlini**, an almond-
flavored biscuit, and **crespelli**, strips of dough that are
deep-fried, then dusted with sugar. But this is only a
start of the wonderful foods of this region.

● TOSCANA (Firenze, Pisa) The food of Tuscany is
hearty and simple. This is the region that produces the
best olive oil in Italy, from Lucca. It is also where the
finest beef in Italy is raised and so you will often see on
a menu their Florentine steak, which is similar to a T-
bone. It is served rare, unless you indicate otherwise.
Chicken is served with a ginger sauce, **pollo alla
diavola**; pork is slowly braised in broth and flavored
with rosemary and garlic. **Stracotto alla fiorentina** is
similar to pot roast, with carrots, celery, onions, and
tomatoes. There aren't any exceptional fish dishes
served here, although **baccalà** (salt cod) is popular,

plumped in a tomato sauce. **Caciucco alla livornese** is a fish soup very similar to bouillabaisse that comes from Leghorn. In Pisa, you can eat **le cieche**, baby eels seared in hot oil. In contrast, **ribollita** is a dish of what is essentially leftovers, perked up with a helping of beans, which are a favorite ingredient in these parts. They can also be found in the minestrone, in their rice dishes, and served along with the steak. For dessert, these Italians like **castagnaccio**, a deep-fried chestnut cake.

- MARCHE (Ancona) This is actually several regions put together, so you won't find many unifying dishes; each area of the Marches has a proud cuisine of its own, mostly not known well outside of the area. Some of the famous foods from this region are the stuffed olives (**olive all'ascolana**) from Ascoli Piceno; the **brodetto** (fish chowder), which must always include the **scorfano** (hog fish); and the **porchetta** (roasted suckling pig). Also notable is **vincisgrassi**, a baked layered dish of lasagna, chicken livers, mushrooms, and onions, graced with a béchamel sauce.

- UMBRIA (Perugia) Saddled between the Marches and Lazio, Umbria has a cuisine that blends the heartiness of the mountains with the sophistication of the cities. The food is prepared fairly simply, but often includes some black truffles, which grow in this region. There are other wild mushrooms too, including the fleshy cèpes. Fennel flavors much of the cooking, including the **porchetta** (roast suckling pig). From here we also get **prosciutto di montagna**, a cured mountain ham, and some sheep's milk cheeses, **ravigiolo** and **caciotto**. From Norcia comes a liver sausage, **mazzafegati**. The sweets likely to be found here are **mostaccioli**, a spiced cake, and **pinoccata**, a chocolate-flavored cake made with pignolis.

- LAZIO (Roma) The food of this region centers on Rome, and in Rome you will find many specialties. One common one is **porchetta**, a spit-roasted suckling pig, and another is **abbacchio**, a baby lamb that is roasted with rosemary. **Saltimbocca** (slices of veal topped with prosciutto, then sautéed and sauced with Marsala) comes from Rome, although it appears on menus now in many parts of Italy. **Coda alla vaccinara** is oxtails in a tomato sauce, while **gnocchi alla romana** is that light dumpling, this time made without potatoes and instead with semolina and cheese. **Fettuccine all'Alfredo** is, of course, from Rome's infamous restaurant; this is tagliatelle noodles in a butter and cheese (Parmesan) sauce. Another popular pasta dish is **spaghetti alla carbonara**, in which spaghetti are tossed with bacon, garlic, oil, and Parmesan cheese. The Romans make a **stracciatelle**, which is a chicken or beef broth into which is beaten strands of egg—sort of an egg-drop soup. On menus you'll see some robust fish soups, plus a lot of other seafood: sardines stuffed with spinach, **baccalà** in a tomato sauce, grilled clams (**vongole**). **Stufatino** is a beef stew, **coppa** is head cheese, **trippa alla romana** is tripe that has been simmered with vegetables in a tomato sauce, along with parsley and mint. Vegetables are varied and plentiful, with several preparations for artichokes (including fried in oil until they are black and opened out as a flower), eggplant, spinach, and peppers. For dessert, you'll probably be offered fruit or **budino di rocotta** (cheese pudding). At Christmastime, you'll see **pangiallo**, a fruit-studded cake, and at Easter, **quaresimali**, dry and crisp cookies. **Maritozzi** are soft breakfast buns with raisins.

● ABRUZZO (Pescara, l'Aquila) This is very rugged country, with a coastline that drops sharply to the Adriatic. Therefore, in the food you'll find an abundance of trout from mountain streams, and **scapece**, a pickled fish, flavored with saffron. **Polpi in purgatorio** is a highly spiced cuttlefish; **triglie ripiene** is red mullet, stuffed and baked. The area produces a **prosciutto aquilano** and also liver sausages (**fegati dolci, fegati pazzi**), one sweet and one hot. **Agnello con sottaceti** is a stewed lamb, done up with rosemary and pickled vegetables. This area is famous for its **panarda**, which is a celebratory meal of at least 30 courses.

- MOLISE (Campobasso) This food follows Abruzzo in style, with a few additional specialties such as **capretti al forno** (roasted kid) and **maccheroni alla chitarra**, a homemade macaroni that is cut into slices with guitar strings. The mozzarella here is made from water buffalo milk. **Picellati** are round, crisp biscuits.

- CAMPANIA (Napoli) Much of the Italian food that has traveled to other countries comes originally from Naples. This is the home of the **pizza**, and also of the **calzoni**, basically a pizza that has been wrapped up and sealed around the edges. Mozzarella cheese comes from here, historically made from water buffalo milk but now more commonly from cow's milk; and also **provolone**, both smoked and fresh. Most of the pasta dishes are based on macaroni, made in factories, and in countless widths and lengths. Other dishes are **mozzarella in carrozza**, a simple sandwich of mozzarella cheese between two pieces of bread that is dipped in beaten egg and fried until crisp. There is little meat but a lot of fish on the menus, including **fritto di pesce**, any kind of seafood that has been breaded and deep-fried. **Zuppa alla marinara** is the fish soup from Naples, spiked with garlic and served over fried bread. Desserts here are plentiful, and include babas, **zeppole** (fritters), and, of course, **spumone** (ice cream).

- PUGLIA (Bari) Part of Apulia is the spur of Italy's boot, jutting into the Adriatic, so much of the food of this region is fish and shellfish. In particular, you'll find many preparations of black mussels (**cozze**), as well as **calamaretti in casseruola** (squid stew), baked anchovies, and fried fishes of many other types. The melons (**poponi**) from this area are wonderfully fragrant. Among the pastries, there are **scatagghiett**, honey-dipped bits of pastry; **castagnedi**, chocolate-iced pastries with almond filling; **fichi confettati**, sugar-coated figs; and **pettole**, fritters dusted with sugar.

- BASILICATA (Potenza) The food of this region follows that of Apulia, although the sausages and sauces here are more heavily spiced. The pasta often is a **fusilli** (corkscrew pasta), served with a meat sauce or ricotta. **Maccheroni alla trainiera** is macaroni with capers, garlic, and ginger. On menus, you'll see lamb dishes, some goat, and also game. There are dishes based on beans and bean purees, others with artichokes.

● CALABRIA (Reggio Calabria) This is a poor region, with many mountainous areas and little land in which to grow crops. Where there is land, fruit is grown, especially citrus fruits such as lemons and oranges, some of which are used to make perfume. Except for some sausages, the food is mostly vegetables and pasta. There is not even much cheese. Soups are very good, usually thick, and the pasta is often served with **soffritto** (usually a sauce base but here it is a sauce itself, made with liver, tripe, garlic, and tomatoes). Many pastas are stuffed and baked, such as cannelloni. Tomatoes are also stuffed, as are eggplants and peppers. Sweets include **crocette** (roasted figs), **turiddu** (almond biscuits), and **cannariculi** (fritters soaked in honey).

● SICILIA (Palermo) An island in the Mediterranean, Sicily has a vast array of seafood upon which to base its cuisine. In addition, the soil around Mount Etna is fertile, allowing the people to grow quantities of fruits. This is where the best oranges in Italy come from, and also where most of the almonds are grown. Among the vegetables, tomatoes, beans, peas, and artichokes are exceptional. Leading cheeses are **pecorino siciliano** (a hard romano type), **caciocaballo** (a spicy cow's milk cheese), and **ragusano** (varying in color, also as smoked). Sicily is a large region, and you'll find that each area has its own specialties. A typical dish for the island, however, is **caponata**, a hearty mixture of vegetables, including especially eggplant, in a pickled mixture with capers, olives, and anchovies. You're also likely to find **couscous**, an obvious import from Arabia, but here it is made with fish. Pasta with sardines (**pasta con sarde**) is popular, as is **farsumagru**, a beef roll stuffed with spices and herbs, hard-cooked eggs, and sausage meat. **Arancine** are meat-and-rice balls, while **braciola** is a roast pork with a sweet stuffing of raisins and pignolis. But perhaps the best of Sicily's offerings is its desserts. Most well known are the **cannoli** (cylinders of pastry filled with sweetened ricotta cheese) and **cassata** (a highly variable cake of sponge layers and sweetened ricotta, studded with candied fruits). There are many pastries, but also notable are the **torrone** (nougat) and **frutta candita** (candied fruits). And, of course, the ice cream in Sicily is unmatched.

- SARDEGNA (Cagliari) Like Sicily, Sardinia is a rugged island. The small number of people who live there raise sheep and goats. It is noted for its **pecorino** (sheep's cheese) and its **fiore sardo** (a grating cheese). Their prosciutto from Ogliastra is highly respected, but they also make a **prosciutto di cinghiale**, from wild boar. There isn't much use made of the fish from the waters that surround the island, although the spiny lobster (**aragosta**) is popular. Rather than pasta, this island's people survive on coarse breads. But perhaps the most typical food of this region is the **cinghiale allo spiedo**, a spit-roasted wild boar.

SELECTING ITALIAN WINES

With the exception of some outstanding restaurants where there is a waiter who really knows wines, the waiter is not an expert. He is likely to ask "red wine or white?" as soon as you sit down and before you have decided what to eat. The rule of "red with dark meats and white with chicken, fish, and egg dishes" applies, of course. Wine is the Italian national drink, and if you want the most economical wine, ask for the local open wine (not in bottles but served from large flasks or pitchers) or **vino della casa**. Vintages also are not very important in Italy. The weather is usually good and, except for some dramatic disaster at harvest time, one year is as good as the other. White wines, however, are best when two years old at most; one year is even better.

TYPE OF WINE	SUGGESTED VARIETIES	REGION OF ORIGIN	MAJOR CITY
White Wines			
Dry light-bodied whites	**Est! Est! Est!** **Frascati** **Marino**	Lazio	Rome
	Lugana	Lombardy	Milan
	Pinot Bianco **Pinot Grigio**	Veneto and Friuli-Venezia Giulia	Venice Trieste
Dry medium-bodied whites	**Orvieto** **Secco**	Umbria	Perugia
	Soave	Veneto	Venezia
	Tocai	Friuli-Venezia Giulia	Trieste
	Trebbiano di Romagna	Emilia-Romagna	Bologna
	Verdicchio	Marche	Ancona
Mellow whites	**Orvieto** **Abboccato**	Umbria	Perugia
	Prosecco	Veneto	Venice

TYPE OF WINE	SUGGESTED VARIETIES	REGION OF ORIGIN	MAJOR CITY
	Red Wines		
Semidry reds	**Lambrusco**	Emilia Romagna	Bologna
Dry light-bodied reds	**Bardolino** **Valpolicella**	Veneto Veneto	Lake Garda
Dry medium-bodied reds	**Castel del Monte Rosso**	Apulia	Bari
	Cabernet	Trentino Alto Adige	Bolzano
	Chianti	Tuscany	Florence
	Dolcetto Freisa Grignolino Nebbiolo	Piedmont	Turin
	Montepulciano d'Abruzzo	Abruzzo and Molise	L'Aquila Campobasso
	Merlot	Friuli-Venezia Giulia	Udine
	Sangiovese di Romagna	Emilia-Romagna	Bologna
	Sassella	Lombardy	Milan
	Torgiano Rosso	Umbria	Perugia

TYPE OF WINE	SUGGESTED VARIETIES	REGION OF ORIGIN	MAJOR CITY
Robust Reds			
	Barbaresco Barbera d'Asti Barolo Carema Gattinara Ghemme	Piedmont	Turin
	Brunello di Montalcino Chianti Riserva Vino Nobile di Montepulciano	Tuscany	Florence
	Inferno	Lombardy	Milan
Rosé Wines			
	Castel del Monte	Apulia	Bari
	Chiaretto	Lombardy	Milan

TYPE OF WINE	SUGGESTED VARIETIES	REGION OF ORIGIN	MAJOR CITY
Dessert Wines			
Caluso Passito		Piedmont	Turin
Marsala **Moscato di** **Pantelleria**		Sicily	Palermo
Vin Santo		Trentino Alto Adige	Bolzano
Moscato **d'Asti**		Piedmont	Asti
Sparkling Wines			
Asti **Spumante** **Nebbiolo** **Spumante**		Piedmont	Turin

MEETING PEOPLE

Italians are hospitable. They are curious and friendly, even desirous of getting acquainted with travelers.

SMALL TALK

My name is ____.	**Il mio nome è ____.** *eel mEE-oh nOH-meh EH*
Do you live here?	**Lei abita qui?** *lEH-ee AH-bee-tah koo-EE*
Where are you from?	**Lei di dov'è?** *lEH-ee dee doh-vEH*
I am ____.	**Vengo ____.** *vEHn-goh*
■ from the United States	**dagli Stati Uniti** *dAH-ly-ee stAH-tee oo-nEE-tee*
■ from Canada	**dal Canadà** *dAHl kah-nah-dAH*
■ from England	**dall'Inghilterra** *dahl-lEEn-gheel-tEHr-rah*
■ from Australia	**dall'Australia** *dahl-lah-oos-trAH-lee-ah*
I like Italy (Rome) very much.	**L'Italia (Roma) mi piace moltissimo.** *lee-tAH-lee-ah (rOH-mah) mee pee-AH-cheh mohl-tEEs-see-moh*
I would like to go there.	**Mi piacerebbe andarci.** *mee pee-ah-cheh-rAYb-beh ahn-dAHr-chee*
How long will you be staying?	**Quanto tempo resterà qui?** *koo-AHn-toh tEHm-poh reh-steh-rAH koo-EE*
I'll stay for a few days (a week).	**Resterò alcuni giorni (una settimana).** *reh-steh-rOH ahl-kOO-nee jee-OHr-nee (OO-nah seht-tee-mAH-nah)*

What hotel are you staying at?	**In quale hotel (albergo) sta?** *een koo-AH-leh oh-tEHl (ahl-bEHr-goh) stAH*
What do you think of it?	**Che ne pensa?** *kay nay pEHn-sah*
I (don't) like it very much.	**(Non) mi piace tanto.** *(nohn) mee pee-AH-cheh tAHn-toh*
I think it's ____.	**Penso che sia ____.** *pEHn-soh kay sEE-ah*
■ beautiful	**bello** *bEHl-loh*
■ interesting	**interessante** *een-teh-rehs-sAHn-teh*
■ magnificent	**splendido (magnifico)** *splEHn-dee-doh (mah-ny-EE-fee-koh)*
■ wonderful	**stupendo** *stoo-pEHn-doh*
May I introduce ____?	**Posso presentarle ____?** *pOHs-soh preh-sehn-tAHr-leh*
■ my brother (sister)	**mio fratello (mia sorella)** *mEE-oh frah-tEHl-loh (mEE-ah soh-rEHl-lah)*
■ my father (mother)	**mio padre (mia madre)** *mEE-oh pAH-dreh (mEE-ah mAH-dreh)*
■ my friend	**il mio amico** *eel mEE-oh ah-mEE-koh*
■ my husband (wife)	**mio marito (mia moglie)** *mEE-oh mah-rEE-toh (mEE-ah mOH-ly-ee-eh)*
■ my sweetheart	**il mio ragazzo (la mia ragazza)** *eel mEE-oh rah-gAH-tsoh (lah mEE-ah rah-gAH-tsah)*
■ my son (daughter)	**mio figlio (mia figlia)** *mEE-oh fEE-ly-ee-oh (mEE-ah fEE-ly-ee-ah)*
Glad to meet you.	**Piacere. Lieto(a) di conoscerla.** *pee-ah-chAY-reh lee-EH-toh(ah) dee koh-nOH-shehr-lah*

How do you do?	**Come sta?** *kOH-meh stah*
I am a(n) _____.	**Sono** _____. *sOH-noh*
■ accountant	**ragioniere** *rah-jee-oh-nee-EH-reh*
■ artist	**artista** *ahr-tEEs-tah*
■ businessperson	**persona d'affari** *pehr-sOH-nah dahf-fAH-ree*
■ construction worker	**operaio edile** *oh-peh-rAH-ee-oh eh-dEE-leh*
■ cook	**cuoco** *koo-OH-koh*
■ dentist	**dentista** *dehn-tEE-stah*
■ doctor	**dottore (dottoressa)** *doht-tOH-reh (doht-toh-rAYs-sah)*
■ firefighter	**vigile del fuoco** *vEE-jee-leh dayl foo-OH-koh*
■ hairdresser	**parrucchiere(a)** *pahr-roo-key-AY-reh(ah)*
■ lawyer	**avvocato (avvocatessa)** *ahv-voh-kAH-toh (ahv-voh-kah-tAYs-sah)*
■ manager	**dirigente (manager)** *dee-ree-jEHn-teh (manager)*
■ nurse	**infermiere(a)** *een-fehr-mee-EH-reh(ah)*
■ police officer	**poliziotto(a)** *poh-lee-tzee-OHt-toh(ah)*
■ salesperson	**commesso(a)** *kohm-mAYs-soh(ah)*
■ secretary	**segretario(a)** *seh-greh-tAH-ree-oh(ah)*
■ student	**studente (studentessa)** *stoo-dEHn-teh (stoo-dehn-tAYs-sah)*
■ teacher	**maestro(a)** *mah-AYs-troh(ah)*
■ waiter (waittress)	**cameriere(a)** *kah-meh-ree-EH-reh(ah)*

Would you like a picture (snapshot)?	**Vuole che le scatti una foto (un'instantanea)?** *voo-OH-leh kay leh skAHt-tee OO-nah fOH-toh (oon-een-stahn-tAH-neh-ah)*
Stand here (there).	**Si metta qui (lì).** *see mAYt-tah koo-EE (lEE)*
Don't move.	**Non si muova.** *nohn see moo-OH-vah*
Smile. That's it.	**Sorrida. Ecco fatto.** *sohr-rEE-dah EH-koh fAHt-toh*
Will you take a picture of me (us)?	**Può farmi (farci) una foto?** *poo-OH fAHr-mee (fAHr-chee) OO-nah fOH-toh*

DATING AND SOCIALIZING

| May I have this dance? | **Le piacerebbe ballare con me?** *leh pee-ah-cheh-rAYb-beh bahl-lAH-reh kohn mAY* |

With pleasure.	**Con piacere.** *kohn pee-ah-chAY-reh*
Would you like a drink (a cigarette)?	**Potrei offrirle da bere (una sigaretta)?** *poh-trEH-ee ohf-frEEr-leh dah bAY-reh (OO-nah see-gah-rAYt-tah)*
Do you have a light (matches)?	**Ha un accendino (un fiammifero)?** *ah oon ah-chayn-dEE-noh (oon fee-ahm-mEE-feh-roh)*
Do you mind if I smoke?	**Le dispiace se fumo?** *leh dee-spee-AH-cheh say fOO-moh*
May I call you?	**Posso telefonarle?** *pOHs-soh teh-leh-foh-nAHr-leh*
May I take you home?	**L'accompagno a casa?** *lahk-kohm-pAH-ny-oh ah kAH-sah*
Are you doing anything tomorrow?	**Che fa domani?** *kay fAH doh-mAH-nee*
Are you free this evening?	**È libero(a) stasera?** *EH lEE-beh-roh(ah) stah-sAY-rah*
Would you like to go to _____ together?	**Le piacerebbe andare insieme a _____?** *leh pee-ah-cheh-rEHb-beh ahn-dAH-reh een-see-EH-meh ah*
I'll wait for you in front of the hotel.	**L'aspetterò davanti all'hotel (all'albergo).** *lah-speht-teh-rOH dah-vAHn-tee ahl-loh-tEHl (ahl-lahl-bEHr-goh)*
I'll pick you up at your house (hotel).	**La verrò a prendere a casa sua (all'hotel).** *lah vehr-rOH ah prAYn-day-reh ah kAH-sah sOO-ah (ahl-loh-tEHl)*
What is your telephone number?	**Qual è il suo numero di telefono?** *koo-ahl-EH eel sOO-oh nOO-meh-roh dee teh-lEH-foh-noh*

Here's my telephone number (address).	**Ecco il mio numero di telefono (indirizzo).** *EHk-koh eel mEE-oh nOO-meh-roh dee teh-lEH-foh-noh (een-dee-rEE-tsoh)*
I'm single (married).	**Sono scapolo nubile (sposato[a]).** *sOH-noh scAH-poh-loh nOO-bih-leh (spoh-sAH-toh[ah])*
Is your husband (wife) here?	**Sta qui suo marito (la signora)?** *stAH koo-EE sOO-oh mah-rEE-toh (lah see-ny-OH-rah)*
I'm here with my family.	**Sono qui con la mia famiglia.** *sOH-noh koo-EE kohn lah mEE-ah fah-mEE-ly-ee-ah*
Do you have any children?	**Ha bambini?** *AH bahm-bEE-nee*
How many?	**Quanti?** *koo-AHn-tee*
How old are they?	**Quanti anni hanno?** *koo-AHn-tee AHn-nee AHn-noh*

SAYING GOOD-BYE

Nice to have met you.	**È stato un piacere conoscerla.** *EH stAH-toh oon pee-ah-chAY-reh koh-nOH-shehr-lah*
The pleasure was mine.	**Il piacere è stato mio.** *eel pee-ah-chAY-reh EH stAH-toh mEE-oh*
Regards to ____.	**Saluti a ____.** *sah-lOO-tee ah*
Thanks for the evening.	**Grazie della serata.** *grAH-tsee-eh dAYl-lah say-rAH-tah*
I must go home now.	**Adesso devo andarmene a casa.** *ah-dEHs-soh dAY-voh ahn-dAHr-meh-neh ah kAH-sah*

| You must come to visit us. | **Deve venire a farci visita.** | *dAY-veh veh-nEE-reh ah fAHr-chee vEE-see-tah* |

Travel Tips Save receipts on foreign purchases for declaring at customs on reentry to the U.S. Some countries return a sales or value-added tax to foreign visitors. Take receipts to a special office at the store or to a tax rebate window at the airport of departure. Americans who buy costly objects abroad may be surprised to get a bill from their state tax collector. Most states with a sales tax levy a "use" tariff on all items bought outside the home state, including those purchased abroad. Most tax agencies in these states will send a form for declaring and paying the assessment.

SHOPPING

Italian retail stores close for the mid-afternoon, usually between 1 and 4 P.M., but the closing hours vary slightly from place to place and according to the season.

Pharmacies (chemists) also observe the middle-of-the-day closing, but they are open on a rotation basis on holidays (see page 239), including Sundays, when the name and address of the nearest one open is posted on the front door of each pharmacy that is closed.

During the summer, especially from July 15 to September 1, most smaller stores close for vacation periods of their own choosing. For this reason, tourists will find that not all stores are open at a given time during the summer vacation period.

TYPICAL ARTS AND CRAFTS

Italy offers a wide range of traditional arts and crafts. Each region, city, village, and town has its own variety of products. Bargaining for the item you wish is apt to be a new experience but the shopkeepers and merchants expect it. Here are some tips on what to look for in Italy's different regions.

- VALLE D'AOSTA (Aosta)—Laces, embossed copper wares, leather articles, and wood-carved jugs.

- PIEMONTE (Torino)—Wood-carved chamois and steenbok, woodworked boxes of Gran San Bernardo, and local pottery.

- LOMBARDIA (Milano)—Pottery of Laveno, printed silk of Como, rubber toys, shoes of Vigevano, laces of Cantù, accordions, and carpets. Best buys: silk dresses, latest fashions in the boutiques, leather goods.

- TRENTINO ALTO ADIGE (Bolzano, Trento)—Woodworks of Val Gardena, cuckoo clocks, knick-knacks made of onyx and horn, straw hats of Bessanone, bowls of Martello.

- VENETO (Venezia)—Glass and crystals of Murano, laces of Burano, wrought iron, mosaics, leather articles, woodworks, kettles, and pipes. Best buys: glassware, antiques.

- FRIULI-VENEZIA GIULIA (Trieste)—Knives, mosaics, hempen clothes, linen, and wooden shoes.

- LIGURIA (Genova)—Embroidered silk shawls, laces of Santa Margherita, bottled miniature vessels, pottery of Albisona and Savona.

- EMILIA-ROMAGNA (Bologna, Ravenna)—Pottery of Faenza, wrought iron and woodwork of Grazzano Visconti, laces of Forlì, and copper engravings of Ravenna.

- TOSCANA (Firenze, Pisa)—Alabaster of Volterra, statuettes made with marble sawdust of Lucca, straw hats, prime light-grain florentine leather goods, pottery, and embroidery. Best buys: shoes, cameos, brushed gold (*satinato*), jewelry, silk.

- MARCHE (Ancona)—Accordions of Castelfidardo, Osimo, Numana, and Recanati; pottery of Urbino, Ascoli, and Pesaro; laces of Offida, in the province of Ascoli Piceno; and articles of straw.

- UMBRIA (Perugia)—Artistic pottery of Orvieto, Gubbio, Deruta, Perugia, Gualdo Tadino, and Città di Castello; textiles and laces of Assisi; inlaid furniture, wood carving, and wrought iron of Perugia, Gubbio, and Todi.

- LAZIO (Roma)—Copper wares of Fiuggi, carpets of Veroli, pottery of Civita Castellana, wrought iron of Ciociaria, and pillow laces. Best buys: luggage, leather goods, shoes, antiques, old books and prints.

- ABRUZZO (Pescara, L'Aquila)—Embossed copper wares, wrought iron, wood carving, carpets, textiles, laces, jeweler's wares, and artistic pottery.

- MOLISE (Campobasso)—Multicolored pottery, laces, dressed stones, wrought iron, watermarked papers, and jeweler's wares.

- CAMPANIA (Napoli)—Porcelain of Capodimonte, leather gloves of Naples, corals of Torre del Greco, pearls, textiles and silk, straw and wicker works, wrought iron and inlaid furniture. Best buys: coral items, cameos. Note: Do not buy tortoiseshell; the U.S. forbids you to bring it in.

- PUGLIA (Bari)—Textiles (particularly woolens), tobacco pipes, embroidery, carpets, and tapestry.
- BASILICATA (Potenza)—Pottery of Potenza, woodworks, copper wares and wrought iron, embroidery, and handwoven textiles.
- CALABRIA (Reggio Calabria, Catanzaro)—Leather articles, laces, inlaid furniture, painted amphorae, and hand-woven textiles; string instruments of Bisignano and gold of Crotone.
- SICILIA (Palermo)—Sicilian handcarts, puppets of Palermo, corals, mandolins and guitars of Catania, marble sculptures, and articles of alabaster.
- SARDEGNA (Cagliari)—Carpets, textiles, blankets of lively colors, baskets made with reeds and rush, laces, earthenware, pottery, and wrought iron.

FLEA MARKETS

- CALABRIA (Cosenza)—in Via Lungo Crati de Seta. Every day.
- CAMPANIA (Benevento)—in Piazza Risorgimento and in Piazza Santa Maria. Wednesdays and Saturdays from 8:00 A.M. to 1 P.M.
- CAMPANIA (Napoli)—The *Weekend Market* in Viale Dohrn of the Villa Comunale. Twice a month.

  The *Crib Figurines Market* in Via San Gregorio Armeno. Year-round.

  The *Food Market* in Porta Nolana. Year-round.
- EMILIA-ROMAGNA (Ferrara)—in Piazza Travaglio. Every Monday.
- EMILIA-ROMAGNA (Modena)—in Via Corso Cavour, Viale Beregario, and Viale Fontanelli. Mondays from 8:00 A.M. to 1:00 P.M.
- LAZIO (Latina)—The *American Market* in Via Ardea, Via Mugilla, Via Quarto, and Via Sulmo. Every Tuesday from 8:00 A.M. to 1:30 P.M.

- LAZIO (Roma)—in Porta Portese. Every Sunday from 8:00 A.M. to 2:00 P.M.
  —in Via Sannio, near Piazza San Giovanni. Every day but Sunday from 8:00 A.M. till sundown.

- LIGURIA (Arma Di Taggia) (Imperia)—Every fourth Saturday and Sunday of the month.

- LIGURIA (Genova)—in Piazzetta Lavagna, off Via Luccoli. Weekdays, mornings and afternoons.

- LOMBARDIA (Milano)—in the *Senigaglia Market* in Via Calatafimi. Every Saturday from 8:00 A.M. to 7:00 P.M. The *Oh Bei! Oh Bei! Market* in Piazza Sant'Ambrogio. Every year from December 5th to December 8th.

- SICILIA (Catania)—in Piazza Carlo Alberto. Every day but Sunday from 8:00 A.M. to 2:00 P.M.

- SICILIA (Messina)—at the intersection of Via La Farina and Viale Europa. Every day during morning hours.

- SICILIA (Palermo)—in Piazza Domenico Peranni. Weekdays from 9:00 A.M. till sundown. Sundays and holidays till 1:00 P.M.

- TOSCANA (Arezzo)—The *Antique Fair* in Piazza Grande. The first Saturday and Sunday of every month from Saturday morning to Sunday evening.

- TOSCANA (Firenze)—in Piazza dei Ciompi. The last Sunday of every month. Open all day as per local shop hours.

- TOSCANA (Forte Dei Marmi) (Lucca)—in Piazza del Mercato. Wednesday mornings from 8:00 A.M.

- TOSCANA (Grosseto)—in Piazza de Maria and beneath the walls.

- TOSCANA (Livorno)—The *American Market* in Piazza XX Settembre. Open every day from 9:00 A.M. to 7:30 P.M.

- TOSCANA (Lucca)—in Piazza del Duomo and nearby Via del Battistero. The third Saturday and Sunday of every month. Closed on religious holidays.

- TOSCANA (Viareggio) (Lucca)—in Piazzetta near the dock. Every Thursday morning.

GOING SHOPPING

Where can I find ____?	**Dove posso trovare ____?** *dOH-veh pOHs-soh troh-vAH-reh*
■ a bakery	**un fornaio** *oon fohr-nAH-ee-oh*
■ a bookstore	**una libreria** *OO-nah lee-bray-rEE-ah*
■ a butcher	**una macelleria** *OO-nah mah-chehl-leh-rEE-ah*
■ a camera shop	**un negozio di fotocine** *oon neh-gOH-tsee-oh dee foh-toh-chEE-neh*
■ a candy store	**un sale e tabacchi** *oon sAH-leh ay tah-bAH-key*
■ a clothing store	**un negozio di abbigliamento** *oon neh-gOH-tsee-oh dee ahb-bee-ly-ee-ah-mEHn-toh*
■ for children's clothes	**per bambini** *pehr bahm-bEE-nee*
■ men's store	**per uomini** *pehr oo-OH-mee-nee*
■ women's boutique	**per signore** *pehr see-ny-OH-reh*
■ a delicatessen	**una salumeria** *OO-nah sah-loo-meh-rEE-ah*
■ a department store	**i grandi magazzini** *ee grAHn-dee mah-gah-tsEE-nee*
■ a pharmacy (chemist)	**una farmacia** *OO-nah fahr-mah-chEE-ah*
■ a florist	**un fioraio** *oon fee-oh-rAH-ee-oh*
■ a gift (souvenir) shop	**un negozio di regali (souvenir)** *oon neh-gOH-tsee-oh dee reh-gAH-lee (soo-vay-nEEr)*
■ a grocery store	**un negozio di alimentari** *oon neh-gOH-tsee-oh dee ah-lee-mehn-tAH-ree*

■ a hardware store (ironmonger)
un negozio di ferramenta *oon neh-gOH-tsee-oh dee fehr-rah-mEHn-tah*

■ a jewelry store
una gioielleria *OO-nah jee-oh-ee-ehl-leh-rEE-ah*

■ a liquor store
una enoteca *OO-nah eh-noh-tEH-kah*

■ a newsstand
un'edicola (il giornalaio) *oo-neh-dEE-koh-lah (eel jee-ohr-nah-lAH-ee-oh)*

■ a record store
un negozio di dischi *oon neh-gOH-tsee-oh dee dEE-skey*

■ a supermarket
un supermercato *oon soo-pehr-mehr-kAH-toh*

■ a tobacco shop
una tabaccherìa *OO-nah tah-bahk-keh-rEE-ah*

■ a toy store
un negozio di giocattoli *oon neh-gOH-tsee-oh dee jee-oh-kAHt-toh-lee*

■ a wine shop
una mescita, una cantina, una enoteca *OO-nah mAY-shee-tah OO-nah kahn-tEE-nah OO-nah eh-noh-tEH-kah*

Young man, can you wait on me?
Giovanotto, può occuparsi di me? *jee-oh-vah-nOHt-toh poo-OH ohk-koo-pAHr-see dee meh*

Miss, can you help me?
Signorina, può aiutarmi? *see-ny-oh-rEE-nah poo-OH ah-ee-oo-tAHr-mee*

Do you take credit cards?
Accettano carte di credito? *ah-chEHt-tah-noh kAHr-teh dee krEH-dee-toh*

Can I pay with a traveler's check?
Posso pagare con un traveler's check? *pOHs-soh pah-gAH-reh kohn oon trAH-veh-lehs chEH-keh*

BOOKS

Is there a store that carries English-language books?	**C'è un negozio dove si vendono libri in lingua inglese?** *chEH oon neh-gOH-tsee-oh dOH-veh see vAYn-doh-noh lEE-bree een lEEn-goo-ah een-glAY-seh*
What is the best (biggest) bookstore here?	**Dov'è la migliore (la più grande) libreria qui?** *doh-vEH lah mee-ly-ee-OH-reh (lah pee-OO grAHn-deh) lee-breh-rEE-ah koo-EE*
I'm looking for a copy of ____.	**M'interessa una copia di ____.** *meen-teh-rEHs-sah OO-nah kOH-pee-ah dee*
The author of the book is ____.	**L'autore del libro è ____.** *lah-oo-tOH-reh dayl lEE-broh EH*
I'm just looking.	**Sto solo guardando.** *stoh sOH-loh goo-ahr-dAHn-doh*
Do you have books (novels) in English?	**Ha libri (romanzi) in inglese?** *ah lEE-bree (roh-mAHn-tsee) een een-glAY-seh*
I want ____.	**Desidero ____.** *deh-sEE-deh-roh*
■ a guide book	**una guida** *OO-nah goo-EE-dah*
■ a map of this city	**una pianta di questa città** *OO-nah pee-AHn-tah dee koo-AYs-tah cheet-tAH*
■ a pocket dictionary	**un dizionario tascabile** *oon dee-tsee-oh-nAH-ree-oh tah-skAH-bee-leh*
■ an Italian-English dictionary	**un dizionario italiano-inglese** *oon dee-tsee-oh-nAH-ree-oh ee-tah-lee-AH-noh een-glAY-seh*
Where can I find ____?	**Dove posso trovare ____?** *dOH-veh pOHs-soh troh-vAH-reh*

■ detective stories	**romanzi gialli**	*roh-mAHn-tsee jee-AHl-lee*
■ comics	**fumetti**	*foo-mAYt-tee*
■ history books	**libri di storia**	*lEE-bree dee stOH-ree-ah*
■ short stories	**una raccolta di novelle**	*OO-nah rahk-kOHl-tah dee noh-vEHl-leh*
■ cookbooks	**libri di cucina**	*lEE-bree dee koo-chEE-nah*

I'll take these books.	**Prendo questi libri.** *prAYn-doh koo-AYs-tee lEE-bree*
Will you wrap them, please?	**Me l'incarta, per favore?** *meh leen-kAHr-tah pehr fah-vOH-reh*

CLOTHING

Is this the _____ department?	**È questo il reparto (la sezione) di _____?** *EH koo-AYs-toh eel ray-pAHr-toh (lah say-tzee-OH-neh) dee*
Would you please show me _____?	**Per favore, può mostrarmi _____?** *pehr fah-vOH-reh poo-OH moh-strAHr-mee*
■ a bathing suit	**un costume da bagno** *oon koh-stOO-meh dah bAH-ny-ee-oh*
■ a man's (lady's) belt	**una cintura per uomo (per signora)** *OO-nah cheen-tOO-rah pehr oo-OH-moh (pehr see-ny-OH-rah)*
■ a blouse	**una blusa (camicetta)** *OO-nah blOO-sah (kah-mee-chAYt-tah)*
■ boots	**degli stivali** *dAY-ly-ee stee-vAH-lee*
■ a bra	**un reggiseno** *oon reh-jee-sAY-noh*
■ a dress	**una veste** *OO-nah vEH-steh*
■ an evening gown	**un abito da sera** *oon AH-bee-toh dah sAY-rah*

■ leather (suede) gloves	**dei guanti di pelle (scamosciata)**	*dAY-ee goo-AHn-tee dee pEHl-leh (skah-moh-shee-AH-tah)*
■ handkerchiefs	**dei fazzoletti**	*dAY-ee fah-tsoh-lAYt-tee*
■ a hat	**un cappello**	*oon kahp-pEHl-loh*
■ a jacket	**una giacca**	*OO-nah jee-AHk-kah*
■ jeans	**dei jeans**	*dAY-ee jeans*
■ a jogging suit	**un completo per jogging**	*oon kohm-plEH-toh pehr jogging*
■ an overcoat	**un soprabito**	*oon soh-prAH-bee-toh*
■ pajamas	**dei pigiama**	*dAY-ee pee-jee-AH-mah*
■ panties	**delle mutandine**	*dAYl-leh moo-tahn-dEE-neh*
■ pants	**dei pantaloni**	*dAY-ee pahn-tah-lOH-nee*
■ panty hose	**un collant**	*oon koh-lAHn*
■ a raincoat	**un impermeabile**	*oon eem-pehr-meh-AH-bee-leh*
■ a robe (for lady)	**una vestaglia**	*OO-nah veh-stAH-ly-ee-ah*
■ a robe (for man)	**una veste da camera**	*OO-nah vEH-steh dah kAH-meh-rah*
■ sandals	**dei sandali**	*dAY-ee sAHn-dah-lee*
■ sneakers	**delle scarpette**	*dAYl-leh skahr-pAYt-teh*
■ a shirt	**una camicia**	*OO-nah kah-mEE-chee-ah*
■ (a pair of) shoes	**un paio di scarpe**	*oon pAH-ee-oh dee skAHr-peh*
■ shorts (briefs)	**dei pantaloncini (delle mutande)**	*dAY-ee pahn-tah-lohn-chEE-nee (dAYl-leh moo-tAHn-deh)*
■ a skirt	**una gonna**	*OO-nah gOHn-nah*

■ a slip	**una sottoveste** *OO-nah soht-toh-vEH-steh*
■ slippers	**delle pantofole** *dAYl-leh pahn-tOH-foh-leh*
■ socks	**dei calzini** *dAY-ee kahl-tsEE-nee*
■ stockings	**delle calze** *dAYl-leh kAHl-tseh*
■ a suit	**un vestito** *oon veh-stEE-toh*
■ a sweater	**una maglia** *OO-nah mAH-ly-ah*
■ a tee-shirt	**una maglietta** *OO-nah mah-ly-ee-AYt-tah*
■ a tie	**una cravatta** *OO-nah krah-vAHt-tah*
■ an undershirt	**una canottiera** *OO-nah kah-noht-tee-EH-rah*
■ underwear	**della biancheria intima** *dAYl-lah bee-ahn-keh-rEE-ah EEn-tee-mah*
■ a wallet	**un portafoglio** *oon pohr-tah-fOH-ly-ee-oh*
Is there a special sale today?	**Oggi c'è una vendita d'occasione?** *OH-jee chEH OO-nah vAYn-dee-tah dohk-kah-see-OH-neh*
I'd like a shirt with short (long) sleeves.	**Vorrei una camicia con le maniche corte (lunghe).** *vohr-rEH-ee OO-nah kah-mEE-chee-ah kohn leh mAH-nee-keh kOHr-teh (lOOn-gheh)*
Do you have anything _____?	**Ha qualche cosa _____?** *AH koo-AHl-keh kOH-sah*
■ else	**d'altro** *dAHl-troh*
■ larger	**più grande** *pee-OO grAHn-deh*
■ less expensive	**meno costoso** *mAY-noh koh-stOH-soh*
■ longer	**più lungo** *pee-OO lOOn-goh*

■ of better quality	**di migliore qualità**	*dee mee-ly-ee-OH-reh koo-ah-lee-tAH*
■ shorter	**più corto**	*pee-OO kOHr-toh*
■ smaller	**più piccolo**	*pee-OO pEE-koh-loh*
I don't like the color.	**Non mi piace il colore.**	*nohn mee pee-AH-cheh eel koh-lOH-reh*
Do you have it in _____?	**Lo ha in _____?**	*loh AH een*
■ black	**nero**	*nAY-roh*
■ blue	**blu**	*blOO*
■ brown	**marrone**	*mahr-rOH-neh*
■ gray	**grigio**	*grEE-jee-oh*
■ green	**verde**	*vAYr-deh*
■ pink	**rosa**	*rOH-sah*
■ red	**rosso**	*rOHs-soh*
■ white	**bianco**	*bee-AHn-koh*
■ yellow	**giallo**	*jee-AHl-loh*

SALE SIGNS

SVENDITA	(sale)
SALDI DI FINE STAGIONE	(end-of-season sale)
LIQUIDAZIONE	(everything must go)
VENDITA TOTALE	
PREZZI FISSI	(fixed prices)

I want something in ____.	**Voglio qualche cosa ____.** *vOH-ly-ee-oh koo-AHl-keh kOH-sah*
■ chiffon	**di chiffon** *dee sheef-fOHn*
■ corduroy	**di velluto a coste** *dee vehl-lOO-toh ah kOH-steh*
■ cotton	**di cotone** *dee koh-tOH-neh*
■ denim	**di denim** *dee dEH-nim*
■ felt	**di feltro** *dee fAYl-troh*
■ flannel	**di flanella** *dee flah-nEHl-lah*
■ gabardine	**di gabardine** *dee gah-bahr-dEE-neh*
■ lace	**in pizzo** *een pEE-tsoh*
■ leather	**in pelle** *een pEHl-leh*
■ linen	**di lino** *dee lEE-noh*
■ nylon	**di nylon** *dee nAH-ee-lohn*
■ permanent press	**con piega permanente** *kohn pee-EH-gah pehr-mah-nEHn-teh*
■ satin	**di raso** *dee rAH-soh*
■ silk	**di seta** *dee sAY-tah*
■ suede	**di renna** *dee rAYn-nah*

■ synthetic (polyester)   **in poliestere**   *een poh-lee-EH-steh-reh*

■ terrycloth   **in tessuto spugnoso**   *een tehs-sOO-toh spoo-ny-OH-soh*

■ velvet   **di velluto**   *dee vehl-lOO-toh*

■ wool   **di lana**   *dee lAH-nah*

■ wash-and-wear   **che non si stira**   *kay nohn see stEE-rah*

Show me something _____.   **Mi faccia vedere qualche cosa _____.**   *mee fAH-chee-ah veh-dAY-reh koo-AHl-kay kOH-sah*

■ in a solid color   **a tinta unita**   *ah tEEn-tah oo-nEE-tah*

■ with stripes   **a righe**   *ah rEE-gheh*

■ with polka dots   **a pallini**   *ah pahl-lEE-nee*

■ in plaid   **a quadri**   *ah koo-AH-dree*

Could you take my measurements?   **Può prendermi le misure?**   *poo-OH prEHn-dayr-mee leh mee-sOO-reh*

I take size (my size is) _____.   **La mia taglia è _____.**   *lah mEE-ah tAH-ly-ee-ah EH*

■ small   **piccola**   *pEEk-koh-lah*

■ medium   **media**   *mEH-dee-ah*

■ large   **grande**   *grAHn-deh*

Can I try it on?   **Posso provarmelo(la)?**   *pOHs-soh proh-vAHr-meh-loh(lah)*

Can you alter it?   **Può aggiustarmelo(la)?**   *poo-OH ah-jee-oo-stAHr-meh-loh(lah)*

Can I return the article (if I change my mind)?   **(Se non mi va), posso portarlo indietro?**   *(say nohn mee vAH) pOHs-soh pohr-tAHr-loh een-dee-EH-troh*

Do you have something handmade?   **Non c'è nulla che sia fatto a mano?**   *nohn chEH nOOl-lah kay sEE-ah fAHt-toh ah mAH-noh*

CLOTHING MEASUREMENTS

WOMEN

Shoes

American	4	5	6	7	8	9
British	3	4	5	6	7	8
Continental	35	36	37	38	39	40

Dresses, suits

American	8	10	12	14	16	18
British	10	12	14	16	18	20
Continental	36	38	40	42	44	46

Blouses, sweaters

American	32	34	36	38	40	42
British	34	36	38	40	42	44
Continental	40	42	44	46	48	50

MEN

Shoes

American	7	8	9	10	11	12
British	6	7	8	9	10	11
Continental	39	41	43	44	45	46

Suits, coats

American	34	36	38	40	42	44	46	48
British	44	46	48	50	54	56	58	60
Continental	44	46	48	50	52	54	56	58

Shirts

American	14	$14\frac{1}{2}$	15	$15\frac{1}{2}$	16	$16\frac{1}{2}$	17	$17\frac{1}{2}$
British	14	$14\frac{1}{2}$	15	$15\frac{1}{2}$	16	$16\frac{1}{2}$	17	$17\frac{1}{2}$
Continental	36	37	38	39	40	41	42	43

The zipper doesn't work.	**La cerniera non funziona.** *lah chehr-nee-EH-rah nohn fOOn-tsee-OH-nah*
It doesn't fit me.	**Non mi sta bene.** *nohn mee stAH bEH-neh*
It fits very well.	**Mi sta molto bene.** *mee stAH mOHl-toh bEH-neh*
I'll take it.	**Lo(la) prendo.** *loh(lah) prAYn-doh*
Will you wrap it?	**Me lo(la) impacchetta?** *meh loh(lah) eem-pahk-kEHt-tah*
I'd like to see the pair of shoes (boots) in the window.	**Vorrei vedere il paio di scarpe (stivali) in vetrina.** *vohr-rEH-ee veh-dAY-reh eel pAH-ee-oh dee skAHr-peh (stee-vAH-lee) een vay-trEE-nah*
They're too narrow (wide).	**Sono troppo strette (larghe).** *sOH-noh trOHp-poh strAYt-teh (lAHr-gheh)*
They pinch me.	**Mi stanno strette.** *mee stAHn-noh strAYt-teh*
They fit me.	**Mi stanno bene.** *mee stAHn-noh bEH-neh*
I'll take them.	**Le compro.** *leh kOHm-proh*
I also need shoe-laces.	**Ho bisogno anche dei lacci.** *oh bee-sOH-ny-oh AHn-keh dAY-ee lAHchee*
That's all I want for now.	**Questo è tutto quello che voglio per ora.** *koo-AYs-toh EH tOOt-toh koo-AYl-loh kay vOH-ly-ee-oh pehr OH-rah*

ELECTRICAL APPLIANCES

Electric current in the U.S. is 110V AC, whereas in Italy it is 220V AC. Unless your electric shaver or alarm clock is able to handle both currents, you will need to purchase an adapter. When making a purchase, please be aware that some Italian products are engineered to work with either system whereas others will require an adapter. When making a purchase, be careful to check the warranty to ensure that the product is covered internationally.

I what to buy ____.	**Vorrei comprare ____.** *vohr-rEH-ee kohm-prAH-reh*
■ an adapter	**un trasformatore** *oon trahs-fohr-mah-tOH-reh*
■ a battery	**una pila** *OO-nah pEE-lah*
■ a blender	**un frullatore** *oon frool-lah-tOH-reh*
■ a curling iron	**una spazzola riscaldante elettrica per fare la messa in piega** *OO-nah spAH-tzoh-lah ree-skahl-dAHn-teh eh-lEHt-tree-kah pehr FAH-reh lah mAYs-sah een pee-EH-gah*
■ an electric shaver	**un rasoio elettrico** *oon rah-sOH-ee-oh eh-lEHt-tree-koh*
■ an electric water pick	**un idropulsore elettronico per la pulizia dei denti** *oon ee-droh-pool-sOH-reh eh-leht-trOH-nee-koh pehr lah poo-lee-tzEE-ah dAY-ee dEHn-tee*
■ a food processor	**un frullatore** *oon frool-lah-tOH-reh*
■ a hair dryer	**un asciugacapelli** *oon ah-shee-OO-gah-kah-pAYl-lee*
■ a headset	**un casco asciugacapelli** *oon kAH-skoh ah-shee-OO-gah-kah-pAYl-lee*
■ a manicure set	**un completo per manicure** *oon kohm-plEH-toh pehr mah-nee-kOO-reh*

- a plug **una spina (elettrica)** *OO-nah spEE-nah eh-lEHt-tree-kah*

- a microwave **un forno a micro onde** *oon fOHr-noh ah mEE-kroh OHn-deh*

- a toaster **un tostapane** *oon toh-stah-pAH-neh*

- a transformer **un trasformatore** *oon trahs-fohr-mah-tOH-reh*

FOODS AND HOUSEHOLD ITEMS

See also pages 114–149 and the dictionary (pages 268–297) for more food words. When you go to a food market or shop, bring your own bag along with you to tote home your groceries. A collapsible net bag is very useful.

I'd like _____.	**Vorrei _____.** *vohr-rEH-ee*	
Could you give me _____?	**Potrebbe darmi _____?** *poh-trAYb-beh dAHr-mee*	

- a bar of soap **una saponetta** *OO-nah sah-poh-nEHt-tah*

- a bottle of juice **un succo di frutta** *oon sOO-koh dee frOOt-tah*

- a box of cereal **una scatola di cereali** *OO-nah skAH-toh-lah dee cheh-reh-AH-lee*

- a can (tin) of tomato sauce **una scatola di conserva di pomodoro** *OO-nah skAH-toh-lah dee kohn-sEHr-vah dee poh-moh-dOH-roh*

- a dozen eggs **una dozzina d'uova** *OO-nah doh-tsEE-nah doo-OH-vah*

- a jar of coffee **un vasetto di caffè** *oon vah-sAYt-toh dee kahf-fEH*

- a kilo of potatoes (just over 2 pounds) **un chilo di patate** *oon kEE-loh dee pah-tAH-teh*

■ a half-kilo of cherries (just over 1 pound) **mezzo chilo di ciliege** *mEH-tsoh kEE-loh dee chee-lee-EH-jeh*

■ a liter of milk (about 1 quart) **un litro di latte** *oon LEE-troh dee lAHt-teh*

■ a package of candies **un pacchetto di caramelle** *oon pah-kAYt-toh dee kah-rah-mEHl-leh*

■ 100 grams of cheese (about $\frac{1}{4}$ pound) **cento grammi di formaggio (un etto)** *chEHn-toh grAHm-mee dee fohr-mAH-jee-oh (oon EHt-toh)*

■ a roll of toilet paper **un rotolo di carta igienica** *oon rOH-toh-loh dee kAHr-tah ee-jee-EH-nee-kah*

I'd like a kilo (about 2 pounds) of oranges. **Vorrei un chilo di arance.** *vohr-rEY-ee oon kEY-loh dee ah-rAHn-chay*

■ a half-kilo of butter **mezzo chilo di burro** *mAY-tsoh kEY-loh dee bOOr-roh*

■ 200 grams (about $\frac{1}{2}$ pound) of cookies **due etti di biscotti** *dOO-eh EHt-tee dee bees-kOHt-tee*

■ 100 grams (about $\frac{1}{4}$ pound) of bologna **un etto di mortadella** *oon EHt-toh dee mohr-tah-dAYl-lah*

NOTE: Common measurements for purchasing foods are a kilo (**chilo**), or fractions thereof, and 100 (**cento**), 200 (**duecento**), and 500 (**cinquecento**) grams (**grammi**). See also the pages on Numbers, 16–18.

What is this (that)? **Che cosa è questo (quello)?** *kay kOH-sah EH koo-AYs-toh (koo-AYl-loh)*

Is it fresh? **È fresco?** *EH frAY-skoh*

METRIC WEIGHTS AND MEASURES

Solid Measures
(approximate measurements only)

OUNCES	GRAMS (GRAMMI)	GRAMS	OUNCES
$\frac{1}{4}$	7	10	$\frac{1}{3}$
$\frac{1}{2}$	14	100	$3\frac{1}{2}$
$\frac{3}{4}$	21	300	$10\frac{1}{2}$
1	28	500	18

POUNDS	KILOGRAMS (CHILI)	KILOGRAMS	POUNDS
1	$\frac{1}{2}$	1	$2\frac{1}{4}$
5	$2\frac{1}{4}$	3	$6\frac{1}{2}$
10	$4\frac{1}{2}$	5	11
20	9	10	22
50	23	50	110
100	45	100	220

Liquid Measures
(approximate measurements only)

OUNCES	MILLILITERS (MILLILITRI)	MILLILITERS	OUNCES
1	30	10	$\frac{1}{3}$
6	175	50	$1\frac{1}{2}$
12	350	100	$3\frac{1}{2}$
16	475	150	5

GALLONS	LITERS (LITRI)	LITERS	GALLONS
1	$3\frac{3}{4}$	1	$\frac{1}{4}$ (1 quart)
5	19	5	$1\frac{1}{3}$
10	38	10	$2\frac{1}{2}$

JEWELRY

I'd like to see ____.	**Vorrei vedere ____.** *vohr-rEH-ee veh-dAY-reh*
■ a bracelet	**un braccialetto** *oon brah-chee-ah-lAYt-toh*
■ a brooch	**un fermaglio (una spilla)** *oon fehr-mAH-ly-ee-oh (OO-nah spEEl lah)*
■ a chain	**una catenina** *OO-nah kay-teh-nEE-nah*
■ a charm	**un ciondolo** *oon chee-OHn-doh-loh*
■ some earrings	**degli orecchini** *dAY-ly-ee oh-rehk-kEE-nee*
■ a necklace	**un monile** *oon moh-nEE-leh*
■ a pin	**una spilla** *OO-nah spEEl-lah*
■ a ring	**un anello** *oon ah-nEHl-loh*
■ a rosary	**una corona del rosario** *OO-nah koh-rOH-nah dayl roh-sAH-ree-oh*
■ a (wrist) watch	**un orologio da polso** *oon oh-roh-lOH-jee-oh dah pOHl-soh*
Is this ____?	**Questo è ____?** *koo-AYs-toh EH*
■ gold	**d'oro** *dOH-roh*
■ platinum	**di platino** *dee plAH-tee-noh*
■ silver	**d'argento** *dahr-jEHn-toh*
■ stainless steel	**d'acciaio inossidabile** *dah-chee-AH-ee-oh ee-nohs-see-dAH-bee-leh*
Is it solid gold or gold plated?	**È oro massiccio oppure oro placcato?** *EH OH-roh mahs-sEE-chee-oh ohp-pOO-reh OH-roh plahk-kAH-toh*
How many carats is it?	**Di quanti carati è?** *dee koo-AHn-tee kah-rAH-tee EH*

What is that (precious) stone?	**Che pietra (preziosa) è?**	*kay pee-EH-trah (preh-tsee-OH-sah) EH*
I want _____.	**Vorrei (voglio) _____.**	*vohr-rEH-ee (vOH-ly-ee-oh)*
◾ an amethyst	**un'ametista**	*oo-nah-meh-tEE-stah*
◾ an aqua-marine	**un'acquamarina**	*oo-nah-koo-ah-mah-rEE-nah*
◾ a coral	**un corallo**	*oon koh-rAHl-loh*
◾ a diamond	**un diamante**	*oon dee-ah-mAHn-teh*
◾ an emerald	**uno smeraldo**	*OO-noh smeh-rAHl-doh*
◾ ivory	**una cosa d'avorio**	*OO-nah kOH-sah dah-vOH-ree-oh*
◾ jade	**una giada**	*OO-nah jee-AH-dah*
◾ onyx	**un'onice**	*oon-OH-nee-cheh*
◾ pearls	**delle perle**	*dAYl-leh pEHr-leh*
◾ a ruby	**un rubino**	*oon roo-bEE-noh*
◾ a sapphire	**uno zaffiro**	*OO-noh tsahf-fEE-roh*
◾ a topaz	**un topazio**	*oon toh-pAH-tsee-oh*
◾ a turquoise	**un turchese**	*oon toor-kAY-seh*
How much is it?	**Quanto costa?**	*koo-AHn-toh kOH-stah*
I'll take it.	**Lo(a) prendo.**	*loh(ah) prAYn-doh*

AUDIOVISUAL EQUIPMENT

Please see the note under Electrical Appliances on page 172. In addition, Europe uses broadcasting and recording systems that are often incompatible with those of the U.S. Unless expressly warranted, Italian TVs, VCRs, VCR tapes, computers, and telephone answering systems will not operate properly in the U.S.

Where is the _____ section?	**Dov'è la sezione _____?**	*doh-vEH lah seh-tsee-OH-neh*
■ classical music	**di musica classica**	*dee mOO-see-kah clAHs-see-kah*
■ popular music	**di musica popolare**	*dee mOO-see-kah poh-poh-lAH-reh*
■ latest hits	**degli ultimi successi**	*dAY-ly-ee OOl-tee-mee soo-chEHs-see*
■ Italian music	**della musica italiana**	*dAYl-lah mOO-see-kah ee-tah-lee-AH-nah*
■ opera	**di musica d'opera**	*dee mOO-see-kah dOH-peh-rah*
Do you have any songs of _____?	**Avete la canzone di _____?**	*ah-vay-teh lah kahn-tzOH-neh dee*
Is it recorded digitally?	**È una registrazione digitale?**	*EH OO-nah reh-jee-strah-tzee-OH-neh dee-jee-tAH-leh*
Is there an audio/video store in the neighborhood?	**C'è qui vicino un negozio di articoli audio/video?**	*chEH koo-ee vee-chEE-noh oon neh-gOH-tsee-oh dee ahr-tEE-koh-lee AH-oo-dee-oh/VEE-deh-oh*
I would like to buy _____.	**Vorrei comprare _____.**	*vohr-rEH-ee kohm-prAH-reh*
■ an analog cassette	**una cassetta analogica**	*OO-nah kahs-sAYt-tah ah-nah-lOH-jee-kah*
■ an analog tape deck	**una piastra di un registratore analogico**	*OO-nah pee-AH-strah dee oon reh-jee-strah-tOH-reh ah-nah-lOH-jee-koh*
■ a portable CD player	**un lettore CD portatile**	*oon leht-tOH-reh see-dEE pohr-tAH-tee-leh*
■ a CD recorder	**un registratore CD**	*oon reh-jee-strah-tOH-reh see-dEE*
■ CDs	**dei CD**	*dAY-ee see-dEE*

■ DAT cassettes	**delle audio cassette digitali** *dAYl-leh AH-oo-dee-oh kahs-sAYt-teh dee-jee-tAH-lee*
■ a digital tape deck	**una piastra di un registratore digitale** *OO-nah pee-AH-strah dee oon reh-jee-strah-tOH-reh dee-jee-tAH-leh*
■ headphones	**una cuffia** *OO-nah kOOf-fee-ah*
■ a minidisk player	**un lettore per minidisk** *oon leht-tOH-reh pehr minidisk*
■ minidisks	**dei minidischetti** (or minidisks) *dAY-ee mee-nee-dee-skAYt-tee*
■ a receiver	**un ricevitore** *oon ree-chay-vee-tOH-reh*
■ recordable CDs	**dei compact disks vuoti (registrabili, vergini)** *dAY-ee compact disks voo-OH-tee (reh-jee-strAH-bee-lee vAYr-jee-nee)*
■ a small cassette player	**un piccolo stereo** *oon pEEk-koh-loh st-EH-reh-oh*
■ a small cassette recorder	**un piccolo registratore a cassetta** *oon pEEk-koh-loh reh-jee-strah-tOH-reh ah kahs-sAYt-tah*
■ a tuner	**un sintonizzatore** *oon seen-toh-nee-tsah-tOH-reh*
■ wireless headphones	**delle cuffie senza filo** *dAYl-leh kOOf-fee-eh sEHn-tsah fEE-loh*
I need ____.	**Ho bisogno di ____.** *oh bee-sOH-ny-oh dee*
■ a (digital) camcorder	**una videocamera (digitale)** *OO-nah vEE-deh-oh-kAH-meh-rah (dee-jee-tAH-leh)*
■ digital videofilm	**un videofilm digitale** *oon vee-deh-oh-fEElm dee-jee-tAH-leh*
■ DVD movies	**dei film DVD** *dAY-ee fEElm dee-vee-dee*

■ a DVD player   **un registratore DVD** *oon reh-jee-strah-tOH-reh dee-vee-dee*

■ videofilm   **un film registrato su nastro video** *oon fEElm reh-jee-strAH-toh soo nAH-stroh vEE-deh-oh*

■ a VCR   **un videoregistratore** *oon vee-deh-oh-rah-jee-strah-tOH-reh*

■ a VCR tape   **una videocassette** *OO-nah vee-deh-oh-kahs-sEHt-teh*

Do you have VCR or DVD movies with subtitles in English?   **Avete film con sottotitolo in inglese per videoregistratore o per DVD?** *ah-vAY-teh fEElm kohn soht-toh-tEE-toh-loh een een-glAY-seh pehr vee-deh-oh-reh-jee-strah-tOH-reh oh pehr dee-vee-dee*

Will the warranty be honored in the U.S.?   **La garanzia sarà valida (accettata) negli Stati Uniti?** *lah gah-rahn-tsEE-ah sah-rAH vAH-lee-dah (ah-cheht-tAH-tah) nAYly-ee stAH-tee oo-nEE-tee*

Whom shall I contact if this malfunctions?   **Chi dovrò contattare se non funziona bene?** *key doh-vrOH kohn-taht-tAH-reh say nohn foon-tsee-OH-nah bEH-neh*

PHOTOGRAPHIC EQUIPMENT

For phrases dealing with camera repairs, see page 197.

Where is there a camera shop?   **Dov'è un negozio di fotocine (machine fotografiche)?** *doh-vEH oon neh-GOH-tsee-oh dee foh-toh-chEE-neh (mAHk-kee-neh foh-toh-grAH-fee-keh)*

I want a roll of color (black and white) film.	**Voglio un rullino a colori (in bianco e nero).** *vOH-ly-ee-oh oon rool-lEE-noh ah koh-lOH-ree (een bee-AHn-koh ay nAY-roh)*
I want a roll of 20 (36) exposures (for slides).	**Vorrei un rullino (per diapositive) di venti (trentasei) pose.** *vohr-rEH-ee oon rool-lEE-noh (pehr dee-ah-poh-see-tEE-veh) dee vAYn-tee (trehn-tah-sEH-ee) pOH-seh*
I want a Polaroid filmpack.	**Vorrei (voglio) un rullino per istantanee (polaroid).** *vohr-rEH-ee (vOH-ly-ee-oh) oon rool-lEE-noh pehr ee-stahn-tAH-neh-eh (polaroid)*
I need _____.	**Ho bisogno di _____.** *oh bee-sOH-ny-oh dee*
■ black and white film	**un film in bianco e nero** *oon fEElm een bee-AHn-koh ay nAY-roh*
■ a camera bag	**una custodia della macchina fotografica** *OO-nah koo-stOH-dee-ah dAYl-lah mAH-key-nah foh-toh-grAH-fee-kah*
■ camera batteries	**pile per la macchina fotografica** *pEE-leh pehr lah mAH-key-nah foh-toh-grAH-fee-kah*
■ digital camera disks	**dischetti digitali per la macchina fotografica** *dee-skAYt-tee dee-jee-tAH-lee pehr lah mAH-key-nah foh-toh-grAH-fee-kah*
■ a disposable camera	**una macchina fotografica usa e getta** *OO-nah mAH-key-nah foh-toh-grAH-fee-kah OO-sah ay jEHt-tah*
■ an expensive (inexpensive) camera	**una buona macchina fotografica (a buon mercato).** *OO-nah boo-OH-nah mAHk-kee-nah foh-toh-grAH-fee-kah (ah boo-OHn mayr-kAH-toh)*

- film **un rullino** *oon rool-lEE-noh*

- a flash **il flash** *eel flash*

- a lens **una lente** *OO-nah lEHn-teh*

- a point-and-shoot camera **una macchina fotografica "vai e clicca"** *OO-nah mAHk-kee-nah foh-toh-grAH-fee-kah vAH-ee ay klEEk-kah*

- slide film **un rullino per diapositive** *oon rool-lEE-noh pehr dee-ah-poh-see-tEE-veh*

- an SLR camera **una macchina fotografica SLR** *OO-nah mAHk-kee-nah foh-toh-grAH-fee-kah EHs-seh Ehl-leh Ehr-reh*

- a tripod **un treppiede** *oon trehp-pee-EH-deh*

- a zoom lens **un obiettivo con zoom** *oon oh-bee-ayt-tEE-voh kohn zoom*

Do they develop film? **Sviluppano i rullini?** *svee-lOOp-pah-noh ee rool-lEE-nee*

How much does it cost to develop a roll? **Quanto costa far sviluppare un rullino?** *koo-AHn-toh kOH-stah fahr svee-loop-pAH-reh oon rool-lEE-noh*

I want one print of each. **Voglio una copia per ogni fotografia.** *vOH-ly-ee-oh OO-nah kOH-pee-ah pehr OH-ny-ee foh-toh-grah-fEE-ah*

I want _____. **Vorrei (voglio) _____.** *vohr-rEH-ee (vOH-ly-ee-oh)*

- an enlargement **un ingrandimento** *oon een-grahn-dee-mEHn-toh*

  with a glossy (matte) finish **su carta lucida (opaca, matta)** *soo kAHr-tah lOO-chee-dah (oh-pAH-kah mAHt-tah)*

When can I pick up the pictures? **Quando vengo a ritirarle?** *koo-AHn-doh vEHn-goh ah ree-tee-rAHr-leh*

NEWSPAPERS AND MAGAZINES

Do you carry English newspapers (magazines)?	**Ha giornali (riviste) in inglese?** *a jee-ohr-nAH-lee (ree-vEE-steh) een een-glAY-seh*
I'd like to buy some (picture) postcards.	**Vorrei comprare delle cartoline (illustrate).** *vohr-rEH-ee kohm-prAH-reh dAYl-leh kahr-toh-lEE-neh (eel-loo-strAH-teh)*

SOUVENIRS, HANDICRAFTS

I'd like _____.	**Vorrei _____.** *vohr-rEH-ee*
■ a pretty gift	**un bel regalo** *oon bEHl reh-gAH-loh*
■ a small gift	**un regalino** *oon reh-gah-lEE-noh*
■ a souvenir	**un souvenir** *oon soo-veh-nEEr*
It's for _____.	**È per _____.** *EH pehr*
I don't want to spend more than 20 (30) dollars.	**Non voglio spendere più di venti (trenta) dollari.** *nohn vOH-ly-ee-oh spEHn-deh-reh pee-OO dee vAYn-tee (trEHn-tah) dOHl-lah-ree*
Could you suggest something?	**Potrebbe suggerirmi qualche cosa?** *poh-trAYb-beh soo-jeh-rEEr-mee koo-AHl-keh kOH-sah*
Would you show me your selection of _____?	**Che cosa potrebbe mostrarmi di _____?** *kay kOH-sah poh-trAYb-beh moh-strAHr-mee dee*
■ blown glass	**vetro soffiato** *vAY-troh sohf-fee-AH-toh*
■ carved objects	**legno intagliato** *lAY-ny-oh een-tah-ly-ee-AH-toh*
■ crystal	**cristallo** *kree-stAHl-loh*

■ earthenware (pottery)	**ceramiche**	*cheh-rAH-mee-keh*
■ fans	**ventagli**	*vehn-tAH-ly-ee*
■ jewelry	**oggetti preziosi**	*oh-jEHt-tee preh-tsee-OH-see*
■ lace	**pizzi**	*pEE-tsee*
■ leather goods	**articoli in pelle**	*ahr-tEE-koh-lee een pEHl-leh*
■ liqueurs	**liquori**	*lee-koo-OH-ree*
■ local handicrafts	**prodotti dell'artigianato locale?**	*proh-dOHt-tee dayl-lahr-tee-jee-ah-nAH-toh loh-kAH-leh*
■ musical instruments	**strumenti musicali**	*stroo-mEHn-tee moo-see-kAH-lee*
■ perfumes	**profumi**	*proh-fOO-mee*
■ (miniature) pictures	**quadretti (in miniatura)**	*koo-ah-drAYt-tee (een mee-nee-ah-tOO-rah)*
■ posters	**affissi, manifesti, poster**	*ahf-fEEs-see mah-nee-fEH-stee pOH-stehr*
■ religious articles	**articoli religiosi**	*ahr-tEE-koh-lee reh-lee-jee-OH-see*

STATIONERY ITEMS

I want to buy _____.	**Voglio comprare** _____.	*vOH-ly-ee-oh kohm-prAH-reh*
■ a ballpoint pen	**una penna a sfera**	*OO-nah pAYn-nah ah sfEH-rah*
■ a deck of cards	**un mazzo di carte**	*oon mAH-tsoh dee kAHr-teh*
■ envelopes	**delle buste**	*dAYl-leh bOO-steh*
■ an eraser	**una gomma per cancellare**	*OO-nah gOHm-mah pehr kahn-chehl-lAH-reh*

■ glue	**della colla**	*dAYl-lah kOHl-lah*
■ a notebook	**un taccuino**	*oon tahk-koo-EE-noh*
■ pencils	**delle matite**	*dAYl-leh mah-tEE-teh*
■ a pencil sharpener	**un temperamatite**	*oon tehm-peh-rah-mah-tEE-teh*
■ a ruler	**una riga**	*OO-nah rEE-gah*
■ Scotch tape	**un nastro adesivo (uno scotch)**	*oon nAH-stroh ah-deh-sEE-voh (OO-noh skO-ch)*
■ some string	**del filo**	*dayl fEE-loh*
■ typing paper	**della carta per battere a macchina**	*dAYl-lah kAHr-tah pehr bAHt-teh-reh ah mAH-kee-nah*
■ wrapping paper	**della carta da imballaggio**	*dAYl-lah kAHr-tah dah eem-bahl-lAH-jee-oh*
■ a writing pad	**un blocchetto di carta**	*oon blohk-kAYt-toh dee kAHr-tah*
■ writing paper	**della carta da scrivere**	*dAYl-lah kAHr-tah dah scrEE-veh-reh*

TOBACCO

You can buy cigarettes and other related items at a **Sale e tabacchi** shop. They also sell postcards and stamps.

A pack (carton) of cigarettes, please.	**Un pacchetto (una stecca) di sigarette, per piacere.** *oon pah-kAYt-toh (OO-nah stAYk-kah) dee see-gah-rAYt-teh pehr pee-ah-chAY-reh*
■ filtered	**con filtro** *kohn fEEl-troh*
■ unfiltered	**senza filtro** *sEHn-tsah fEEl-troh*
■ menthol	**alla menta** *ahl-lah mEHn-tah*
■ king-size	**lunghe** *lOOn-gheh*

| Are these cigarettes (very) strong (mild)? | **Sono (molto) forti (leggere) queste sigarette?** *sOH-noh (mOHl-toh) fOHr-tee (leh-jEH-reh) koo-AYs-teh see-gah-rAYt-teh* |

| Do you have American cigarettes? | **Ha sigarette americane?** *AH see-gah-rAYt-teh ah-meh-ree-kAH-neh* |

| What brand? | **Di che marca?** *dee kay mAHr-kah* |

| Please give me a pack of matches also. | **Mi dia anche una scatola di fiammiferi, per piacere.** *mee dEE-ah AHn-kay OO-nah skAH-toh-lah dee fee-ahm-mEE-fay-ree pehr pee-ah-chAY-reh* |

Do you sell _____?	**Vendono _____?** *vAYn-doh-noh*
■ chewing tobacco	**tabacco da masticare** *tah-bAHk-koh dah mah-stee-kAH-reh*
■ cigars	**sigari** *sEE-gah-ree*
■ flints	**pietrine** *pee-eh-trEE-neh*
■ lighter fluid	**benzina per accendini?** *behn-tsEE-nah pehr ah-chen-dEE-nee*
■ pipes	**pipe** *pEE-peh*
■ pipe tobacco	**tabacco da pipa** *tah-bAHk-koh dah pEE-pah*

TOILETRIES

In Italy, drugstores (chemists) carry mostly actual drugs and medicines. For toiletries and perfumes, you would go to a **profumeria**.

| Do you have _____? | **Ha _____?** *ah* |
| ■ bobby pins | **delle forcine** *dAYl-leh fohr-chEE-neh* |

■ a brush	**una spazzola**	*OO-nah spAH-tsoh-lah*
■ cleansing cream	**della crema detergente**	*dAYl-lah crEH-mah day-tehr-jEHn-teh*
■ a comb	**un pettine**	*oon pEHt-tee-neh*
■ a deodorant	**un deodorante**	*oon deh-oh-doh-rAHn-teh*
■ (disposable) diapers	**dei pannolini usa e getta**	*dAY-ee pahn-noh-lEE-nee OO-sah ay jEHt-tah*
■ emery boards	**delle limette per le unghie**	*dAYl-leh lee-mEHt-teh pehr leh OOn-ghee-eh*
■ eyeliner	**un eye liner**	*oon eye liner*
■ eye shadow	**l'ombretto**	*lohm-brAYt-toh*
■ eyebrow pencil	**una matita per le sopracciglia**	*OO-nah mah-tEE-tah pehr leh soh-prah-chEE-ly-ee-ah*
■ hair spray	**della lacca per capelli**	*dAYl-la lAHk-kah pehr kah-pAYl-lee*
■ lipstick	**il lipstick (rossetto per le labbra)**	*eel lipstick (rohs-sEHt-toh pehr leh lAHb-brah)*
■ make-up	**il make-up (trucco)**	*eel make up (trOOk-koh)*
■ mascara	**del mascara**	*dAYl mah-skAH-rah*
■ a mirror	**uno specchio**	*OO-noh spEHk-key-oh*
■ mouthwash	**del disinfettante per la bocca**	*dayl dee-seen-feht-tAHn-teh pehr lah bOHk-kah*
■ nail clippers	**dei tagliaunghie**	*dAY-ee tah-ly-ee-ah-OOn-ghee-eh*
■ a nail file	**una limetta per le unghie**	*OO-nah lee-mAYt-tah pehr leh OOn-ghee-eh*

■ nail polish	**dello smalto per le unghie** *dAYl-loh smAHl-toh pehr leh OOn-ghee-eh*
■ nail polish remover	**dell'acetone** *dayl-lah-cheh-tOH-neh*
■ a razor	**un rasoio di sicurezza** *oon rah-sOH-ee-oh dee see-koo-rAY-tsah*
■ razor blades	**delle lamette** *dAYl-leh lah-mAYt-teh*
■ rouge	**il rossetto (belletto)** *eel rohs-sEHt-toh (behl-lEHt-toh)*
■ sanitary napkins	**degli assorbenti (igienici)** *dAY-ly-ee ahs-sohr-bEHn-tee (ee-jee-EH-nee-chee)*
■ (cuticle) scissors	**delle forbicine** *dAYl-leh fohr-bee-chEE-neh*
■ shampoo	**dello shampoo** *dAYl-loh ShAHm-poh*
■ shaving lotion	**un dopobarba** *oon doh-poh-bAHr-bah*
■ soap	**del sapone** *dayl sah-pOH-neh*
■ a sponge	**una spugna** *OO-nah spOO-ny-ah*
■ tampons	**dei tamponi** *dAY-ee tahm-pOH-nee*
■ tissues	**dei fazzolettini di carta** *dAY-ee fah-tsoh-leht-tEE-nee dee kAHr-tah*
■ toilet paper	**della carta igienica** *dAYl-lah kAHr-tah ee-jee-EH-nee-kah*
■ a toothbrush	**uno spazzolino per i denti** *OO-noh spah-tsoh-lEE-noh pehr ee dEHn-tee*
■ toothpaste	**un dentifricio** *oon dEHn-tee-frEE-chee-oh*
■ tweezers	**delle pinzette** *dAYl-leh peen-tsEHt-teh*

PERSONAL CARE AND SERVICES

If your hotel doesn't offer these services, ask the attendant at the desk to recommend someone nearby.

AT THE BARBER

Where is there a good barbershop?	**Dove potrei trovare (una buona barberia) un buon parrucchiere?** *dOH-veh poh-trEH-ee troh-vAH-reh (OO-nah boo-OH-nah bahr-beh-rEE-ah) oon boo-OHn pahr-rook-key-EH-reh*
Do I have to wait long?	**C'è da aspettare molto?** *chEH dah-speht-tAH-reh mOHl-toh*
Am I next?	**È arrivato il mio turno?** *EH ahr-ree-vAH-toh eel mEE-oh tOOr-noh*
I want a shave.	**Voglio farmi la barba.** *vOH-ly-ee-oh fAHr-mee lah bAHr-bah*
I want a haircut.	**Voglio un taglio di capelli.** *vOH-ly-ee-oh oon tAH-ly-ee-oh dee kah-pAYl-lee*
Short in back, long in front.	**Corti dietro, lunghi davanti.** *kOHr-tee dee-EH-troh lOOn-ghee dah-vAHn-tee*
Leave it long.	**Me li lasci lunghi.** *meh-lee lAH-shee lOOn-ghee*
I want it (very) short.	**Li voglio (molto) corti.** *lee vOH-ly-ee-oh (mOHl-toh) kOHr-tee*

You can cut a little _____.	**Me li può tagliare un po' _____.** *meh lee poo-OH tah-ly-ee-AH-reh oon pOH*	

- in back **di dietro** *dee dee-EH-troh*
- in front **sul davanti** *sool dah-vAHn-tee*
- off the top **sopra** *sOH-prah*

I part my hair _____. **Porto la riga _____.** *pOHr-toh lah rEE-gah*

- on the left **a sinistra** *ah see-nEE-strah*
- on the right **a destra** *ah dEH-strah*
- in the middle **al centro** *ahl chEHn-troh*

I comb my hair straight back. **Porto i capelli pettinati all'indietro.** *pOHr-toh ee kah-pAYl-lee peht-tee-nAH-tee ahl-leen-dee-EH-troh*

Cut a little bit more here. **Tagli un po'di più qui (per favore).** *tAH-ly-ee oon pOH dee pee-OO koo-EE (pehr fah-vOH-reh)*

That's enough. **Basta così.** *bAH-stah koh-sEE*

It's fine that way. **Così è magnifico.** *Koh-sEE EH mah-ny-EE-fee-koh*

I (don't) want _____. **(Non) voglio _____.** *(nohn) vOH-ly-oh*

- hair spray **la lacca** *lah lAHk-kah*
- lotion **la lozione** *lah loh-tzee-OH-neh*
- shampoo **lo shampoo** *loh shAHm-poh*

Please trim _____. **Può spuntarmi _____.** *poo-OH spoon-tAHr-mee*

- my beard **il pizzo (la barba)** *eel pEE-tsoh (lah bAHr-bah)*
- my moustache **i baffi** *ee bAHf-fee*
- my sideburns **le basette** *leh bah-sAYt-teh*

Where's the mirror?	**Dov'è lo specchio?**	*doh-vEH loh spEHK-key-oh*
How much do I owe you?	**Quanto le devo?**	*koo-AHn-toh leh dAY-voh*
Is service included?	**È incluso il servizio?**	*EH een-klOO-soh eel sehr-vEE-tsee-oh*

AT THE BEAUTY PARLOR

Is there a beauty parlor (hairdresser) near the hotel?	**C'è una parrucchiera vicino all'albergo?**	*chEH OO-nah pahr-rook-key-EH-rah vee-chEE-noh ahl-lahl-bEHr-goh*
I'd like an appointment for this afternoon (tomorrow).	**Vorrei un appuntamento per questo pomeriggio (per domani).**	*vohr-rEH-ee oon ahp-poon-tah-mEHn-toh pehr koo-AYs-toh poh-meh-rEE-jee-oh (pehr doh-mAH-nee)*
Can you give me ____?	**Può farmi ____?**	*poo-OH fAHr-mee*
▪ a color rinse	**un cachet**	*oon kah-shEH*
▪ a facial massage	**un massaggio facciale**	*oon mahs-sAH-jee-oh fah-chee-AH-leh*
▪ a haircut	**un taglio di capelli**	*oon tAH-ly-oh dee kah-pAYl-lee*
▪ a blunt haircut	**una spuntatina**	*OO-nah spoon-tah-tEE-nah*
▪ a layered haircut	**un taglio scalato**	*oon tAH-ly-oh skah-lAH-toh*
▪ a manicure	**la manicure**	*lah mah-nee-kOO-reh*
▪ a pedicure	**il pedicure**	*eel peh-dee-kOO-reh*
▪ a permanent	**una permanente**	*OO-nah pehr-mah-nAYn-teh*

■ a shampoo	**lo shampoo**	*loh shAHm-poh*
■ a shave	**una depilazione**	*OO-nah deh-pee-lah-tzee-OH-neh*
■ a tint	**una tintura**	*OO-nah teen-tOO-rah*
■ a touch-up	**una ritoccatina**	*OO-nah ree-tohk-kah-tEE-nah*
■ a trim	**una spuntatina**	*OO-nah spoon-tah-tEE-nah*
■ a wash and set	**shampoo e messa in piega**	*shAHm-poh ay mAYs-sah een pee-AY-gah*
■ a waxing	**una depilazione mediante ceretta**	*OO-nah deh-pee-lah-tzee-OH-neh meh-dee-AHn-teh cheh-rAYt-tah*

I'd like to see a color chart.	**Vorrei vedere il cartellino dei colori.**	*vohr-rEH-ee veh-dAY-reh eel kahr-tehl-lEE-noh dAY-ee koh-lOH-ree*
I want _____.	**Voglio _____.**	*vOH-ly-ee-oh*
■ auburn	**un color rame**	*oon koh-lOHr rAH-meh*
■ (light) blond	**un biondo (chiaro)**	*oon bee-OHn-doh (key-AH-roh)*
■ brunette	**un bruno**	*oon brOO-noh*
■ a darker color	**un colore più scuro**	*oon koh-lOH-reh pee-OO skOO-roh*
■ a lighter color	**un colore più chiaro**	*oon koh-lOH-reh pee-OO key-AH-roh*
■ the same color	**lo stesso colore**	*loh stAYs-soh koh-lOH-reh*
■ highlights	**i colpi di sole**	*ee kOHl-pee dee sOH-leh*

Don't apply any hair spray.	**Non mi metta nessuna lacca.**	*nohn mee mEHt-tah nays-sOO-nah lAHk-kah*

Not too much hair spray.	**Non troppa lacca.** *nohn trOHp-pah lAHk-kah*
I want my hair ____.	**Vorrei (voglio) i capelli ____.** *vohr-rEH-ee (vOH-ly-ee-oh) ee kah-pEHl-lee*
■ with bangs	**con la frangia** *kohn lah frAHn-jee-ah*
■ in a bun	**a nodo (a crocchia)** *ah nOH-doh (ah krOHk-key-ah)*
■ in curls	**a boccoli** *ah bOHk-koh-lee*
■ with waves	**ondulati** *ohn-doo-lAH-tee*
Where's the mirror?	**Dov'è lo specchio?** *doh-vEH loh spEHk-key-oh*
How much do I owe you?	**Quanto le devo?** *koo-AHn-toh leh dAY-voh*
Is service included?	**È incluso il servizio?** *EH een-klOO-soh eel sehr-vEE-tsee-oh*

LAUNDRY AND DRY CLEANING

Where is the nearest laundry (dry cleaner's)?	**Dov'è la lavanderia (la tintoria) più vicina?** *doh-vEH lah lah-vahn-deh-rEE-ah (lah teen-toh-rEE-ah) pee-OO vee-chEE-nah*
I have a lot of (dirty) clothes to be ____.	**Ho molta biancheria (sporca) da ____.** *oh mOHl-tah bee-ahn-keh-rEE-ah (spOHr-kah) dah*
■ dry-cleaned	**lavare a secco** *lah-vAH-reh ah sAYk-koh*
■ washed	**lavare** *lah-vAH-reh*
■ mended	**rammendare** *rahm-mehn-dAH-reh*
■ ironed	**stirare** *stee-rAH-reh*
Here's the list:	**Ecco l'elenco:** *EHk-koh leh-lEHn-koh*
■ 3 shirts (men's)	**tre camicie (da uomo)** *tray kah-mEE-chee-eh (dah oo-OH-moh)*
■ 12 handkerchiefs	**dodici fazzoletti** *dOH-dee-chee fah-tsoh-lAYt-tee*
■ 6 pairs of socks	**sei paia di calzini** *sAY-ee pAH-ee-ah dee kahl-tsEE-nee*
■ 1 blouse (nylon)	**una blusa (di nylon)** *oo-nah blOO-sah (dee nAH-ee-lohn)*
■ 4 shorts	**quattro mutande** *koo-AHt-tro moo-tAHn-deh*
■ 2 pajamas	**due pigiama** *dOO-eh pee-jee-AH-mah*
■ 2 suits	**due vestiti** *dOO-eh veh-stEE-tee*
■ 3 ties	**tre cravatte** *tray krah-vAHt-teh*
■ 2 dresses (cotton)	**due vesti (di cotone)** *dOO-eh vEH-stee (dee koh-tOH-neh)*
■ 2 skirts	**due gonne** *dOO-eh gOHn-neh*
■ 1 sweater (wool)	**una maglia (di lana)** *OO-nah mAH-ly-ah (dee lAH-nah)*

■ 1 pair of gloves	**un paio di guanti** *oon pAH-ee-oh dee goo-AHn-tee*	

I need them (for) _____. **Mi occorrono (per) _____.** *mee ohk-kOHr-roh-noh (pehr)*

■ as soon as possible **al più presto possibile** *ahl pee-OO prEH-stoh pohs-sEE-bee-leh*

■ tonight **stasera** *stah-sAY-rah*

■ tomorrow **domani** *doh-mAH-nee*

■ next week **la settimana prossima** *lah seht-tee-mAH-nah prOHs-see-mah*

■ the day after tomorrow **dopodomani** *doh-poh-doh-mAH-nee*

When will you bring it (them) back? **Quando lo (li) riporterà?** *koo-AHn-doh loh (lee) ree-pohr-teh-rAH*

When will it be ready? **Quando sarà pronto?** *koo-AHn-doh sah-rAH prOHn-toh*

There's a button missing. **Manca un bottone.** *mAHn-kah oon boht-tOH-neh*

Can you sew it on? **Può riattaccarlo?** *poo-OH ree-aht-tahk-kAHr-loh*

This isn't my laundry. **Questa non è la mia biancheria.** *koo-AYs-tah nohn EH lah mEE-ah bee-ahn-keh-rEE-ah*

SHOE REPAIRS

Can you fix these shoes (boots)? **Può ripararmi queste scarpe (questi stivali)?** *poo-OH ree-pah-rAHr-mee koo-AYs-teh skAHr-peh (koo-AYs-tee stee-vAH-lee)*

Put on (half) soles and rubber heels. **Ci metta le (mezze) suole e i tacchi di gomma.** *chee mEHt-tah leh (mEH-tseh) soo-OH-leh ay ee tAH-key dee gOHm-mah*

I'd like to have my shoes shined too.	**Vorrei anche che mi lucidasse le scarpe.** *vohr-rEH-ee AHn-keh kay mee loo-chee-dAHs-seh leh skAHr-peh*
When will they be ready?	**Quando saranno pronte?** *koo-AHn-doh sah-rAHn-noh prOHn-teh*
I need them by Saturday (without fail).	**Mi occorrono per sabato (assolutamente).** *mee ohk-kOHr-roh-noh pehr sAH-bah-toh (ahs-soh-loo-tah-mEHn-teh)*

WATCH REPAIRS

Can you fix this watch (alarm clock) (for me)?	**(Mi) può aggiustare quest'orologio (questa sveglia)?** *(mee) poo-OH ah-jee-oo-stAH-reh koo-ay-stoh-roh-lOH-jee-oh (koo-AYs-tah svAY-ly-ee-ah)*
Can you clean it?	**Può pulirlo(la)?** *poo-OH poo-lEEr-loh(lah)*
I dropped it.	**L'ho lasciato(a) cadere.** *lOH lah-shee-AH-toh(tah) kah-dAY-reh*
It's running slow (fast).	**Va piano (in anticipo).** *vAH pee-AH-noh (een ahn-tEE-chee-poh)*
It's stopped.	**S'è fermato(a).** *sEH fehr-mAH-toh(tah)*
I wind it every day.	**Lo (la) carico ogni giorno.** *loh (lah) kAH-ree-koh OH-ny-ee jee-OHr-noh*
I need _____.	**Ho bisogno di _____.** *oh bee-sOH-ny-oh dee*
■ a crystal, glass	**un vetro** *oon vAY-troh*
■ an hour hand	**una lancetta delle ore** *OO-nah lahn-chAYt-tah dAYl-leh OH-reh*
■ a minute hand	**una lancetta dei minuti** *OO-nah lahn-chAYt-tah dAY-ee mee-nOO-tee*

■ a second hand	**una lancetta dei secondi** *OO-nah lahn-chAYt-tah dAY-ee seh-kOHn-dee*
■ a stem	**una vite** *oo-nah vEE-teh*
■ a battery	**una pila** *oo-nah pEE-lah*
When will it be ready?	**Quando sarà pronto?** *koo-AHn-doh sah-rAH prOHn-toh*
May I have a receipt?	**Posso avere la ricevuta?** *pOHs-soh ah-vAY-reh lah ree-cheh-vOO-tah*

CAMERA REPAIRS

Can you fix this camera (movie camera)?	**Può aggiustare questa macchina fotografica (questa cinepresa)?** *poo-OH ah-jee-oo-stAH-reh koo-AYs-tah mAH-kee-nah foh-toh-grAH-fee-kah (koo-AYs-tah chee-neh-prAY-sah)*
The film doesn't advance.	**Si è bloccato il rullino.** *see EH bloh-kAH-toh eel rool-lEE-noh*
I think I need new batteries.	**Penso di aver bisogno delle pile nuove.** *pEHn-soh dee ah-vAYr bee-sOH-ny-oh dAYl-leh pEE-leh noo-OH-veh*
How much will the repair cost?	**Quanto mi costerà farla aggiustare?** *koo-AHn-toh mee koh-steh-rAH fAHr-lah ah-jee-oo-stAH-reh*
When can I come and get it?	**Quando posso venire a ritirarla?** *koo-AHn-doh pOHs-soh veh-nEE-reh ah ree-tee-rAHr-lah*
I need it as soon as possible.	**Ne ho bisogno al più presto possibile.** *nay oh bee-sOH-ny-oh ahl pee-OO prEH-stoh pohs-sEE-bee-leh*

MEDICAL CARE

THE PHARMACY (CHEMIST)

When you need immediate medical attention, go to the **Pronto Soccorso** *(prOHn-toh soh-kOHr-soh)*, the Emergency or First Aid Service. It is located at airports, hospitals, ports, and railway stations. Pharmacies carry various medical products and homeopathic supplies. The pharmacies may be open 24 hours in order to provide **servizio notturno** *(sehr-vEE-tsee-oh noht-tOOr-noh)* or night services. Their time schedules are displayed on the pharmacy door and their names and time schedules are listed in the local newspapers.

Where is the nearest (all-night) pharmacy (chemist)?	**Dov'è la farmacia (notturna) più vicina?** *doh-vEH lah fahr-mah-chEE-ah (noht-tOOr-nah) pee-OO vee-chEE-nah*
At what time does the pharmacy open (close)?	**A che ora apre (chiude) la farmacia?** *ah kay OH-rah AH-preh (key-OO-deh) lah fahr-mah-chEE-ah*
I need something for ____.	**Ho bisogno di qualche cosa per ____.** *oh bee-sOH-ny-oh dee koo-AHl-keh kOH-sah pehr*

- a cold — **il raffreddore** *eel rahf-frehd-dOH-reh*
- constipation — **la stitichezza** *lah stee-tee-kAY-tsah*
- a cough — **la tosse** *lah tOHs-seh*
- diarrhea — **la diarrea** *lah dee-ahr-rEH-ah*
- a fever — **la febbre** *lah fEHb-breh*
- hay fever — **una rinite da fieno** *OO-nah ree-nEE-teh dah fee-EH-noh*
- a headache — **il mal di testa** *eel mAHl dee tEHs-tah*
- insomnia — **l'insonnia** *leen-sOHn-nee-ah*

- motion sickness (seasickness) — **il mal d'auto (di mare)** *eel mAHl dAH-oo-toh (dee mAH-reh)*

- sunburn — **la scottatura solare** *lah skoht-tah-tOO-rah soh-lAH-reh*

- a toothache — **il mal di denti** *eel mAHl dee dEHn-tee*

- an upset stomach — **il mal di stomaco** *eel mAHl dee stOH-mah-koh*

I do not have a prescription. — **Non ho la ricetta medica.** *nohn OH lah ree-chEHt-tah mEH-dee-kah*

May I have it right away? — **Posso averla subito?** *pOHs-soh ah-vAYr-lah sOO-bee-toh*

It's an emergency. — **È un'emergenza.** *eh oo-neh-mehr-jEHn-tsah*

How long will it take? — **Quanto tempo ci vorrà?** *koo-AHn-toh tEHm-poh chee vohr-rAH*

When can I come for it? — **Quando potrò venire a prenderla?** *koo-AHn-doh poh-trOH veh-nEE-reh ah prAYn-dehr-lah*

I would like _____. — **Vorrei _____.** *vohr-rEH-ee*

- adhesive tape — **un nastro adesivo** *oon nAH-stroh ah-deh-sEE-voh*

- alcohol — **dell'alcool** *dayl-lAHl-koh-ohl*

- an antacid — **un antiacido** *oon ahn-tee-AH-chee-doh*

- an antiseptic — **un antisettico** *oon ahn-tee-sEHt-tee-koh*

- aspirins — **delle aspirine** *dAYl-leh ah-spee-rEE-neh*

- Band-Aids — **dei cerotti** *dAY-ee cheh-rOHt-tee*

- contraceptives — **dei contraccettivi** *dAY-ee kohn-trah-cheht-tEE-vee*

- corn plasters — **dei callifughi** *dAY-ee kahl-lEE-foo-ghee*

- cotton balls   **del cotone idrofilo** *dayl koh-tOH-neh ee-drOH-fee-loh*

- cough drops (syrup)   **delle pasticche (dello sciroppo) per la tosse** *dAYl-leh pahs-tEEk-keh (dAHl-loh shee-rOHp-poh) pehr lah tOHs-seh*

- eardrops   **delle gocce per gli orecchi** *dAYl-leh gOH-cheh pehr ly-ee oh-rAYk-key*

- eyedrops   **del collirio** *dayl kohl-lEE-ree-oh*

- iodine   **della tintura di iodio** *dAYl-lah teen-tOO-rah dee ee-OH-dee-oh*

- a (mild) laxative   **un lassativo (leggero)** *oon lahs-sah-tEE-voh (lay-jEH-roh)*

- milk of magnesia   **della magnesia** *dAYl-lah mah-ny-ee-EH-see-ah*

- prophylactics   **dei profilattici** *dAY-ee proh-fee-lAHt-tee-chee*

- sanitary napkins   **degli assorbenti (igienici)** *dAY-ly-ee ahs-sohr-bEHn-tee (ee-jee-EH-nee-chee)*

- suppositories   **delle supposte** *dAYl-leh soop-pOH-steh*

- talcum powder   **del borotalco** *dayl boh-roh-tAHl-koh*

- tampons   **dei tamponi** *dAY-ee tahm-pOH-nee*

- a thermometer   **un termometro** *oon tehr-mOH-meh-troh*

- vitamins   **delle vitamine** *dAYl-leh vee-tah-mEE-neh*

WITH THE DOCTOR

I don't feel well.	**Non mi sento bene.** *nohn mee sEHn-toh bEH-neh*
I feel sick.	**Mi sento male.** *mee sEHn-toh mAH-leh*

I need a doctor right away.	**Ho bisogno urgente del medico.** *oh bee-sOH-ny-oh oor-jEHn-teh dayl mEH-dee-koh*
Do you know a doctor who speaks English?	**Conosce un dottore che parla inglese?** *koh-nOH-sheh oon doht-tOH-reh kay pAHr-lah een-glAY-seh*
Where is his office (surgery)?	**Dov'è il suo ambulatorio?** *doh-vEH eel sOO-oh ahm-boo-lah-tOH-ree-oh*
Will the doctor come to the hotel?	**Il dottore potrà venire all'hotel?** *eel doht-tOH-reh poh-trAH veh-NEE-reh ahl-loh-tEHl*
I feel dizzy.	**Mi gira la testa (ho le vertigini).** *mee jEE-rah lah tEHs-tah (oh leh vehr-tEE-jee-nee)*
I feel weak.	**Mi sento debole.** *mee sEHn-toh dAY-boh-leh*
I want to sit down for a while.	**Vorrei sedermi un poco.** *vohr-rEH-ee seh-dAYr-mee oon pOH-koh*
My temperature is normal (37°C) (high).	**La temperatura è normale (trenta sette gradi)(alta).** *lah tehm-peh-rah-tOO-rah EH nohr-mAH-leh (trEHn-tah sEHt-teh grAH-dee) (AHl-tah)*
I (think I) have ____.	**(Credo che) ho ____.** *(kreh-doh kay) oh*
■ an abscess	**un ascesso** *oon ah-shEHs-soh*
■ a broken bone	**una frattura** *OO-nah frat-tOO-rah*
■ a bruise	**una contusione** *OO-nah kohn-too-see-OH-neh*
■ a burn	**un'ustione** *oo-noo-stee-oH-neh*
■ the chills	**i brividi** *ee brEE-vee-dee*
■ a cold	**un raffreddore** *oon rahf-frehd-dOH-reh*

◼ constipation	**stitichezza**	*stee-tee-kAY-tsah*
◼ a cut	**una ferita (un taglio)**	*OO-nah feh-rEE-tah (oon tAH-ly-ee-oh)*
◼ diarrhea	**la diarrea**	*lah dee-ahr-rEH-ah*
◼ a fever	**la febbre**	*la fEHb-breh*
◼ a headache	**un mal di testa**	*oon mAHl dee tEHs-tah*
◼ an infection	**un'infezione**	*oo-neen-feh-tsee-OH-neh*
◼ a lump	**un gonfiore**	*oon gohn-fee-OH-reh*
◼ rheumatism	**i reumatismi**	*ee reh-oo-mah-tEE-smee*
◼ something in my eye	**qualche cosa nell'occhio**	*koo-AHl-keh kOH-sah nayl-lOHk-key-oh*
◼ a sore throat	**un mal di gola**	*oon mAHl dee gOH-lah*
◼ stomach cramps	**crampi allo stomaco**	*krAHm-pee AHl-loh stOH-mah-koh*
◼ a stomachache	**un mal di stomaco**	*oon mAHl dee stOH-mah-koh*

TELLING THE DOCTOR

It hurts me here.	**Mi fa male qui.**	*mee fah mAH-leh koo-EE*
My whole body hurts.	**Mi fa male dappertutto.**	*Mee fah mAH-leh dahp-pehr-tOOt-toh*
I'm presently taking antibiotics.	**Sto prendendo degli antibiotici.**	*stoh prayn-dEHn-doh dAY-ly-ee ahn-tee-bee-OH-tee-chee*
I'm constipated.	**Soffro di stitichezza.**	*sOHf-froh dee stee-tee-kAY-tsah*
I'm flatulent.	**Ho gas intestinali.**	*oh gAHs een-teh-stee-nAH-lee*
I need a laxative.	**Ho bisogno di un lassativo.**	*oh bee-sOH-ny-oh dee oon lahs-sah-tEE-voh*

I have (hay) fever.	**Ho la febbre (da fieno).**	*oh lah fEHb-breh (dah fee-EH-noh)*
My _____ hurts.	**Mi fa male _____.**	*mee fah mAH-leh*
■ appendix	**l'appendicite**	*lahp-pehn-dee-chEE-teh*
■ ankle	**la caviglia**	*lah kah-vEE-ly-ah*
■ arm	**il braccio**	*eel brAH-chee-oh*
■ back	**la schiena**	*lah skey-EH-nah*
■ breast	**il petto**	*eel pEHt-toh*
■ cheek	**la guancia**	*lah goo-AHn-chee-ah*
■ ear	**l'orecchio**	*loh-rAY-key-oh*
■ elbow	**il gomito**	*eel gOH-mee-toh*
■ eye	**l'occhio**	*lOH-key-oh*
■ face	**la faccia**	*lah fAH-chee-ah*
■ finger	**il dito**	*eel dEE-doh*
■ foot	**il piede**	*eel pee-EH-deh*
■ hand	**la mano**	*lah mAH-noh*
■ head	**la testa**	*lah tEHs-tah*
■ heart	**il cuore**	*eel koo-OH-reh*
■ hip	**l'anca**	*lAHn-kah*
■ knee	**il ginocchio**	*eel jee-nOH-key-oh*
■ leg	**la gamba**	*lah gAHm-bah*
■ lip	**il labbro**	*eel lAHb-broh*
■ mouth	**la bocca**	*lah bOH-kah*
■ neck	**il collo**	*eel kOHl-loh*
■ nose	**il naso**	*eel nAH-soh*
■ shoulder	**la spalla**	*lah spAHl-lah*
■ throat	**la gola**	*lah gOH-lah*
■ thumb	**il pollice**	*eel pOHl-lee-cheh*

■ toe **l'alluce** *lAHl-loo-cheh*

■ tooth **il dente** *eel dEHn-teh*

■ wrist **il polso** *eel pOHl-soh*

I've had this pain since yesterday. **Ho questo dolore da ieri.** *oh koo-AYs-toh doh-lOH-reh dah ee-EH-ree*

There's a (no) history of asthma (diabetes, heart problems) in my family. **(Non) c'è anamnesi di asma (diabete, problemi cardiaci) nella mia famiglia.** *(nohn) chEH ah-nahm-nEH-see dee AH-smah (dee-ah-bEH-teh proh-blEH-mee kahr-dEE-ah-chee) nAYl-lah mEE-ah fah-mEE-ly-ee-ah*

I'm (not) allergic to antibiotics (penicillin). **(Non) sono allergico agli antibiotici (alla penicillina).** *(nohn) sOH-noh ahl-lEHr-jee-koh AH-ly-ee ahn-tee-bee-OH-tee-chee (AHl-lah peh-nee-cheel-lEE-nah)*

I have chest pains. **Ho dolori al petto.** *oh doh-lOH-ree ahl pEHt-toh*

I had a heart attack _____. **Ho avuto un attacco cardiaco _____.** *oh ah-vOO-toh oon aht-tAHk-koh kahr-dEE-ah-koh*

■ last year **l'anno scorso** *lAHn-noh skOHr-soh*

■ (three) years ago **(tre) anni fa** *trEH AHn-nee fah*

I'm taking this medicine (insulin). **Sto prendendo questa medicina (insulina).** *stOH prehn-dEHn-doh koo-AYs-tah meh-dee-chEE-nah (een-soo-lEE-nah)*

I'm pregnant. **Sono incinta.** *sOH-noh een-chEEn-tah*

I feel faint. **Mi sento svenire.** *mee sEHn-toh sveh-nEE-reh*

I feel all right now. **Mi sento bene adesso.** *mee sEHn-toh bEH-neh ah-dEHs-soh*

I feel better (worse).	**Mi sento meglio (peggio).** *mee sEHn-toh mEH-ly-ee-oh (pEH-jee-oh)*
Do I have _____?	**Ho _____?** *OH*
■ appendicitis	**l'appendicite** *lahp-pehn-dee-chEE-teh*
■ the flu	**l'influenza** *leen-floo-EHn-tzah*
■ tonsilitis	**una tonsillite** *OO-nah tohn-seel-lEE-teh*
Is it serious (contagious)?	**È serio (contagioso)?** *EH sEH-ree-oh (kohn-tah-jee-OH-soh)*
Do I have to go to the hospital?	**Devo andare in ospedale?** *dAY-voh ahn-dAH-reh een oh-speh-dAH-leh*
When can I continue my trip?	**Quando potrò continuare la mia gita?** *koo-AHn-doh poh-trOH kohn-tee-noo-AH-reh lah mEE-ah jEE-tah*

QUESTIONS

Are you giving me a prescription?	**Mi darà una ricetta?** *mee dah-rAH OO-nah ree-chEHt-tah*
How often must I take this medicine (these pills)?	**Quante volte devo prendere questa medicina (queste pillole)?** *koo-AHn-teh vOHl-teh dAY-voh prAYn-deh-reh koo-AYs-tah meh-dee-chEE-nah (koo-AYs-teh pEEl-loh-leh)*
(How long) do I have to stay in bed?	**(Quanto) devo rimanere a letto?** *(koo-AHn-toh) dAY-voh ree-mah-nAY-reh ah lEHt-toh*
Thank you (for everything) doctor.	**Grazie (di tutto), dottore.** *grAH-tsee-eh (dee tOOt-toh) doht-tOH-reh*
How much do I owe you for your services?	**Quanto le devo per la visita?** *koo-AHn-toh leh dAY-voh pehr lah vEE-see-tah*

May I have a receipt?	**Può darmi la ricevuta?** *poo-OH dAHr-mee lah ree-chay-vOO-tah*
I have medical insurance.	**Ho l'assicurazione (l'assistenza) medica.** *oh lahs-see-koo-rah-tsee-OH-neh (lahs-sees-stEHn-tsah) mEH-dee-kah*
Will you accept my medical insurance?	**Accetta la mia assicurazione (assistenza) medica?** *ah-chEHt-tah lah mEE-ah ahs-see-koo-rah-tsee-OH-neh (ahs-see-stEHn-tsah) mEH-dee-kah*
Is there a co-payment?	**C'è qualche pagamento a carica del paziente?** *chEH koo-AHl-kay pah-gah-mEHn-toh ah kaH-ree-kah dayl pah-tsee-EHn-teh*

IN THE HOSPITAL (ACCIDENTS)

Help!	**Aiuto!** *ah-ee-OO-toh*
Get a doctor, quick!	**Chiamate un medico, subito!** *key-ah-mAH-teh oon mEH-dee-koh sOO-bee-toh*
Call an ambulance!	**Chiamate un'ambulanza!** *key-ah-mAH-teh oo-nahm-boo-lAHn-tsah*
Take him to the hospital.	**Portatelo in ospedale.** *pohr-tAH-teh-loh een oh-speh-dAH-leh*
I've fallen.	**Sono caduto(a).** *sOH-noh kah-dOO-toh(ah)*
I was knocked down.	**Mi hanno buttato(a) a terra.** *mee AHn-noh boot-tAH-toh(ah) ah tEHr-rah*
She was run over.	**È stata investita.** *EH stAH-tah een-veh-stEE-tah*
I think I've had a heart attack.	**Credo che ho avuto un collasso cardiaco.** *krEH-do kay oh ah-vOO-toh oon kohl-lAHs-soh kahr-dEE-ah-koh*

I burned myself.	**Mi sono ustionato(a).** *mee sOH-noh oo-stee-oh-nAH-toh(ah)*
I cut myself.	**Mi sono tagliato(a).** *mee sOH-noh tah-ly-ee-AH-toh(ah)*
I'm bleeding.	**Sto sanguinando.** *stOH sahn-goo-ee-nAHn-doh*
He's lost a lot of blood.	**Ha perduto molto sangue.** *ah pehr-dOO-toh mOHl-toh sAHn-goo-eh*
I think the bone is broken (dislocated).	**Penso che mi si sia fratturato (lussato) l'osso.** *pEHn-soh kay mee see sEE-ah fraht-too-rAH-toh (loos-sAH-toh) lOHs-soh*
The leg is swollen.	**La gamba è gonfia.** *lah gAHm-bah EH gOHn-fee-ah*
The wrist is sprained (twisted).	**Mi si è slogato (storto) il polso.** *mee see-EH sloh-gAH-toh (stOHr-toh) eel pOHl-soh*
The ankle is sprained (twisted).	**Mi si è slogata (storta) la caviglia.** *mee see-EH sloh-gAH-tah (stOHr-tah) lah kah-vEE-ly-ee-ah*

I can't move my elbow (knee).	**Non posso muovere il gomito (il ginocchio).** *nohn pOHs-soh moo-OH-veh-reh eel gOH-mee-toh (eel jee-nOHk-key-oh)*

AT THE DENTIST

I have to go to the dentist.	**Devo andare dal dentista.** *dAY-voh ahn-dAH-reh dAHl dehn-tEEs-tah*
Can you recommend a dentist?	**Può raccomandarmi un dentista?** *poo-OH rahk-koh-mahn-dAHr-mee oon dehn-tEEs-tah*
I have a toothache that's driving me crazy.	**Ho un mal di denti che mi fa impazzire.** *oh oon mAHl dee dEHn-tee kay mee fah eem-pah-tsEE-reh*
I have a cavity that's giving me a lot of pain.	**Ho una carie che mi fa molto male.** *oh OO-nah kAH-ree-eh kay mee fah mOHl-toh mAH-leh*
I've lost a filling.	**Ho perduto l'otturazione.** *oh payr-dOO-toh loht-too-rah-tsee-OH-neh*
I've a broken tooth.	**Mi son rotto un dente.** *mee sOHn rOHt-toh oon dEHn-teh*
My gums hurt me.	**Mi fanno male le gengive.** *mee fAHn-noh mAH-leh leh jehn-jEE-veh*
Is there an infection?	**C'è un'infezione?** *chEH oo-neen-feh-tsee-OH-neh*
Will you have to extract the tooth?	**Deve estrarre il dente?** *dAY-veh ehs-trAHr-reh eel dEHn-teh*
I'd prefer you filled it _____.	**Preferisco farlo otturare _____.** *preh-feh-rIH-skoh fAHr-loh oht-too-rAH-reh*
■ with amalgam	**con l'algama** *kohn lAHl-gah-mah*

■ with gold	**con oro**	*kohn OH-roh*
■ with silver	**con argento**	*kohn ahr-jEHn-toh*
■ for now (temporarily)	**provvisoriamente**	*prohv-vee-soh-ree-ah-mEHn-teh*

Can you fix _____?	**Può riparare _____?** *poo-OH ree-pah-rAH-reh*
■ this bridge	**questo ponte** *koo-AYs-toh pOHn-teh*
■ this crown	**questa corona** *koo-AYs-tah koh-rOH-nah*
■ these dentures	**questi denti finti** *koo-AYs-tee dEHn-tee fEEn-tee*

When should I come back?	**Quando dovrei ritornare?** *koo-AHn-doh doh-vrEH-ee ree-tohr-nAH-reh*
How much do I owe you for your services?	**Quanto le devo per la visita?** *koo-AHn-toh leh dAY-voh pehr lah vEE-see-tah*

WITH THE OPTICIAN

Can you repair these glasses (for me)?	**Può aggiustar(mi) questi occhiali?** *poo-OH ah-jee-oo-stAHr (mee) koo-AYs-tee oh-key-AH-lee*
I've broken a lens (the frame).	**Mi si è rotta una lente (la montatura).** *mee see-EH rOHt-tah OO-nah lEHn-teh (lah mohn-tah-tOO-rah)*
Can you put in a new lens?	**Può metterci una lente nuova?** *poo-OH mAYt-tehr-chee OO-nah lEHn-teh noo-OH-vah*
I do not have a prescription.	**Non ho la ricetta medica.** *nohn oh lah ree-chEHt-tah mEH-dee-kah*

Can you tighten the screw?	**Può stringere la vite?** *poo-OH strEEn-jeh-rEH lah vEE-teh*
I need the glasses as soon as possible.	**Ho bisogno degli occhiali al più presto possibile.** *oh bee-sOH-ny-oh dAY-ly-ee oh-key-AH-lee ahl pee-OO prEH-stoh pohs-sEE-bee-leh*
I don't have any others.	**Non ne ho altri.** *nohn nay-OH AHl-tree*
Do you sell ____?	**Vende ____?** *vAYn-deh*
■ contact lenses	**lenti a contatto** *lEHn-tee ah kohn-tAHt-toh*
■ sunglasses	**occhiali da sole** *oh-key-AH-lee dah sOH-leh*
■ transition lenses	**lenti fotocromatiche** *lEHn-tee fOH-toh-kroh-mAH-tee-keh*
■ progressive lenses	**lenti progressive** *lEHn-tee proh-grehs-sEE-veh*
■ bifocal lenses	**lenti bifocali** *lEHn-tee bee-foh-kAH-lee*
■ (disposable) contact lenses	**lenti a contatto (usa e getta)** *lEHn-tee ah kohn-tAHt-toh (OO-sah ay jEHt-tah)*
■ color contact lenses	**lenti a contatto cromate** *lEHn-tee ah kohn-tAHt-toh kroh-mAH-teh*
■ hearing aids	**apparecchi acustici per l'udito** *ah-pah-rAY-key ah-kOO-stee-chee pehr loo-dEE-toh*
I'm ____.	**Sono ____.**
■ astigmatic	**astigmatico** *ah-steeg-mAH-tee-koh*
■ farsighted	**presbiope** *prEH-sbee-oh-peh*
■ nearsighted	**miope** *mEE-oh-peh*
I have lost a contact lens.	**Ho perduto una lente a contatto.** *oh pehr-dOO-toh oo-nah lEHn-teh ah kohn-tAHt-toh*

Can you replace it quickly?	**Può darmene un'altra subito?** *poo-OH dAHr-meh-neh oo-nAHl-trah sOO-bee-toh*

PHARMACEUTICALS—MINIDICTIONARY

amphetamine	**l'anfetamina** *lahn-feh-tah-mEE-nah*
anaesthetic	**l'anestetico** *lah-neh-stEG-tee-koh*
analgesic	**l'analgesico** *lah-nahl-jEH-see-koh*
antacid	**l'antiacido** *lahn-tee-AH-chee-doh*
anti-inflammatory	**l'antiflogistico** *lahn-tee-floh-jEE-stee-koh*
antibiotic	**l'antibiotico** *lahn-tee-bee-OH-tee-koh*
antidepressant	**l'antidepressivo** *lahn-tee-deh-prehs-sEE-voh*
antiseptic	**l'antisettico** *lahn-tee-sEHt-tee-koh*
aspirin	**l'aspirina** *lah-spee-rEE-nah*
blood pressure monitoring kit	**un monitore per la pressione** *oon moh-nee-tOH-reh pehr lah prehs-see-OH-neh*
cough drop	**la pastiglia per la tosse** *lah pah-stEE-ly-ah pehr lah tOHs-seh*
cough syrup	**lo sciroppo per la tosse** *loh shee-rOHp-poh pehr lah tOHs-seh*
diuretic	**il diuretico** *eel dee-oo-rEH-tee-koh*
dose	**la dose** *lah dOH-seh*
drop	**la goccia** *lah gOH-chee-ah*
drug	**il fàrmaco** *eel fAHr-mah-koh*

eyedrop	**il collirio** *eel kohl-lEE-ree-oh*
injection	**l'iniezione (la puntura)** *lee-nee-eh-tzee-OH-neh (lah poon-tOO-rah)*
laxative	**il lassativo (il purgante)** *eel lahs-sah-tEE-voh (eel poor-gAHn-teh)*
ointment	**l'unguento (la pomata)** *loon-goo-EHn-toh (lah poh-mAH-tah)*
pill	**la pillola** *lah pEEl-loh-lah*
saccharin	**la saccarina** *lah sahk-kah-rEE-nah*
sedative	**il calmante** *eel kahl-mAHn-teh*
sleeping pill	**il sonnifero** *eel sohn-nEE-feh-roh*
stimulant	**lo stimolante** *loh stee-moh-lAHn-teh*
syringe	**la siringa** *lah see-rEEn-gah*
tablet	**la pastiglia (la compressa)** *lah pahs-tEE-ly-ah (lah kohm-prEHs-sah)*
thermometer	**il termometro** *eel tehr-mOH-meh-troh*
tranquilizer	**il tranquillante** *eel trahn-koo-eel-lAIIn toh*
vaccine	**il vaccino** *eel vah-chEE-noh*
vitamin	**la vitamina** *lah vee-tah-mEE-ah*

Travel Tips   Every traveler needs to carry a few small items for emergencies. Skip Swiss army knives or any objects that could be considered a weapon by airport security guards.

COMMUNICATIONS

POST OFFICE

Post offices in Italy can be identified by a sign, **Poste e Telecomunicazioni**, or the initials **PT**. All post offices are generally open on weekdays from 8:00 A.M. to 1:30 or 2:00 P.M., and Saturdays from 8:00 A.M. to 11:45 A.M. In the largest cities (Rome, Milan, Turin, Naples, etc.) the central post office **(posta centrale)** is open until 9 P.M. Some counters (registered mail, telegrams, etc.) may have different hours and in the main cities they may also be open in the afternoon.

Stamps are sold at windows usually marked **Raccomandate/ Francobolli** (Registered Letters/Stamps). Always have the clerk weigh airmail letters since overweight letters will be sent surface mail rather than returned to the sender. Urgent letters may be sent **espresso** (special delivery) with additional postage.

Italian post offices are often very crowded because **conti correnti** (current bills for taxes, electricity and gas, and telephone) are paid at the post office.

Stamps for letters of normal weight and postcards can be purchased more conveniently at a tobacco shop **(tabaccheria)**. The tobacconist has a schedule of postal rates. There are no stamp-dispensing machines in Italy.

Letter boxes, which are red and attached to the wall rather than freestanding, are found in front of post offices and in the vicinity of tobacco shops. If there are two letter boxes side by side, be sure *not* to put letters and postcards for other destinations, including overseas, in the box marked **Città** (City).

General delivery letters should be addressed as follows:
Name of addressee
c/o Ufficio Postale Centrale
Fermo Posta
City

I want to mail a letter.	**Voglio spedire una lettera.** *vOH-ly-ee-oh speh-dEE-reh OO-nah lAYt-teh-rah*
Where's the post office?	**Dov'è l'ufficio postale?** *doh-vEH loof-fEE-chee-oh poh-stAH-leh*
Where's a letter box?	**Dov'è una cassetta postale?** *doh-vEH OO-nah kas-sAYt-tah poh-stAH-leh*
What is the postage on _____ to the United States (Canada, England, Australia)?	**Qual è l'affrancatura per _____ per gli Stati Uniti (Canadà, Inghilterra, Australia)?** *koo-ah-lEH lahf-frahn-kah-tOO-rah pehr _____ pehr ly-ee stAH-tee oo-nEE-tee (kah-nah-dAH een-gheel-tEHr-rah ahoo-strAH-lee-ah)*
■ a letter	**una lettera** *OO-nah lAYt-teh-rah*
■ an airmail letter	**una lettera via aerea** *OO-nah lAYt-teh-rah vEE-ah ah-EH-reh-ah*
■ an insured letter	**una lettera assicurata** *OO-nah lAYt-teh-rah ahs-see-koo-rAH-tah*
■ a registered letter	**una lettera raccomandata** *OO-nah lAYt-teh-rah rahk-koh-mahn-dAH-tah*
■ a special delivery letter	**una lettera espresso** *OO-nah lAYt-teh-rah ehs-prEHs-soh*
■ a package	**un pacco** *oon pAHk-koh*
■ a postcard	**una cartolina postale** *OO-nah kahr-toh-lEE-nah poh-stAH-leh*
When will it arrive?	**Quando arriverà?** *koo-AHn-doh ahr-ree-veh-rAH*
Which is the _____ window?	**Qual è lo sportello per _____?** *koo-ah-lEH loh spohr-tEHl-loh pehr*
■ general delivery	**il fermo posta** *eel fAYr-moh pOH-stah*

| money order | **i vaglia postali**   *ee vAH-ly-ee-ah poh-stAH-lee* |
| stamp | **i francobolli**   *ee frahn-koh-bOHl-lee* |

Are there any letters for me? My name is _____.

Ci sono lettere per me? Il mio nome è _____. *chee sOH-noh lAYt-teh-reh pehr mAY eel mEE-oh nOH-meh EH*

I'd like _____.

Vorrei _____. *vohr-rEH-ee*

| 10 postcards | **dieci cartoline postali** *dee-EH-chee kahr-toh-lEE-neh poh-stAH-lee* |
| 5 (airmail) stamps | **cinque francobolli (via aerea)** *chEEn-koo-eh frahn-koh-bOHl-lee (vEE-ah ah-EH-reh-ah)* |

Do I fill out a customs receipt?

Devo compilare una ricevuta? *dAY-voh kohm-pee-lAH-reh OO-nah ree-cheh-vOO-tah*

TELEPHONES

You'll find public telephones in cafés, bars, and station terminals. Obtain a prepaid phone card at a minimum charge of L 5,000 (five thousand liras). It can be bought almost everywhere (automatic distributors, Telecom shops, public phone locations, bars, newspaper stands, post offices, and tobacco shops). You may want to use a **tèlemat** (a public telephone that operates with coins and magnetic cards). As soon as you pick up the receiver, the directions for proper use will appear on the screen. You'll be able to select among four languages: Italian, English, French, and German. Remember to dial the area code for local calls, long-distance domestic, international, and intercontinental calls. To obtain information on rates, area codes, and phone numbers for foreign subscribers, dial **176**. (This service is on-line 24 hours a day.) You can access **Countrydirect** by dialing **172** + country code. (The identity codes for various countries are listed in the official phone directories.) With this service, you can call abroad from Italy with assistance in your own language. Dial **800-020020** (Monday to Friday from 8:30 A.M. to 4:30 P.M.) to reach the International Contact Point Service for information in Italian or English on networks, telecommunication services, and relative charges. At several telephone centers there are "clicking" timers. You will pay after having completed the phone call and will be charged by the number of **scatti** *(skAHt-tee)* or "clicks" marked by the timer.

While the telephone is ringing, you'll be able to hear two different signals. The long *too, too* sounds signify that the line is free and the bell is ringing; the short and repeated *too, too, too* sounds signify that the line is busy.

If you have difficulty operating the telephone or feel you will not be able to understand the person who answers the call, ask the clerk at your hotel to make the call for you.

USEFUL NUMBERS

112 & 113	EMERGENCY ASSISTANCE NUMBERS
112	POLICE **carabinieri** *(kah-rah-bee-nee-EH-ree)*.
113	POLICE/STATE POLICE **Polizia Urbana/ Pubblica Sicurezza** *(poh-lee-tzEE-ah oor-bAH-nah/pOO-blee-kah see-koo-rAY-tzah)*. Usually has an English interpreter.
115	FIRE DEPARTMENT **Vigili del Fuoco** *(vEE-jee-lee dAYl foo-OH-koh)*.
116	EMERGENCY ROAD SERVICE
	ACI (Italian Automobile Club). ACI also has a 24-hour-a-day Multilingual Phone Service Center **(CAT = Centro Assistanza Telefonica)** for motorists in English, French, German, Spanish, Portuguese, and Dutch. Call 06 4477 to receive information on automotive procedures, currency, customs formalities, ferries, highway tolls, mileage distances, roads, tourist itineraries, and weather conditions.
117	AMBULANCE/HEALTH EMERGENCY

176	INTERNATIONAL INQUIRIES
12	PHONE DIRECTORY ASSISTANCE
17 90	ITALCABLE (for reverse charge and calling card calls).
172 15 98	AT&T
172 10 11	MCI
172 10 22	SPRINT

You may get additional useful data by calling the local tourist offices and youth information centers in the major cities.

ACI = Automobile Club d'Italia. Italian Automobile Club.

AIG = Associazione Italiana Alberghi per la Gioventù. Italian Youth Hostels Association.

ATG = Associazione Turismo Giovanile. Youth Tourist Association.

C.R.U.E.I. = Centro Relazioni Universitarie. University Relations Center.

CIT = Compagnia Italiana Turismo. The official Italian travel agency.

CTS = Centro Turistico Studentesco. Tourist Center for Students. (See page 31.)

ENIT = Ente Nazionale per il Turismo. Italian State Tourist Office.

EPT = Ente Provinciale per il Turismo. Provincial Tourist Information Office.

Pro Loco = Local Tourist Information Office.

AREA CODES
Here are the dialing/area codes, **prefissi telefonici** (*preh-fEEs-see teh leh-phOH-nee-chee*), for some of the principal cities in Italy. When you make a call from New York to Naples, you should dial as follows: 011 + 39 + 081 + phone number. When you call New York (Manhattan) from Italy, you dial 001 + 212 + phone number.

Ancona	071	Leghorn	0586
Aosta	0165	Messina	090
Assisi	075	Milan	02
Bari	080	Naples	081
Benevento	0824	Palermo	091
Bologna	051	Perugia	075
Bolzano	0471	Pisa	050
Brindisi	0831	Potenza	0971
Cagliari	070	Reggio Calabria	0965
Campobasso	0874	Rimini	0541
Capri	081	Rome	06
Catania	095	San Marino	0541
Catanzaro	0961	Siena	0577
Cortina d'Ampezzo	0436	Trento	0461
Florence	055	Turin	011
Genoa	010	Trieste	040
Ischia	081	Venice	041
L'Aquila	0862	Verona	045
Lipari Islands	090	Viareggio	0584

Where is _____?	**Dov'è _____?** *doh-vEH*
■ a public telephone	**un telefono pubblico** *oon teh-lEH-foh-noh-pOOb-blee-koh*
■ a telephone booth	**una cabina telefonica** *OO-nah kah-bEE-nah teh-leh-fOH-nee-kah*
■ a telephone directory	**un elenco telefonico** *oon eh-lEHn-koh teh-leh-fOH-nee-koh*
May I use your phone?	**Posso usare il suo telefono?** *pOHs-soh oo-sAH-reh eel sOO-oh teh-lEH-foh-noh*
Can I call direct?	**Posso telefonare direttamente?** *pOHs-soh teh-leh-foh-nAH-reh dee-reht-tah-mEHn-teh*
I want to reverse the charges.	**Desidero fare una riversibile.** *deh-sEE-deh-roh fAH-reh OO-nah ree-vehr-sEE-bee-leh*

I'd like a three-way call.	**Vorrei un collegamento in simultanea a tre.** *vohr-rEH-ee oon kohl-lay-gah-mEHn-toh een see-mool-tAH-neh-ah ah trAY*
Do I need a magnetic phone card?	**Occorre una scheda magnetica?** *ohk-kOHr-reh oo-nah skEH-dah mah-nyEH-tee-kah*
Can you give me a phone card, please?	**Può darmi una scheda telefonica?** *poo-OH dAHr-mee OO-nah skEH-dah teh-leh-fOH-nee-kah*
I want to make a ____ to ____.	**Vorrei fare una ____ a ____.** *vohr-rEH-ee fAH-reh OO-nah____ ah ____*

■ local call   **telefonata urbana** *teh-leh-foh-nAH-tah oor-bAH-nah*

■ long-distance call   **una telefonata in teleselezione (interurbana, internazionale)** *OO-nah teh-leh-foh-nAH-tah een teh-leh-seh-leh-tsee-OH-neh (een-tehr-oor-bAH-nah een-tehr-nah-tsee-oh-nAH-leh)*

■ person-to-person call   **una telefonata diretta con preavviso** *OO-nah teh-leh-foh-nAH-tah dee-rEHt-tah kohn preh-ahv-vEE-soh*

| How do I get the operator? | **Come si ottiene il centralino?** *kOH-meh see oht-tee-EH-neh eel chehn-trah-lEE-noh* |
| Operator, can you give me ____? | **Signorina (signore, centralino), può darmi ____?** *see-ny-oh-rEE-nah (see-ny-OH-reh chehn-trah-lEE-noh) poo-OH dAHr-mee* |

■ number 23 345   **il ventitrè trecentoquarantacinque** *eel vayn-tee-trEH treh-chEHn-toh-koo-ah-rahn-tah-chEEn-koo-eh*

■ extension 19 **interno diciannove** *een-tEHr-noh dee-chee-ahn-nOH-veh*

■ area code ____ **prefisso numero ____** *preh-fEEs-soh nOO-meh-roh*

■ country code ____ **prefisso internazionale ____** *preh-fEEs-soh een-tehr-nah-tzee-oh-nAH-leh*

■ city code ____ **prefisso interurbano ____** *preh-fEEs-soh een-tehr-oor-bAH-noh*

My number is ____. **Il mio numero è ____.** *eel mEE-oh nOO-meh-roh EH*

May I speak to ____? **Potrei parlare con ____?** *poh-trEH-ee pahr-lAH-reh kohn*

Is ____ in? **C'è ____?** *chEH*

■ Mr. ____ **il signor ____** *EEl sy-nee-Ohr*

■ Mrs. ____ **la signora ____** *lah sy-nee-OH-rah*

■ Miss ____ **la signorina ____** *lah sy-nee-oh-rEE-nah*

Speaking. **Sono io.** *sOH-noh EE-oh*

Hello. **Pronto.** *prOHn-toh*

Who is it? **Chi è?** *key EH*

PROBLEMS ON THE LINE

I can't hear. **Non si sente bene.** *nohn see sEHn-teh bEH-neh*

Speak louder (please). **Parli più forte (per favore).** *pAHr-lee pee-OO fOHr-teh (pehr fah-vOH-reh)*

Don't hang up. **Non appenda il ricevitore.** *nohn ahp-pEHn-dah eel ree-cheh-vee-tOH-reh*

This is ____. **Parla ____.** *pAHr-lah*

Do you have an answering machine?	**Ha una segreteria telefonica?** *ah OO-nah seh-greh-teh-rEE-ah teh-leh-fOH-nee-kah*
The line is busy.	**La linea è occupata.** *lah lEE-neh-ah EH ohk-koo-pAH-tah*
You gave me (that was) a wrong number.	**Mi ha dato (era) un numero sbagliato.** *mee ah dAH-toh (EH-rah) oon nOO-meh-roh sbah-ly-ee-AH-toh*
I was cut off.	**È caduta la linea.** *EH kah-dOO-tah lah lEE-neh-ah*
Please dial it again.	**Per favore, rifaccia il numero.** *pehr fah-vOH-reh ree-fAH-chee-ah eel nOO-meh-roh*
I want to leave a message.	**Voglio lasciare un (messaggio) appunto.** *vOH-ly-ee-oh lah-shee-AH-reh oon (mehs-sAH-jee-oh) ahp-pOOn-toh*

PAYING UP

How much do I have to pay?	**Quanto devo pagare?** *koo-AHn-toh dEH-voh pah-gAH-reh*
How many clicks did I have?	**Quanti scatti sono?** *koo-AHn-tee skAHt-tee sOH-noh*

FAXES

Do you have a fax machine?	**Ha un fax?** *ah oon fahcs*
What is your fax number?	**Qual è il numero del fax?** *koo-ahl-EH eel nOO-meh-roh dayl fahcs*
I'd like to fax _____.	**Vorrei faxare _____.** *vohr-rEH-ee fahc-sAH-reh*
■ a document	**un documento** *oon doh-koo-mEHn-toh*
■ an invoice	**una fattura** *OO-nah faht-tOO-rah*
■ a letter	**una lettera** *OO-nah lAYt-teh-rah*
■ a receipt	**una ricetta** *OO-nah ree-chEHt-tah*
May I fax it to you?	**Glielo posso faxare?** *ly-ay-loh pOHs-soh fahc-sAH-reh*
Fax it to me.	**Me lo faxi.** *may-loh fAHc-see*
I didn't get your fax.	**Non ho ricevuto il suo fax.** *nohn oh ree-cheh-vOO-toh eel sOO-oh fahcs*
Did you receive my fax?	**Ha ricevuto il mio fax?** *ah ree-cheh-vOO-toh eel mEE-oh fahcs*
Your fax is illegible.	**Il suo fax è illegibile.** *eel sOO-oh fahcs EH eel-leh-jEE-bee-leh*
Please, send it again.	**Per favore, me lo(la) faxi di nuovo.** *pAYr fah-vOH-reh may-loh(lah) fahc-see dee noo-OH-voh*

PHOTOCOPIES

Do you have a photocopier?	**C'è una fotocopiatrice?** *chEH OO-nah foh-toh-koh-pee-ah-trEE-ceh*
I would like to make a photocopy of this _____.	**Vorrei fare una fotocopia di _____.** *vohr-rEH-ee fAH-reh OO-nah foh-toh-kOH-pee-ah dee*
■ page	**questa pagina** *koo-AYs-tah pAH-jee-nah*
■ document	**questo documento** *koo-AYs-toh doh-koo-mEH-ntoh*
What is the cost per page?	**Quanto costa per pagina?** *koo-AHn-toh kOH-stah pehr pAH-jee-nah*
Can you enlarge it (by 25%)?	**Può ingrandirlo (del 25%)?** *poo-OH een-grahn-dEEr-loh (dayl vayn-tee-chEEn-koo-eh pehr chEHn-toh)*
Can you reduce it (by 50%)?	**Può ridurlo (del 50%)?** *poo-OH ree-dOOr-loh (dayl cheen-koo-AHn-tah pehr chEHn-toh)*
Can you make a color copy?	**Può fare una copia a colori?** *poo-OH fAH-reh OO-nah kOH-pee-ah ah koh-lOH-ree*

COMPUTERS

To get information on the internet:
- Go to the location box on your web browser
- Type *http://www.altavista.digital.com* or *www.hotbot.com*
- Click *Enter*
- You will see a search screen. Click on *"any language"*
- Select *Italian*
- You can search for any subject

What kind of computer do you have?	**Che sistema (tipo di computer) ha?** *kay see-stEH-mah (tEE-poh dee computer) ah*
What operating system are you using?	**Che sistema operativo usa?** *kay see-stEH-mah oh-peh-rah-tEE-voh OO-sah*
What word processing program are you using?	**Quale software applicativo usa?** *koo-AH-leh software ahp-plee-kah-tEE-voh OO-sah*
Are our systems compatible?	**Sono compatibili i nostri sistemi?** *sOH-noh kohm-pah-tEE-bee-lee ee nOHs-tree see-stEH-mee*
Do you have (use) an e-mail address?	**Ha (usa) un indirizzo di posta elettronica?** *ah (OO-sah) oon een-dee-rEE-tzoh dee pOH-stah eh-leht-trOH-nee-kah*
What is your e-mail address?	**Qual è il suo indirizzo e-mail?** *koo-ah-lEH eel sOO-oh een-dee-rEE-tzoh E-mail*

COMPUTER TERMS—MINIDICTIONARY

access	**accèsso (connessione)** *ah-chEH-soh (kohn-nehs-see-OH-neh)*
boot, to	**accendere** *ah-chEHn-deh-reh*
brand name	**la marca (il nome di marca)** *lah mAHr-kah (eel nOH-meh dee mAHr-kah)*
cable	**cavo** *kAH-voh*
CD-ROM disk	**same as English**
chip	**(micro) chip** *(mEE-kroh) cheep*
click, to	**cliccare** *kleek-kAH-reh*
computerize, to	**computerizzare** *kohm-poo-teh-ree-tzAH-reh*

cursor	**il cursore**	*eel koor-sOH-reh*
database	**same as English**	
disk drive	**same as English**	
diskette	**dischetto (floppy disk)**	*dee-skAEt-toh*
DOS	**same as English**	
download, to	**scaricare**	*skah-ree-kAH-reh*
e-mail	**la posta elettronica**	*lah pOH-stah eh-leht-trOH-nee-kah*
file	**i file**	*ee fAH-eel*
graphics	**la grafica**	*lah grAH-fee-kah*
home page	**l'home page**	*lOH-m page*
internet	**same as English**	
joystick	**same as English**	
key	**chiave**	*key-AH-veh*
keyboard	**tastiera**	*tah-stee-EH-rah*
laptop computer	**pc portatile**	*pee-see pohr-tAH-tee-lee*
link	**same as English**	
memory	**la memoria**	*lah meh-mOH-ree-ah*
modem	**il modem**	*eel mOH-dehm*
monitor	**same as English**	
mouse	**same as English**	
navigate, to	**navigare**	*nah-vee-gAH-reh*
network	**same as English**	
online service	**servizio in rete**	*sayr-vEE-tsee-oh een rAY-teh*
printer	**la stampante**	*lah stahm-pAHn-teh*
■ laser	**(il) laser**	*eel laser*
■ ink jet	**l'ink jet**	*leenk jeht*

scanner	**lo scanner** *loh skAHn-neehr*
search engine	**sistema di ricerca** *see-stEH-mah dee ree-chAYr-kah*
site	**il sito** *eel sEE-toh*
software	**il software** *eel software*
speed	**la velocità** *lah veh-loh-chee-tAH*
spell checker	**il controllo ortografico** *eel cohn-trOHl-loh ohrtoh-grAH-fee-koh*
web page	**pagina web** *pAH-jee-nah web*

BUSINESS SERVICES

I need to send a telex (fax).	**Devo mandare un telex (fax).** *dAY-voh mahn-dAH-reh oon telex (fahcs)*
Are there telephone lines for computers in the rooms?	**Ci sono linee telefoniche per computers in camera?** *chee sOH-noh lEE-neh-eh teh-leh-fOH-nee-keh pehr computers een kAH-meh-rah*
Is there a (laptop) computer available?	**C'è un computer (pc portatile) disponibile?** *chee oon computer (pee-see pohr-tAH-tee-leh) dees-poh-nEE-bee-leh*
Does it have a ____?	**Ha ____?** *ah*
▪ floppy disk	**un floppy?** *oon floppy*
▪ CD-ROM/DVD drive	**un porto di CD-ROM e di DVD?** *oon pOHr-toh dee cd-rom ay dee dee-vee-dee*
▪ modem	**un modem** *oon modem*
▪ printer (in color)?	**una stampante (a colore)?** *OO-nah stahm-pAHn-teh (ah koh-lOH-reh)*

| scanner | **uno scanner** *OO-noh scanner* |
| an anti-virus program | **un programma antivirus?** *oon proh-grAHm-mah antivirus* |

| What is the speed of the modem? | **Qual è la velocità del modem?** *koo-ahl-EH lah vay-loh-chee-tAH dayl modem* |

| Is it possible to get on the internet? | **È possibile collegarsi ad internet?** *EH pohs-sEE-bee-leh kohl-lay-gAHr-see ahd internet* |

| Is there a local provider? | **C'è un POP (Point Of Presence) (provider) in questa città?** *chEH oon pOHp (provider) een koo-AYs-tah cheet-tAH* |

| Who is the provider? | **Chi è il provider?** *key EH eel provider* |

| What is the access code? | **C'è un codice segreto (una password)?** *chEH oon kOH-dee-cheh say-grEH-toh (OO-nah password)* |

| May I have my own access code? | **È possibile avere un codice segreto privato (mio) (una password mia)?** *EH pohs-sEE-bee-leh ah-vAY-reh oon KOH-dee-ceh say-grEH-toh pree-vAH-toh (mEE-oh) (OO-nah password mEE-ah)* |

| Is the phone call charged as a local call? | **Si può usufruire della tariffa telefonica urbana?** *see poo-OH oo-soo-froo-EE-reh dAYl-lah tah-rEEf-fah teh-leh-fOH-nee-kah oor-bAH-nah* |

| Is the phone connection quick or slow? | **Il collegamento è veloce o lento?** *eel kohl-lay-gah-mEHn-toh EH vay-lOH-cheh oh lEHn-toh* |

| Is there an e-mail address? | **C'è un indirizzo di posta elettronica?** *chEH oon een-dee-rEE-tzoh dee pOHs-tah eh-leht-trOH-nee-kah* |

How can I send (receive) an e-mail?	**Come posso spedire (ricevere) una e-mail?** *kOH-meh pOHs-soh speh-dEE-reh (ree-chAY-vay-reh) OO-nah e-mail*
Is the telephone wireless?	**È un telefono senza fili?** *EH oon teh-lEH-foh-noh sEHn-tsah fEE-lee*
Does the telephone come with an answering machine?	**Il telefono ha anche la segreteria telefonica?** *eel teh-lEH-foh-noh ah AHn-keh lah seh-greh-teh-rEE-ah teh-leh-fOH-nee-kah*
Does the answering machine cost extra?	**C'è un costo extra (un supplemento) per la segreteria telefonica?** *chEH oon kOHs-toh EH-kstrah (oon soop-pleh-mAYn-toh) pehr lah seh-greh-teh-rEE-ah teh-leh-fOH-nee-kah*
Where can I rent (buy) _____?	**Dove posso noleggiare (comprare) _____?** *doH-veh pOHs-soh noh-lay-jee-AH-reh (kohm-prAH-reh)*
■ a cellular phone	**un cellulare** *oon chehl-loo-lAH-reh*
■ a beeper	**un beeper (cercapersona)** *oon bee-pehr (chayr-kah-pehr-sOH-nah)*
■ a dictation machine	**una dictation machine (registratore)** *OO-nah dictation machine (reh-jee-strah-tOH-reh)*
■ an electronic translator	**un traduttore elettronico** *oon trah-doot-tOH-reh eh-leht-trOH-nee-koh*
■ a palm organizer	**un computer palmare (un organizer)** *oon computer pahl-mAH-reh (oon organizer)*
Does it have voice-mail?	**Ha l'accesso voce?** *AH lah-chEHs-soh vOH-cheh*
Does it have a pager service?	**Può ricevere, scrivere e inviare messaggi?** *poo-OH ree-chAY-vay-reh skrEE-vay-reh ay een-vee-AH-reh mehs-sAH-jee*

How much does it cost per ____?	**Quanto costa ____?** *koo-AHn-toh kOHs-tah*
■ day	**al giorno** *ahl jee-OHr-noh*
■ week	**alla settimana** *ahl-lah seht-tee-mAH-nah*
■ month	**al mese** *ahl mAY-seh*
■ year	**all'anno** *ahl-lAHn-noh*
Is there a nearby copy center for ____?	**Qui vicino, c'è un posto dove ____?** *koo-EE vee-chEE-noh chEH oon POHs-toh dOH-veh*
■ printing	**stampano** *stAHm-pah-noh*
■ making copies	**copiano** *kOH-pee-ah-noh*
■ faxing	**faxano** *fAHc-sah-noh*
■ scanning	**scansiscono** *skahn-sEEs-koh-noh*
■ internet access	**si collegano in rete** *see kohl-lAY-gah-noh een rAY-teh*

PROBLEMS

The computer (modem) doesn't work.	**Il computer (modem) non funziona.** *eel computer (modem) nohn foon-tzee-OH-nah*
What do I do if the line is busy?	**Che devo fare se la linea è occupata?** *kay dAY-voh fAH-reh say lah lEE-neh-ah EH oh-koo-pAH-tah*
Are there other telephone numbers available?	**Ci sono altri numeri di telefono disponibili?** *chee sOH-noh AHl-tree nOO-meh-ree dee teh-lEH-foh-noh dees-poh-nEE-bee-lee*
Who can I call for assistance?	**A chi posso rivolgermi per l'assistenza?** *ah key pOHs-soh ree-vOHl-jehr-mee pehr lahs-sees-tEHn-tzah*

TELEGRAMS

Where is the telegraph window?

Dov'è il finestrino per i telegrammi? *doh-vEH eel fee-neh-strEE-noh pehr ee teh-leh-grAHm-mee*

How late is the telegraph window open (till what time)?

L'ufficio Poste e Telegrafi sta aperto fino a tardi (fino a che ora)? *loof-fEE-chee-oh pOHs-teh ay teh-lEH-grah-fee stah ah-pEHr-toh fEE-noh ah tAHr-dee (fEE-noh ah kay OH-rah)*

I'd like to send a telegram to _____.

Vorrei spedire un telegramma a _____. *vohr-rEH-ee speh-dEE-reh oon teh-leh-grAHm-mah ah*

How much is it per word?

Quanto costa per parola? *koo-AHn-toh kOH-stah pehr pah-rOH-lah*

Where are the forms?

Dove sono i moduli (le schede)? *dOH-veh sOH-noh ee mOH-doo-lee (leh skEH-deh)*

May I please have a form?

Potrei avere un modulo (una scheda) per favore? *poh-trEH-ee ah-vAY-reh oon mOH-doo-loh (OO-nah skEH-dah) pehr fah-vOH-reh*

I want to send it collect.

Voglio spedirlo(la) a carico del destinatario. *vOH-ly-ee-oh speh-dEEr-loh(lah) ah kAH-ree-koh dayl deh-stee-nah-tAH-ree-oh*

When will it arrive?

Quando sarà recapitato(a)? *koo-AHn-doh sah-rAH reh-kah-pee-tAH-toh(ah)*

Travel Tips There was a time when buying an airline ticket was simple. Since the airline industry was deregulated, however, travelers must shop and compare prices, buy charter or discount tickets far in advance, and join frequent flyer clubs to become eligible for free tickets. Read the fine print in ads and ask questions when making reservations. Often, discount fare tickets cannot be exchanged for cash or another ticket if travel plans must be changed. If you must change plans en route, talk to an airline ticket agent. Sometimes they have soft hearts!

GENERAL INFORMATION

TELLING TIME

What time is it?	**Che ora è?** *kay OH-rah EH*

When telling time in Italian, *it is* is expressed by **è** for 1:00, noon, and midnight; **sono** is used for all other numbers.

It's 1:00.	**È l'una.** *EH lOO-nah*
It's 12 o'clock (noon).	**È mezzogiorno.** *EH meh-tsoh-jee-OHr-noh*
It's midnight.	**È mezzanotte.** *EH meh-tsah-nOHt-teh*
It's early (late).	**È presto (tardi).** *EH prEH-stoh (tAHr-dee)*
It's 2:00.	**Sono le due.** *sOH-noh leh dOO-eh*
It's 3:00, etc.	**Sono le tre.** *sOH-noh leh trAY*

The number of minutes after the hour is expressed by adding **e** ("and"), followed by the number of minutes.

It's 4:10.	**Sono le quattro e dieci.** *sOH-noh leh koo-AHt-roh ay dee-EH-chee*
It's 5:20.	**Sono le cinque e venti.** *sOH-noh leh chEEn-koo-eh ay vAYn-tee*

Fifteen minutes after the hour and half past the hour are expressed by placing **e un quarto** and **e mezzo** after the hour.

It's 6:15.	**Sono le sei e un quarto.** *sOH-noh leh sEH-ee ay oon koo-AHr-toh*

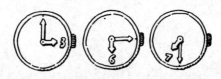

It's 7:30.	**Sono le sette e mezzo.** *sOH-noh leh sEHt-teh ay mEH-tsoh*

After passing the half-hour point on the clock, time is expressed in Italian by *subtracting* the number of minutes to the *next* hour.

It's 7:40.	**Sono le otto meno venti.** *sOH-noh leh OHt-toh mEH-noh vAYn-tee*
It's 8:50.	**Sono le nove meno dieci.** *sOH-noh leh nOH-veh mAY-noh dee-EH-chee*
At what time?	**A che ora?** *ah kay OH-rah*
At 1:00.	**All'una.** *ahl-lOO-nah*
At 2:00 (3:00, etc.).	**Alle due (tre, . . .).** *AHl-leh dOO-eh (trAY)*
A.M. (in the morning)	**del mattino** *dayl maht-tEE-noh*
P.M. (in the afternoon)	**del pomeriggio** *dayl poh-meh-rEE-jee-oh*
At night.	**della notte.** *dAYl-lah nOHt-teh*

Official time is based on the 24-hour clock. You will find train schedules and other such times expressed in terms of a point within a 24-hour sequence.

The train leaves at 15.30.	**Il treno parte alle quindici a trenta.** *eel trEH-noh pAHr-teh AHl-leh koo-EEn-dee-chee ay treHn-tah*

The time is now 21.15.	**Ora sono le ventuno e quindici.** *OH-rah sOH-noh leh vayn-tOO-noh ay koo-EEn-dee-chee.*	

DAYS OF THE WEEK

What day is it?	**Che giorno è oggi?**	*kAY jee-OHr-noh EH OH-jee*

The days of the week are *not* capitalized in Italian.

Today is ____.	**Oggi è ____.**	*OH-jee EH*
■ Monday	**lunedì**	*loo-neh-dEE*
■ Tuesday	**martedì**	*mahr-teh-dEE*
■ Wednesday	**mercoledì**	*mehr-koh-leh-dEE*
■ Thursday	**giovedì**	*jee-oh-veh-dEE*
■ Friday	**venerdì**	*veh-nehr-dEE*
■ Saturday	**sabato**	*sAH-bah-toh*
■ Sunday	**domenica**	*doh-mAY-nee-kah*
■ Yesterday	**Ieri**	*ee-EH-ree*
■ Tomorrow	**Domani**	*doh-mAH-nee*
■ The day after tomorrow	**Dopodomani**	*doh-poh-doh-mAH-nee*
■ Last week	**La settimana passata**	*lah seht-tee-mAH-nah pahs-sAH-tah*
■ Next week	**La settimana prossima**	*lah seht-tee-mAH-nah prOHs-see-mah*

■ Tonight	**Questa notte (stanotte)**	*koo-AYs-tah nOHt-teh (stah-nOHt-teh)*
■ Last night	**La notte passata**	*lah nOHt-teh pahs-sAH-tah*

MONTHS OF THE YEAR

The months of the year are *not* capitalized in Italian.

January	**gennaio**	*jehn-nAH-ee-oh*
February	**febbraio**	*fehb-brAH-ee-oh*
March	**marzo**	*mAHr-tsoh*
April	**aprile**	*ah-prEE-leh*
May	**maggio**	*mAH-jee-oh*
June	**giugno**	*jee-OO-ny-ee-oh*
July	**luglio**	*lOO-ly-ee-oh*
August	**agosto**	*ah-gOH-stoh*
September	**settembre**	*seht-tEHm-breh*
October	**ottobre**	*oht-tOH-breh*
November	**novembre**	*noh-vEHm-breh*
December	**dicembre**	*dee-chEHm-breh*
What's today's date?	**Che data è oggi?**	*kay dAH-ta EH OH-jee*

The first of the month is *il primo* (an ordinal number). All other dates are expressed with *cardinal* numbers.

Today is August *first*.	**Oggi è *il primo* di agosto.**	*OH-jee EH eel prEE-moh dee ah-gOH-stoh*
■ second	**il due**	*eel dOO-eh*

■ fourth	**il quattro**	*eel koo-AHt-troh*
■ 25th	**il venticinque**	*eel vayn-tee-chEEn-koo-eh*
This month	**Questo mese**	*koo-AYs-toh mAY-seh*
Last month	**Il mese scorso**	*eel mAY-seh skOHr-soh*
Next month	**Il mese prossimo**	*eel mAY-seh prOHs-see-moh*
Last year	**L'anno scorso**	*lAHn-noh skOHr-soh*
Next year	**L'anno prossimo**	*lAHn-noh prOHs-see-moh*
May 1, 1876	**Il primo maggio, mille ottocento settanta sei**	*eel prEE-moh mAH-jee-oh mEEl-leh oht-toh-chEHn-toh seht-tAHn-tah sEH-ee*
July 4, 1984	**Il quattro luglio, mille novecento ottanta quattro**	*eel koo-AHt-troh lOO-ly-ee-oh mEEl-leh noh-veh-chEHn-toh oht-tAHn-tah koo-AHt-troh*

THE FOUR SEASONS

Spring	**la primavera**	*lah pree-mah-vEH-rah*
Summer	**l'estate**	*leh-stAH-teh*
Fall	**l'autunno**	*lah-oo-tOOn-noh*
Winter	**l'inverno**	*leen-vEHr-noh*

THE WEATHER

How is the weather today?	**Che tempo fa oggi?**	*kay tEHm-poh fAH OH-jee*
It's good (bad) weather.	**Fa bel (cattivo) tempo.**	*fah behl (kaht-tEE-voh) tEHm-poh*

It's hot.	**Fa caldo.**	*fah kAHl-doh*
■ cold	**freddo**	*frAYd-doh*
■ cool	**fresco**	*frAY-skoh*
It's windy.	**Tira vento.**	*tEE-rah vEHn-toh*
It's sunny.	**C'è il sole.**	*chEH eel sOH-leh*
It's raining.	**Piove.**	*pee-OH-veh*
It's snowing.	**Nevica.**	*nAY-vee-kah*
It's drizzling.	**Pioviggina.**	*pee-oh-vEE-jee-nah*

TEMPERATURE CONVERSIONS

To change Fahrenheit to Centigrade, subtract 32 and multiply by $\frac{5}{9}$.

To change Centigrade to Fahrenheit, multiply by $\frac{9}{5}$ and add 32.

Gradi

Centigradi   Fahrenheit

Termòmetro

CLIMATE

CITIES FROM N TO S IN ORDER OF LATITUDE	COLD MONTHS (JAN.–FEB.)		HOT MONTHS (JULY–AUG.)		AVERAGE ANNUAL TEMPERATURE	
	°C	°F	°C	°F	°C	°F
Bolzano	–1	30	23	72	12	54
Trento	–3	23.5	23	72	11.5	53
Trieste	4	39	23.5	74	13.5	57
Milan	–2	29	24	75	12.5	55
Venice	2.5	37	24.5	76	13.5	57
Turin	–6	21	23	72	12	55
Bologna	1.5	35	24.5	76	13	56
Genoa	7.5	45	24	75	15.5	60
Florence	5	41	24.5	76	14.5	58
Pisa	6	43	23.5	74	14.5	58
Ancona	5.5	52	25.5	78	15.5	60
Iesi	6	43	26	79	16	61
Siena	4.5	40	23.5	74	13.6	57
Perugia	4	39	23	72	13	56
L'Aquila	1	34	21.5	71	11	52
Rome	6.5	43	25	77	15.5	60
Sassari	8.5	47	24	75	15	59
Naples	8	40	25	77	16	61
Foggia	6.5	43	26	79	16	61
Bari	8	46	24	75	16	61
Potenza	3	38	20.5	69	11	52
Lecce	9	48	25	77	16.5	62
Cagliari	9.5	49	25	77	16.5	62
Reggio C.	11.5	53	25	77	18	65
Palermo	10.5	51	25	77	17.5	64
Catania	11	52	26.5	80	18.5	66

NATIONAL HOLIDAYS

Banks, post offices, retail stores, and public offices are closed on national holidays.

January 1	New Year's Day	**Capodanno**
January 6	Epiphany	**Epifania**
Varies	Easter Monday	**Lunedí dopo Pasqua**
April 25	Liberation Day (1945)	**Festa della Resistenza**
May 1	Labor Day	**Festa del Lavoro**
August 15	Assumption Day (known as Ferragosto)	**Assunzione**
November 1	All Saints Day	**Ognissanti**
December 8	Immaculate Conception	**Immacolata Concezione**
December 25	Christmas	**Natale**
December 26	Saint Stephen	**Santo Stefano**

LOCAL HOLIDAYS

Stores and offices in some cities are closed on feast days honoring their patron saints.

Bari	December 6	San Nicola
Bologna	October 4	San Petronio
Cagliari	October 30	San Saturnino
Florence and Genoa	June 24	San Giovanni Battista (John the Baptist)
Milan	December 7	Sant'Ambrogio
Naples	September 19	San Gennaro
Palermo	July 15	Santa Rosalia
Rome	June 29	Santi Pietro e Paolo
Trieste	November 3	San Giusto
Turin	June 24	San Giovanni Battista
Venice	April 25	San Marco

COUNTRIES AND NATIONALITIES

Where are you from?	**Di dov'è lei?**	dee doh-vEH leh-ee
I'm from ____.	**Vengo ____.**	vEHn-goh
I'm ____.	**Sono ____.**	sOH-noh

	COUNTRY	NATIONALITY
Argentina	**dall'Argentina** *dahl-lahr-jehn-tEE-nah*	**argentino(a)** *ahr-jehn-tEE-noh (ah)*
Bolivia	**dalla Bolivia** *dAHl-lah boh-lEE-vee-ah*	**boliviano(a)** *boh-lee-vee-AH-noh(ah)*
Brazil	**dal Brasile** *dahl brah-sEE-leh*	**brasiliano(a)** *brah-see-lee-AH-noh(ah)*
Canada	**dal Canadà** *dahl kah-nah-dAH*	**canadese** *kah-nah-dAY-seh*
Chile	**dal Cile** *dahl chEE-leh*	**cileno(a)** *chee-lAY-noh(ah)*
China	**dalla Cina** *dAHl-lah chEE-nah*	**cinese** *chee-nAY-seh*
Colombia	**dalla Colombia** *dAHl-lah koh-lOHm-bee-ah*	**colombiano(a)** *koh-lohm-bee-AH-noh(ah)*
Costa Rica	**da Costa Rica** *dah koh-stah-rEE-kah*	**costaricense** *koh-stah-ree-chEHn-seh*
Cuba	**da Cuba** *dah kOO-bah*	**cubano(a)** *koo-bAH-noh(ah)*
Denmark	**dalla Danimarca** *dAHl-lah dah-nee-mAHr-kah*	**danese** *dah-nAY-seh*
Ecuador	**dall'Ecuador** *dahl-leh-koo-ah-dOHr*	**ecuadoriano(a)** *eh-koo-ah-doh-ree-AH-noh(ah)*
Egypt	**dall'Egitto** *dahl-lay-jEEt-toh*	**egiziano(a)** *ay-jee-tsee-AH-noh(ah)*

	COUNTRY	NATIONALITY
El Salvador	**dal Salvador** *dahl sahl-vah-dOHr*	**salvadoregno(a)** *sahl-vah-doh-rAY-ny-ee-oh(ah)*
England	**dall'Inghilterra** *dahl-lEEn-gheel-tEHr-ah*	**inglese** *een-glAY-seh*
Europe	**dall'Europa** *dahl-leh-oo-rOH-pah*	**europeo(a)** *eh-oo-roh-pEH-oh(ah)*
Finland	**dalla Finlandia** *dAHl-lah feen-lAHn-dee-ah*	**finlandese** *feen-lahn-dAY-seh*
France	**dalla Francia** *dAHl-lah frAHn-chee-ah*	**francese** *frahn-chAY-seh*
Germany	**dalla Germania** *dAHl-la jehr-mAH-nee-ah*	**tedesco(a)** *tay-dAYs-koh(ah)*
Greece	**dalla Grecia** *dAHl-lah grEH-chee-ah*	**greco(a)** *grEH-koh(ah)*
Guatemala	**dal Guatemala** *dahl goo-ah-teh-mAH-lah*	**guatemalteco(a)** *goo-ah-teh-mahl-tAY-koh(ah)*
Holland	**dall'Olanda** *dahl-loh-lAHn-dah*	**olandese** *oh-lahn-dAY-seh*
Iceland	**dall'Islanda** *dahl-lees-lAHn-dah*	**islandese** *ees-lahn-dAY-seh*
Ireland	**dall'Irlanda** *dahl-leer-lAHn-dah*	**irlandese** *eer-lahn-dAY-seh*
Israel	**da Israel** *dah EE-srah-EHl*	**israeliano(a)** *ee-srah-eh-lee-AH-noh(ah)*
Italy	**dall'Italia** *dahl-lee-tAH-lee-ah*	**italiano(a)** *ee-tah-lee-AH-noh(ah)*
Japan	**dal Giappone** *dahl jee-ahp-pOH-neh*	**giapponese** *jee-ahp-poh-nAY-seh*
Mexico	**dal Messico** *dahl mEHs-see-koh*	**messicano(a)** *mehs-see-kAH-noh(ah)*

	COUNTRY	NATIONALITY
Nicaragua	**dal Nicaragua** *dahl nee-kah-rAH-goo-ah*	**nicaraguese** *nee-kah-rah-goo-AY-seh*
Norway	**dalla Norvegia** *dAHl-lah nohr-vEH-jee-ah*	**norvegese** *nohr-veh-jAY-seh*
Panama	**da Panama** *dah pAH-nah-mah*	**panamegno(a)** *pah-nah-mAY-ny-ee-oh(ah)*
Paraguay	**dal Paraguay** *dahl pah-rah-goo-AH-ee*	**paraguaiano(a)** *pah-rah-goo-ah-ee-AH-noh(ah)*
Peru	**dal Perù** *dahl peh-rOO*	**peruviano(a)** *peh-roo-vee-AH-noh(ah)*
Poland	**dalla Polonia** *dAHl-lah poh-lOH-nee-ah*	**polacco(a)** *poh-lAH-koh(ah)*
Portugal	**dal Portogallo** *dAHl pohr-toh-gAHl-loh*	**portoghese** *pohr-toh-ghAY-seh*
Puerto Rico	**dal Porto Rico** *dAHl pOHr-toh rEE-koh*	**portoricano(a)** *pohr-toh-ree-kAH-noh(ah)*
Russia	**dalla Russia** *dAHl-lah rOOs-see-ah*	**russo(a)** *rOOs-soh(ah)*
Spain	**dalla Spagna** *dAHl-lah spAH-ny-ee-ah*	**spagnolo(a)** *spah-ny-ee-OH-loh(ah)*
Sweden	**dalla Svezia** *dAHl-lah svEH-tsee-ah*	**svedese** *svay-dAY-seh*
Switzerland	**dalla Svizzera** *dAHl-lah svEE-tseh-rah*	**svizzero(a)** *svEE-tseh-roh(ah)*
Turkey	**dalla Turchia** *dAHl-lah toor-kEE-ah*	**turco(a)** *tOOr-koh(ah)*

	COUNTRY	NATIONALITY
United States	**dagli Stati Uniti** *dAH-ly-ee stAH-tee oo-nEE-tee*	**americano(a)** *ah-meh-ree-kAH-noh(ah)*
Uruguay	**dall'Uruguay** *dahl-loo-roo-goo-AH-ee*	**uruguaiano(a)** *oo-roo-goo-ah-ee-AH-noh(ah)*
Venezuela	**dalla Venezuela** *dAHl-lah veh-neh-tsoo-EH-lah*	**venezuelano(a)** *veh-neh-tsoo-EH-lAH-noh(ah)*

IMPORTANT SIGNS

Acqua (non) potabile	(Not) drinking water
Alt	Stop
Aperto	Open
Ascensore	Elevator (Lift)
Attenzione	Caution, watch out
Avanti	Enter (come in, go, walk [at the lights])
Caldo or **"C"**	Hot
Cassa	Cashier
Chiuso	Closed
Divieto di sosta	No parking
Divieto di transito	No entrance, keep out
Freddo or **"F"**	Cold
Gabinetti (WC)	Toilets
Ingresso	Entrance
Libero	Vacant
Non calpestare le aiuole	Keep off the grass

Non ostruire l'ingresso	Don't block entrance
Non toccare	Hands off, don't touch
Occupato	Occupied
Pericolo	Danger
Riservato	Reserved
Si affitta (si loca)	For rent
Si vende	For sale
Donne	Women's room
Uomini	Men's room
Spingere	Push
Strada privata	Private road
Tirare	Pull
Uscita	Exit
Vietato fumare	No smoking
Vietato nuotare	No bathing
Vietato sputare	No spitting

COMMON ABBREVIATIONS

AA	**Azienda Autonoma di Soggiorno e Turismo**	Local Tourist Information Center
ACI	**Automobile Club d'Italia**	Automobile Club of Italy
Cap.	**Capoluogo**	Province
C.P.	**Casella Postale**	Post Office Box
CAP	**Codice Postale**	Zip Code
ENIT	**Ente Nazionale per il Turismo**	Italian State Tourist Office
EPT	**Ente Provinciale per il Turismo**	Provincial Tourist Information Center

F.lli	Brothers	Inc.
FS	Ferrovie dello Stato	Italian State Railways
IVA	Imposte sul Valore Aggiunto	Italian State Tax
L.	Lire	Italian currency
N., n°	Numero	Number
Pro Loco	Ente Locale per il Turismo	Local Tourist Information Office
Prov.	Provincia	Province
P.za	Piazza	(City) Square
S.	San, Santo(a)	Saint
S.A.	Società Anonima	Inc.
Sig.	Signor	Mr.
Sig.na	Signorina	Miss
Sig.ra	Signora	Mrs.
TCI	Touring Club Italiano	Italian Touring Club
v.	Via	Street
v.le	Viale	Boulevard

CENTIMETERS/INCHES

It is usually unnecessary to make exact conversions from your customary inches to the metric system used in Italy, but to give you an approximate idea of how they compare, we have supplied the following guide.

To convert **centimetri** into inches, multiply by .39.
To convert inches into **centimetri**, multiply by 2.54.

METERS/FEET

1 meter (metro) = 39.37 inches   1 foot = 0.3 meters
              = 3.28 feet   1 yard = 0.9 meters
              = 1.09 yards

How tall are you in meters? See for yourself.

FEET-IN.	METERS-CM.	FEET-IN.	METERS-CM.
5-0	1.52	5-7	1.70
5-1	1.54	5-8	1.73
5-2	1.57	5-9	1.75
5-3	1.59	5-10	1.78
5-4	1.62	5-11	1.80
5-5	1.64	6-0	1.83
5-6	1.68	6-1	1.85

WHEN YOU WEIGH YOURSELF

KILOS	POUNDS	KILOS	POUNDS
40	88	75	165
45	99	80	176
50	110	85	187
55	121	90	198
60	132	95	209
65	143	100	220
70	154	105	231

LIQUID MEASUREMENTS

1 liter = 1.06 quarts
4 liters = 1.06 gallons

For quick approximate conversion, multiply the number of gallons by 4 to get liters **(litri)**. Divide the number of liters by 4 to get gallons.

NOTE: You will find other conversion charts on pages 82, 84, 170, 175, 237, 238, and 245.

MINIDICTIONARY FOR BUSINESS TRAVELERS

For other commercial terms, see Money and Banking, pages 25–30 and Abbreviations, pages 244–245.

amount	**ammontare, somma, totale** *ahm-mohn-tAH-reh sOHm-mah toh-tAH-leh*
appraise (to)	**stimare, valutare** *stee-mAH-reh, vah-loo-tAH-reh*
authorize (to)	**autorizzare** *ah-oo-toh-ree-tsAH-reh*
■ authorized edition	**edizione autorizzata** *ay-dee-tsee-OH-neh ah-oo-toh-ree-tsAH-tah*
bill	**fattura** *faht-tOO-rah*
■ bill of exchange	**cambiale** *kahm-bee-AH-leh*
■ bill of lading	**polizza di carico** *poh-lEE-tsah dee kAH-ree-koh*
■ bill of sale	**atto di vendita** *AHt-toh dee vAYn-dee-tah*
business operations	**attività commerciali** *aht-tee-vee-tAH kohm-mehr-chee-AH-lee*

cash	**denaro, contanti** *deh-nAH-roh kohn-tAHn-tee*
▪ to buy, sell, for cash	**comprare, vendere in contanti** *kohm-prAH-reh vAYn-deh-reh een kohn-tAHn-tee*
cash a check (to)	**riscuotere un assegno** *ree-skoo-OH-teh-reh oon ahs-sAY-ny-oh*
certified check	**assegno vistato, autenticato** *ahs-sAY-ny-oh vees-tAH-toh ah-oo-tehn-tee-kAH-toh*
Chamber of Commerce	**Camera di Commercio** *kAH-meh-rah dee kohm-mEHr-chee-oh*
compensation for damage	**compenso (risarcimento) dei danni** *kohm-pEHn-soh (ree-sahr-chee-mEHn-toh) dAY-ee dAHn-nee*
competition	**concorrenza** *kohn-kohr-rEHn-tsah*
competitive price	**prezzo di concorrenza** *prEH-tsoh dee kohn-kohr-rEHn-tsah*
contract	**contratto** *kohn-trAHt-toh*
contractual obligation	**obbligazione (obbligo) contrattuale** *ohb-blee-gah-tsee-OH-neh (OHb-blee-goh) kohn-traht-too-AH-leh*
controlling interest	**controllo delle azioni** *kohn-trOHl-loh dAYl-leh ah-tsee-OH-nee*
co-owner	**comproprietario(a)** *kohm-proh-pree-eh-tAH-ree-oh(ah)*
co-partner	**consocio(a)** *kohn-sOH-chee-oh(ah)*
down payment	**acconto, anticipo, caparra** *ahk-kOHn-toh ahn-tEE-chee-poh kah-pAHr-rah*
due	**dovuto** *doh-vOO-toh*

enterprise	**impresa, iniziativa** *eem-prAY-sah ee-nee-tsee-ah-tEE-vah*
expedite delivery (to)	**sollecitare la consegna** *sohl-lay-chee-tAH-reh lah kohn-sAY-ny-ah*
expenses	**spese, indennità** *spAY-seh een-dehn-nee-tAH*
goods	**merci** *mEHr-chee*
infringement of patent	**contraffazione di brevetto** *kohn-trahf-fah-tsee-OH-neh dee breh-vAYt-toh*
■ rights	**usurpazione di diritti** *oo-soor-pah-tsee-OH-neh dee dee-rEEt-tee*
insurance against all risks	**assicurazione comprendente tutti i rischi** *ahs-see-koo-rah-tsee-OH-neh kohm-prehn-dEHn-teh tOOt-tee ee rEEs-key*
international law	**legge internazionale** *lAY-jeh een-tehr-nah-tsee-oh-nAH-leh*
lawful possessor	**legittimo proprietario** *leh-jEEt-tee-moh proh-pree-eh-tAH-ree-oh*
lawsuit	**causa, processo** *kAHw-sah proh-chEHs-soh*
lawyer	**avvocato (avvocatessa)** *ahv-voh-kAH-toh (ahv-voh-kah-tAYs-sah)*
mail-order business	**ordinazione (di merci) per corrispondenza** *ohr-dee-nah-tsee-OH-neh (dee mEHr-chee) pehr kohr-rees-pohn-dEHn-tsah*
market value	**valore di mercato** *vah-lOH-reh dee mehr-kAH-toh*
manager	**direttore (direttrice)** *dee-reht-tOH-reh (dee-reht-trEE-cheh)*

payment	**pagamento**	*pah-gah-mEHn-toh*
■ part payment	**pagamento parziale**	*pah-gah-mEHn-toh pahr-tsee-AH-leh*
past due	**arretrato**	*ahr-reh-trAH-toh*
post office box	**casella postale**	*kah-sEHl-lah pohs-tAH-leh*
property	**proprietà**	*proh-pree-eh-tAH*
purchasing agent	**agente compratore**	*ah-jEHn-teh kohm-prah-tOH-reh*
put (to) on the American market	**mettere in vendita sul mercato americano**	*mAYt-teh-reh een vAYn-dee-tah sool mehr-kAH-toh ah-meh-ree-kAH-noh*
sale	**vendita, liquidazione, saldi**	*vAYn-dee-tah, lee-koo-ee-dah-tsee-OH-neh, sAHl-dee*
sell (to)	**vendere**	*vAYn-deh-reh*
send (to)	**mandare, inviare, spedire**	*mahn-dAH-reh een-vee-AH-reh speh-dEE-reh*
■ send back	**rinviare, mandare indietro**	*reen-vee-AH-reh mahn-dAH-reh een-dee-AY-troh*
■ send C.O.D.	**spedire contro assegno**	*speh-dEE-reh kOHn-troh ahs-sEH-ny-oh*
shipment	**spedizione (di merci), carico**	*speh-dee-tsee-OH-neh (dee mEHr-chee) kAH-ree-koh*
tax	**tassa, imposta**	*tAHs-sah eem-pOHs-tah*
■ tax-exempt	**esente da tasse**	*ay-sEHn-teh dah tAHs-seh*
■ sales tax	**imposta sulle vendite**	*eem-pOHs-tah sOOl-leh vAYn-dee-teh*

■ value-added tax **imposta sui valori aggiunti** *eem-pOHs-tah sOO-ee vah-lOH-ree ah-jee-OOn-tee*

trade (n.) **commercio** *kohm-mEHr-chee-oh*

■ trade (to) **commerciare** *kohm-mehr-chee-AH-reh*

transact business (to) **trasferire** *trahs-feh-rEE-reh*

transportation charges **spese di trasporto** *spAY-seh dee trahs-pOHr-toh*

via **per, via** *pehr, vEE-ah*

yield a profit (to) **rendere interesse, fruttare un guadagno** *rEHn-deh-reh een-teh-rEHs-seh froot-tAH-reh oon goo-ah-dAH-ny-oh*

QUICK GRAMMAR GUIDE

Your facility with Italian will be greatly enhanced if you know a little of its grammar. Here are a few simple rules governing the use of the various parts of speech.

NOUNS

In contrast with English, in which inanimate objects are considered neuter, Italian nouns are designated either masculine or feminine. In the singular, you'll find that feminine nouns often end in *a* while masculine nouns often end in *o*. Other nouns, which can be either masculine or feminine, often end in *e*. There are still others, however, that you simply have to learn as either masculine or feminine because their endings give you no clue as to their gender. With this in mind, you can follow these simple rules to make a singular noun plural.

1. When a feminine noun ends in *a*, make it plural by changing the *a* to *e*.
2. When a masculine noun ends in *o*, make it plural by changing the *o* to *i*.
3. For masculine or feminine nouns ending in *e*, make them plural by changing the *e* to *i*.
4. For masculine or feminine nouns with endings different from those above, keep the same ending for both singular and plural forms.

GENDER	SINGULAR	PLURAL
feminine	cas*a* (house)	cas*e* (houses)
masculine	libr*o* (book)	libr*i* (books)
masculine or	pied*e* (foot)	pied*i* (feet)
feminine	vest*e* (dress)	vest*i* (dresses)
masculine or	bar (bar)	bar (bars)
feminine	metropoli (city)	metropoli (cities)

Some nouns end in *co* or *go*; these change to *chi* and *ghi* in the plural. Other nouns ending in *ca* or *ga* change to *che* and *ghe* in the plural.

banco (desk)	**banchi** (desks)
fungo (mushroom)	**funghi** (mushrooms)
barca (boat)	**barche** (boats)
alga (alga)	**alghe** (algae)

ARTICLES

Articles (*the*, *a*, *an*) agree in gender (masculine or feminine) and number (singular or plural) with the nouns they modify. Separate rules apply to the definite and indefinite articles.

The **definite article** (*the*) is different in both the singular and plural forms, depending on the noun it is being paired with. Select the proper word for *the*, depending on the sounds that are part of the noun.

il (plural, **i**)	Use before consonants (except *s* followed by another consonant, *z*, *gn*, *ps*, and *x*): **il libro** (the book), **i libri** (the books); **il soldato** (the soldier), **i soldati** (the soldiers).
lo (**gli**)	Use before *z*, *gn*, *ps*, *x*, and *s* followed by another consonant: **lo zio** (the uncle), **gli zii** (the uncles); **lo stadio** (the stadium), **gli stadi** (the stadiums).
lo (**gli**)	Drops the *o* and becomes *l'* before vowels in the singular: **l'amico** (the friend), **gli amici** (the friends); **l'elefante** (the elephant), **gli elefanti** (the elephants).
la (**le**)	Use before consonants: **la casa** (the house), **le case** (the houses); **la ragazza** (the girl), **le ragazze** (the girls).
la (**le**)	Drops the *a* and becomes *l'* before vowels in the singular: **l'ora** (the hour), **le ore** (the hours); **l'edizione** (the edition), **le edizioni** (the editions).

The **indefinite articles** (*a*, *an*) also follow certain rules. Use *un* or *uno* for masculine forms and *una* and *un'* for feminine ones. Use *qualche* to indicate the plural forms (*some*, *any*).

un	Use before vowels and consonants (except *s* followed by another consonant, *z*, *gn*, *ps*, and *x*): **un amico** (a friend), **qualche amico** (some friends); **un dollaro** (a dollar), **qualche dollaro** (some dollars).
uno	Use before *s* followed by another consonant, *z*, *gn*, *ps*, and *x*: **uno specchio** (a mirror), **qualche specchio** (some mirrors); **uno zaino** (a knapsack), **qualche zaino** (some knapsacks).
una	Use before consonants: **una casa** (a house), **qualche casa** (some houses); **una chiesa** (a church), **qualche chiesa** (some churches).
un'	Use before vowel(s): **un'idea** (an idea), **qualche idea** (some ideas); **un'amica** (a girlfriend), **qualche amica** (some girlfriends).

Some and *any* are often also expressed by *alcuni(e)* + the plural of the noun.

un piatto (a dish)	**alcuni piatti** (some dishes)
una ragazza (a girl)	**alcune ragazze** (some girls)

Some and *any* can also be indicated by using *di* + the definite article in a contracted form.

una macchina (a car) **delle macchine** (some cars)

To determine which contracted form is appropriate, use the following guide:

	MASCULINE			FEMININE	
singular	di+il ↓ del	di+lo dello	di+l' dell'	di+la della	di+l' dell'
plural	di+i dei	di+gli degli		di+le delle	

del (dei) — Use before consonants (except *x* followed by another consonant, *z*, *gn*, *ps*, and *x*): **del vino** (some wine), **dei vini** (some wines).

dello (degli) — Use before *s* followed by another consonant, *z*, *gn*, *ps*, and *x*: **dello zucchero** (some sugar), **degli zuccheri** (some sugars).

dello (degli) — Drops the *o* and becomes *dell'* before vowels in the singular: **dell'olio** (some oil), **degli olii** (some oils).

della (delle) — Use before consonants: **della birra** (some beer), **delle birre** (some beers).

della (delle) — Use before vowels: **dell'aranciata** (some orangeade), **delle aranciate** (some orangeades).

ADJECTIVES

Adjectives agree in gender and in number with the nouns they modify. Descriptive adjectives are generally placed after the noun.

la casa bianca (the white house)

il ragazzo alto (the tall boy)

le signore belle (the pretty women)

i libri costosi (the expensive books)

The plurals of adjectives are formed following the same rules as for nouns.

1. For adjectives ending in *a*, change *a* to *e*.

2. For adjectives ending in *o*, change *o* to *i*.

3. For adjectives ending in *e*, change *e* to *i*.

The following show the adjectives in their singular and plural forms.

la carta azzurra (the blue paper)   **le carte azzurre** (the blue papers)

il vestito rosso (the red dress)   **i vestiti rossi** (the red dresses)

l'abito verde (the green suit)   **gli abiti verdi** (the green suits)

Articles, possessives, and limiting adjectives agree in number and gender with the nouns they modify. Usually they are placed before the noun.

molte cose (many things)

pochi americani (few Americans)

In English, the possessive adjective agrees with the person who possesses the object, but in Italian, the possessive adjective agrees in gender and number with the object possessed. The possessive adjective is usually placed alongside the article.

il mio libro (my book)   **i miei libri** (my books)

la mia amica (my girl - friend)   **le mie amiche** (my girlfriends)

Use the following table to determine the correct form of the possessive, both for masculine and feminine forms and also for singular and plural forms.

POSSESSIVE	MASCULINE	FEMININE
my	il mio (i miei)	la mia (le mie)
your	il tuo (i tuoi)	la tua (le tue)
his/her/your (formal)	il suo (i suoi)	la sua (le sue)
our	il nostro (i nostri)	la nostra (le nostre)
your	il vostro (i vostri)	la vostra (le vostre)
their/your (formal)	il loro (i loro)	la loro (le loro)

There are a few exceptions to the above rules.

mio padre (my father)   **mio zio** (my uncle)

mia madre (my mother)   **mia zia** (my aunt)

mio fratello (my brother)   **mio nonno** (my grandfather)

mia sorella (my sister)   **mia nonna** (my grandmother)

Demonstrative adjectives (*this, these*) are placed in front of the nouns they modify. They agree in number and gender with the nouns that they modify. The adjective *this* has the following forms: **questo** (masculine singular), **questa** (feminine singular), **questi** (masculine plural), **queste** (feminine plural).

questo libro (this book)   **questi libri** (these books)

questa casa (this house)   **queste case** (these houses)

The demonstrative adjectives *that* and *those* are handled differently. **Quello** (that) has the following forms, depending on the article of the nouns being modified.

	MASCULINE			FEMININE	
singular	que+il	que+lo	que+l'	que+la	que+l'
	quel	quello	quell'	quella	quell'
plural	que+i	que+gli		que+le	
	quei	quegli		quelle	

For example, the singular forms.

il ragazzo (the boy)   **quel ragazzo** (that boy)

lo zio (the uncle)   **quello zio** (that uncle)

l'albero (the tree)   **quell'albero** (that tree)

l'oca (the goose)   **quell'oca** (that goose)

la casa (the house)   **quella casa** (that house)

Now the plural forms.

i ragazzi (the boys)   **quei ragazzi** (those boys)

gli zii (the uncles)   **quegli zii** (those uncles)

gli alberi (the trees)   **quegli alberi** (those trees)

le oche (the geese)   **quelle oche** (those geese)

le case (the houses)   **quelle case** (those houses)

PRONOUNS

Subject pronouns (*I, you, he, she,* etc.) have both singular and plural forms.

io (I)   **noi** (we)

tu (you, familiar)   **voi** (you, familiar)

Lei (you, polite)   **Loro** (you, polite)

egli, lui (he)   **loro, essi** (they, masculine)

ella, lei (she)   **loro, esse** (they, feminine)

Direct object pronouns (*me, you, him, it, us, them*) are used as direct objects of verbs. They have both singular and plural forms, and their placement before or after the verb varies. Italians usually place the direct object pronouns before the verb except for emphasis.

SINGULAR		PLURAL	
(me)	(You love me)	(us)	(You love us)
after verb	Tu ami *me*	after verb	Tu ami *noi*
before verb	Tu *mi* ami	before verb	Tu *ci* ami
(you)	(I love you)	(you)	(I love you)
after verb	Io amo *te*	after verb	Io amo *voi*
before verb	Io *ti* amo	before verb	Io *vi* amo

SINGULAR		PLURAL	
(him/it)	(I love him)	(them, masc./ you, polite)	(I love them)
after verb	Io amo *lui*	after verb	Io amo *loro*
before verb	Io *lo* amo	before verb	Io *li* amo
(her/it/you, polite)	(I love her/ it/you)	(them, fem./ you, polite)	(I love them)
after verb	Io amo *lei/essa*	after verb	Io amo *loro*
before verb	Io *la* amo	before verb	Io *le* amo

Indirect object pronouns are pronouns replacing nouns as indirect objects. They take the following forms, depending upon whether they are placed before or after the verb.

SINGULAR		PLURAL	
(to me)	(You give me a kiss)	(to us)	(You give us a kiss)
after verb	Tu dai un bacio *a me*	after verb	Tu dai un bacio *a noi*
before verb	Tu *mi* dai un bacio	before verb	Tu *ci* dai un bacio
(to you)	(I give you a kiss)	(to you)	(I give you a kiss)
after verb	Io do un baci *a te*	after verb	Io do un bacio *a voi*
before verb	Io *ti* do un bacio	before verb	Io *vi* do un bacio
(to him)	(I give him a kiss)	(to them/you, polite)	(I give them/ you a kiss)
after verb	Io do un bacio *a lui*	after verb	Io do un bacio *a loro*
before verb	Io *gli* do un bacio	after verb	Io do *loro* un bacio

SINGULAR		PLURAL	
(to her/you, polite)	(I give her/it a kiss)	(to them/you, polite)	(I give them/ you a kiss)
after verb	Io do un bacio *a lei*	after verb	Io do un bacio *a loro*
before verb	Io *le* do un bacio	after verb	Io do *loro* un bacio

VERBS

In this phrase book, we limit the use of verbs to the present tense, since this is the most likely one for you to use as a tourist. Most Italian verbs in the infinitive end in either *are, ere,* or *ire.*

parlare (to speak)

vedere (to see)

partire (to leave)

In order to conjugate a verb, this infinitive ending must be removed and replaced by the appropriate ending found in the following table.

PARLARE (TO SPEAK)	
io parlo (I speak)	noi parliamo (we speak)
tu parli (you speak, familiar)	voi parlate (you speak, familiar)
Lei parla (you speak, polite)	Loro parlano (you speak, polite)
egli parla (he speaks) lui	loro parlano (they speak, essi masculine)
ella parla (she speaks) lei	loro parlano (they speak, esse masculine)

Two other examples of verbs with regular conjugations are:

VEDERE (TO SEE)	
vedo (I see)	vediamo (we see)
vedi (you see)	vedete (you see)
vede (he, she, you see(s))	vedono (they, you see)
PARTIRE (TO LEAVE)	
parto (I leave)	partiamo (we leave)
parti (you leave)	partite (you leave)
parte (he, she, you leave(s))	partono (they, you leave)

Some *ire* verbs add *sc* to the stem before the endings in the *io*, *tu*, *egli*, *essi* forms. For example, with the verb **finire** (to finish):

io finisco	**egli finisce**
tu finisci	**essi finiscono**

Not all verbs are regular. Here are some of the common irregular ones, with their conjugations.

ANDARE (TO GO)	
vado (I go)	andiamo (we go)
vai (you go)	andate (you go)
va (he, she, you go)	vanno (they, you go)
DARE (TO GIVE)	
do (I give)	diamo (we give)
dai (you give)	date (you give)
da (he, she, you give)	danno (they, you give)
FARE (TO DO/TO MAKE)	
faccio (I do/make)	facciamo (we do/make)
fai (you do/make)	fate (you do/make)
fa (he, she, you do/make)	fanno (they, you do/make)
BERE (TO DRINK)	
bevo (I drink)	beviamo (we drink)
bevi (you drink)	bevete (you drink)
beve (he, she, you drink(s))	bevono (they, you drink)

DOVERE (TO HAVE TO)	
devo (I have to)	dobbiamo (we have to)
devi (you have to)	dovete (you have to)
deve (he, she, you has (have) to)	devono (they, you have to)

POTERE (TO BE ABLE TO/CAN)	
posso (I am able to)	possiamo (we are able to)
puoi (you are able to)	potete (you are able to)
può (he, she you is (are) able to)	possono (they, you are able to)

RIMANERE (TO STAY)	
rimango (I stay)	rimaniamo (we stay)
rimani (you stay)	rimanete (you stay)
rimane (he, she, you stay(s))	rimangano (they, you stay)

SAPERE (TO KNOW)	
so (I know)	sappiamo (we know)
sai (you know)	sapete (you know)
sa (he, she, you know(s))	sanno (they, you know)

VOLERE (TO WANT)	
voglio (I want)	vogliamo (we want)
vuoi (you want)	volete (you want)
vuole (he, she, you want(s))	vogliono (they, you want)

USCIRE (TO GO OUT)	
esco (I go out)	usciamo (we go out)
esci (you go out)	uscite (you go out)
esce (he, she, you go(es) out)	escono (they, you go out)

VENIRE (TO COME)	
vengo (I come)	veniamo (we come)
vieni (you come)	venite (you come)
viene (he, she, you come(s))	vengono (they, you come)

CONOSCERE (TO KNOW A PERSON)	
conosco (I know)	conosciamo (we know)
conosci (you know)	conoscete (you know)
conosce (he, she, you know(s))	conoscono (they, you know)

The verb **piacere** means to like something, but how it is conjugated depends on whether you like one thing or several. This is best shown as follows.

mi piace (I like—one thing)   **mi piacciono** (I like—several things)

Thus, the forms of **piacere** are as follows:

	ONE THING	SEVERAL THINGS
I	mi piace	mi piacciono
you (familiar)	ti piace	ti piacciono
he she you (formal)	gli le piace	gli le piacciono
we	ci piace	ci piacciono
you (familiar)	vi piace	vi piace
they you (formal)	piace a loro	piacciono a loro

Used in sentences, they would be as follows:

Le piace Venezia? (Do you like Venice?)

Le piace ballare? (Do you like dancing?)

Le piace Roma? (Do you like Rome?)

Le piacciono i monumenti? (Do you like the monuments?)

Note the following constructions, which vary depending on the meaning intended.

Ti piaccio? (Am I pleasing to you?—familiar form of singular *you*)

Le piaccio? (Am I pleasing to you?—polite form of singular *you*)

Vi piaccio? (Am I pleasing to you?—familiar form of plural *you*)

Piaccio a loro? (Am I pleasing to them?—plural form of third person, polite form of plural *you*)

Or, in the form of a statement.

Mi piaci. (You are pleasing to me, I like you.—familiar form of singular *you*)

Mi piace. (You are pleasing to me. I like her/him.—singular form of third person, polite form of singular *you*)

Mi piacete. (You are pleasing to me, I like you.—familiar form of plural *you*)

Mi piacciono. (They are pleasing to me. I like them.—plural form of third person, polite form of plural *you*)

As in English, many verbs are used in conjunction with auxiliary verbs. Three of the most common are given below, with their conjugations.

AVERE (TO HAVE)	
ho (I have)	abbiamo (we have)
hai (you have)	avete (you have)
ha (he, she, you has(have))	hanno (they, you have)
ESSERE (TO BE)	
sono (I am)	siamo (we are)
sei (you are)	siete (you are)
è (he, she, you is (are))	sono (they, you are)
STARE (TO BE)	
sto (I am)	stiamo (we are)
stai (you are)	state (you are)
sta (he, she, you is (are))	stanno (they, you are)

Stare is used when expressing an action in progress.

Che cosa sta facendo? (What are you doing?)

Io sto camminando. (I am walking.)

Essere is used mostly with intransitive verbs denoting motion such as *to go*. (The past participle with which it is linked agrees with its subject in gender and number.)

Sono andato a fare la spesa. (I have gone shopping.)

Maria è appena arrivata. (Mary has just arrived.)

Avere is used with verbs that may take an object, such as *to buy*.

> **Che cosa ha comprato?** (What have you bought?)

> **Ho comprato un regalo.** (I have bought a gift.)

To form the past participle of a verb, use the following patterns for all regular verbs.

parlare: parl + ato (spoken)	**ho parlato** (I have spoken)
vedere: ved + uto (seen)	**ha veduto** (he, she, you has (have) seen)
partire: part + ito (left)	**sono partiti** (they, you have left)

There are several idiomatic uses of the verb avere (*to have*), in which the verb is being used to express the English *to be*:

> **aver freddo** (to be cold)

> **aver sete** (to be thirsty)

> **aver fame** (to be hungry)

> **aver sonno** (to be sleepy)

> **aver caldo** (to be hot)

> **aver fretta** (to be in a hurry)

> **aver paura** (to be afraid)

> **aver ragione** (to be right)

> **aver torto** (to be wrong)

Used in context, we have some examples of **avere**.

> **Non ho caldo, ho freddo.** (I'm not hot, I'm cold.)

> **Ha fame?** (Are you hungry?)

> **No, ho sete.** (No, I am thirsty.)

> **Abbiamo fretta.** (We're in a hurry.)

> **Egli ha venti anni.** (He's 20 years old.)*

> **Ho ragione.** (I'm right.)

*NOTE: In Italian, to express your age, you use the verb **avere**: to have _____ years.

PREPOSITIONS

The following most common Italian prepositions are listed in the alphabetical order of their English equivalents.

after	**dopo**	*(dOH-poh)*
before (in time)	**prima**	*(prEE-mah)*
before, in front of	**davanti**	*(dah-vAHn-tee)*
behind, in back of	**dietro**	*(dee-AY-troh)*
down	**giù**	*(jee-oo)*
during	**durante**	*(doo-rAHn-tay)*
for, through	**per**	*(pehr)*
from	**da**	*(dah)*
in	**in**	*(een)*
in, into	**a**	*(ah)*
inside	**dentro**	*(dEHn-troh)*
outside	**fuori**	*(foo-OH-ree)*
toward	**verso**	*(vEHr-soh)*
through, across	**attraverso**	*(aht-trah-vEHr-soh)*
until	**fino a**	*(fEE-noh ah)*
up	**su**	*(soo)*
without	**senza**	*(sEHn-tsah)*

TO FORM NEGATIVE EXPRESSIONS

The most common negative word in Italian is *non*. It always precedes the verb.

Io non ho soldi. (I have no money; I don't have any money.)

Other negative words are:

nessuno (no one)	**Nessuno viene.** (No one is coming.)

niente (nothing)	**Non vedo niente.** (I don't see anything; I see nothing.)
mai (never)	**Mai mangiamo in casa.** (We never eat at home.)
neppure (neither)	**Lei non ha soldi e neppure io.** (She has no money and neither do I.)

Any one of the negative words except *non* may be used either before or after the verb. If one is used after the verb, *non* is also used before the verb (forming double negative).

Nessuno parla.
Non parla nessuno. (Nobody is speaking.)
Mai vado da solo(a). (I never go alone.)
Non vado mai da solo(a).

TO FORM QUESTIONS

Some common interrogative words in Italian are the following:

Dove? (Where?)	**Per che cosa?** (What for?)
Come? (How?)	**Perché?** (Why?)
Quale? (Which?)	**Che (cosa)?** (What?)
Quanto? (How much?)	**Chi?** (Who?)
Quanti? (How many?)	

To form a question in Italian, place the subject **after** the verb or raise your intonation at the end of the sentence.

Lei parla italiano. (You speak Italian.)
Parla lei italiano? (Do you speak Italian?)

Maria ha il biglietto. (Mary has the ticket.)
Ha Maria il biglietto? (Does Mary have the ticket?)

Voi andate al cinema. (You are going to the movies.)
Andate voi al cinema? (Are you going to the movies?)

ENGLISH-ITALIAN DICTIONARY

A

a, an un, uno, una *oon, OO-noh, OO-nah*

about circa *chEEr-kah*

above sopra *sOH-prah*

abscess ascesso *ash-EHs-soh*

to accept accettare *ah-cheht-tAH-reh*

accountant ragioniere(a) *rah-jee-oh-nee-EH-reh (ah)*

ace asso *AHs-soh*

across attraverso *aht-trah-vEHr-soh*

address indirizzo *een-dee-rEE-tsoh*

adhesive tape nastro adesivo *nAHs-troh ah-day-sEE-voh*

advance anticipo *ahn-tEE-chee-poh*

adventure avventura *ahv-vehn-tOO-rah*

to adore adorare *ah-doh-rAH-reh*

after dietro *dee-AY-troh;* dopo *dOH-poh*

afternoon pomeriggio *poh-may-rEE-jee-oh*

again ancora *ahn-kOH-rah*

agency agenzia *ah-jehn-tsEE-ah*

air aria *AH-ree-ah;*
    air-conditioned aria condizionata *AH-ree-ah kohn-dee-tsee-oh-nAH-tah;*
    airmail posta aerea *pOHs-tah ah-EH-reh-ah*

airplane aereo *ah-EH-reh-oh*

airport aeroporto *ah-eh-roh-pOHr-toh*

aisle corridoio *kohr-ree dOH-ee-oh*

album album *AHl-boom*

alcohol alcool *AHl-koh-ohl*

all tutto *tOOt-toh*

allergic allergico *ahl-lEHr-jee-koh*

to allow permettere *pehr-mAYt-teh-reh*

almond mandorla *mAHn-dohr-lah*

almost quasi *kwAH-zee*

alone solo *sOH-loh*

also anche *AHn-keh*

always sempre *sEHm-preh*

amalgam amalgama *ah-mAHl-gah-mah*

ambulance autoambulanza *ah-oo-toh-ahm-boo-lAHn-tsah*

American americano *ah-may-ree-kAH-noh*

amethyst ametista *ah-may-tEEs-tah*

among fra *frAH;* tra *trAH*

amount ammontare *ahm-mohn-tAH-reh;* somma *sOHm-mah*

anchovy acciuga *ah-chee-OO-gah*

and e *ay*

ankle caviglia *kah-vEE-ly-ee-ah*

another un altro *oon AHl-troh*

to answer rispondere *rees-pOHn-day-reh*

answering machine segreteria telefonica *seh-greh-teh-rEE-ah teh-leh-fOH-nee-kah*

antacid antiacido *ahn-tee-AH-chee-doh*

antibiotic antibiotico *ahn-tee-bee-OH-tee-koh*

antiseptic antisettico *ahn-tee-sEHt-tee-koh*

apartment appartamento *ahp-pahr-tah-mEHn-toh*

apéritif aperitivo *ah-peh-ree-tEE-voh*

appendicitis appendicite *ahp-payn-dee-chEE-teh*

appetizer antipasto *ahn-tee-pAHs-toh*

apple mela *mAY-lah*

appointment appuntamento *ahp-poon-tah-mEHn-toh*

apricot albicocca *ahl-bee-kOH-kah*

April aprile *ah-prEE-leh*

aquamarine acquamarina *ah-koo-ah-mah-rEE-nah*

Arab arabo *AH-rah-boh*

area code prefisso *pray-fEEs-soh*

Argentinian argentino *ahr-jehn-tEE-noh*

arm braccio *brAH-chee-oh*

around attorno *aht-toHr-noh*

to arrive arrivare *ahr-ree-vAH-reh*

arrival arrivo *ahr-rEE-voh*

article articolo *ahr-tEE-koh-loh*

artificial sweetener dolcificante artificiale *dohl-chee-fee-kAHn-teh ahr-tee-fee-chee-AH-leh*

ashtray portacenere *pohr-tah-chAY-nay-reh*

to ask chiedere *kay-AY-day-reh*

asparagus asparagi *ahs-pAH-ra-jee*

aspirin aspirina *ahs-pee-rEE-nah*

to assist assistere *ahs-sEEs-teh-reh*

assistant assistente *ahs-see-stEHn-teh*

asthma asma *AHs-mah*

at a *ah;* **at least** almeno *ahl-mAY-noh;* **at once** subito *sOO-bee-toh*

attention attenzione *aht-tehn-tsee-OH-neh*

attentive attento *aht-tEHn-toh*

attraction attrazione *aht-trah-tsee-OH-neh*

auburn castano *kahs-tAH-noh*

August agosto *ah-gOHs-toh*

aunt zia *tsEE-ah*

Austrian austriaco *ah-oos-trEE-ah-koh*

author autore *ah-oo-tOH-reh*

automatic automatico *ah-oo-toh-mAH-tee-koh*

autumn autunno *ah-oo-tOOn-noh*

available disponibile *dees-poh-nEE-bee-leh*

awful terribile *tehr-rEE-bee-leh*

away via *vEE-ah*

B

baby bambino *bahm-bEE-noh*

bachelor scapolo *skAH-poh-loh*

back schiena *skee-AY-nah*

backwards dietro *dee-AY-troh*

bacon pancetta *pahn-chAYt-tah*

bad cattivo *kaht-tEE-voh*

bag (handbag) borsa *bOHr-sah;* borsetta *bohr-sAYt-tah;* **(suitcase)** valigia *vah-lEE-jee-ah;* **bag snatching** scippo *shEEp-poh*

baggage bagaglio *bah-gAH-ly-ee-oh*

baked al forno *ahl-fOHr-noh*

bakery fornaio *fohr-nAH-ee-oh*

balcony (house) balcone *bahl-kOH-neh;* **(theater)** galleria *gahl-leh-rEE-ah*

ball (play ball) palla *pAHl-lah*

banana banana *bah-nAH-nah*

bandage fascia *fAH-shee-ah*

Band-Aid cerotto *chay-rOHt-toh*

bang(s) (hair) frangia *frAHn-jee-ah*

bangle bracciale *brah-chee-AH-leh*

bank banca *bAHn-kah*

bank note banconota *bahn-koh-nOH-tah*

barber barbiere *bahr-bee-AY-reh;* parrucchiere *pahr-roo-key-AY-reh*

baritone baritono *bah-rEE-toh-noh*

barley orzo *OHr-tsoh*

barn stalla *stAHl-lah*

bass (singer) basso *bAHs-soh;* **(fish)** branzino *brahn-tsEE-noh*

bath bagno *bAH-ny-oh*

bathing suit costume da bagno *kohs-tOO-may dah bAH-ny-oh*

bathrobe accappatoio *ah-kahp-pah-tOH-ee-oh*

bathroom bagno *bAH-ny-oh*

bathtub vasca *vAHs-kah*

battery batteria *baht-teh-rEE-ah;* pila *pEE-lah* (for radio, camera, etc.)

to be essere *EHs-seh-reh;* stare *stAH-reh*

beach spiaggia *spee-AH-jee-ah*

bean (shell) fagiolo *fah-jee-OH-loh*

beard barba *bAHr-bah*

beautiful bello *bEHl-loh*

because perché *pehr-kAY*

bed letto *lEHt-toh;* **bedroom** camera da letto *kAH-meh-rah dah lEHt-toh*

beef manzo *mAHn-tsoh;* **(beef) steak** bistecca *bees-tAY-kah;* **(grilled)** ai ferri *ah-ee fEHr-ree;* **(medium)** a puntino *ah poon-tEE-noh;* **(rare)** al sangue *ahl sAHn-goo-eh;* **(well-done)** ben cotta *behn kOHt-tah*

beer birra *bEEr-rah;* **beer on tap** birra alla spina *bEEr-rah ahl-lah spEE-nah*

before prima *prEE-mah*

to begin cominciare *koh-meen-chee-AH-reh*

behind dietro *dee-AY-troh*

Belgian belga *bEHl-gah*

to believe credere *krAY-deh-reh*

below sotto *sOHt-toh*

belt cintura *cheen-tOO-rah*

berth cuccetta *koo-chAYt-tah*

beside accanto *ahk-kAHn-toh*

best il migliore *eel-mee-ly-ee-OH-reh*

better meglio *mEh-ly-ee-oh;* migliore *mee-ly-ee-OH-reh*

between fra *frAH;* tra *trAH*

bicycle bicicletta *bee-chee-klAYt-tah*

bifocal lenses lenti bifocali *lEHn-tee bee-foh-kAH-lee*

big grande *grAHn-deh;* grosso *grOHs-soh*

bill conto *kOHn-toh*

bird uccello *oo-chEHl-loh*

birth nascita *nAH-shee-tah*

bite boccone *boh-kOH-neh;* **to have a bite** mangiare un boccone *mahn-jee-AH-reh oon boh-kOH-neh*

bitter amaro *ah-mAH-roh*

black nero *nAY-roh*

blade lama *lAH-mah;* **razor blades** lamette *lah-mAYt-teh*

blank modulo *mOH-doo-loh*

blanket coperta *koh-pEHr-tah*

blender frullatore *frool-lah-tOH-reh*

blond biondo *bee-OHn-doh*

blood sangue *sAHn-goo-eh;* **I'm bleeding** sto sanguinando *stOH sahn-goo-ee-nAHn-doh*

blood test analisi del sangue *ah-nAH-lee-see dAYl sAHn-goo-eh*

blood pressure la pressione *lah prehs-see-OH-neh*

blouse blusa *blOO-sah;* camicetta *kah-mee-chAYt-tah*

blue blu *blOO;* azzurro *ah-tsOOr-roh*

body corpo *kOHr-poh*

boiled bollito *bohl-lEE-toh*

bolt bullone *bool-lOH-neh*

book libro *lEE-broh;* **bookstore** libreria *lee-breh-rEE-ah*

boot stivale *stee-vAH-leh*

booth cabina telefonica *kah-bEE-nah teh-leh-fOH-nee-kah*

botanic botanico *boh-tAH-nee-koh*

both tutti e due *toot-tee ay dOO-eh*

to bother seccare *say-kAH-reh;* dare fastidio *dAH-reh fas-tEE-dee-oh;* **don't bother me!** non darmi fastidio! *nohn dAHr-mee fahs-tEE-dee-oh*

bottle bottiglia *boht-tEE-ly-ee-ah*

box scatola *skAH-toh-lah*

bowling bowling

boy ragazzo *rah-gAH-tsoh*

bra, brassiere reggiseno *reh-jee-SAY-noh*

bracelet bracciale *brah-chee-AH-leh*

brain cervello *chehr-vEHl-loh*

brakes freni *frAY-nee*

Brazilian brasiliano *brah-see-lee-AH-noh*

bread pane *pAH-neh;* **soft part of bread** mollica *mohl-lEE-kah;* **toasted bread** pan tostato *pAHn tohs-tAH-toh*

to break rompere *rOHm-pay-reh*

breakdown (car) guasto *goo-AHs-toh*

breakfast colazione *koh-lah-tsee-OH-neh*

to breathe respirare *rays-pee-rAH-reh*

bridge ponte *pOHn-teh*

to bring portare *pohr-tAH-reh;* **bring me . . .** mi porti . . . *mee pOHr-tee*

broken rotto *rOHt-toh*

brooch fermaglio *fehr-mAH-ly-ee-oh;* spilla *spEEl-lah*

brook ruscello *roo-shEHl-loh*

broth brodo *brOH-doh*

brother fratello *frah-tEHl-loh*

brown marrone *mahr-rOH-neh*

bruise contusione *kohn-too-see-OH-neh*

brunette bruna *brOO-nah;* brunetta *broo-nAYt-tah*

brush spazzola *spAH-tsoh-lah*

bulb (light) lampadina *lahm-pah-dEE-nah*

bumper paraurti *pah-rah-OOr-tee*

bun (bread) rosetta *roh-sAYt-tah;* **(hair)** crocchia *krOH-key-ah*

to burn bruciare *broo-chee-AH-reh*

burn ustione *oos-tee-OH-neh*

burnt ustionato *oos-tee-oh-nAH-toh*

bus autobus *ah-oo-toh-bOOs*

business affare *ahf-fAH-reh*

busy occupato *oh-koo-pAH-toh*

but ma *mah;* però *peh-rOH*

butcher shop macelleria *mah-chehl-leh-rEE-ah*

butter burro *bOOr-roh*

button bottone *boht-tOH-neh*

to buy comprare *kohm-prAH-reh*

C

cabbage cavolo *kAH-voh-loh*

cabin cabina *kah-bEE-nah*

CD player lettore CD *leht-tOH-reh see-dEE*

cake torta *tOHr-tah*

calf vitello *vee-tEHl-loh*

to call chiamare *key-ah-mAH-reh;* telefonare *teh-leh-foh-nAH-reh*

camera macchina fotografica *mAH-kee-nah foh-toh-grAH-fee-kah;* **camera store** negozio fotocine *neh-gOH-tsee-oh fOH-toh-chEE-neh;* negozio di articoli fotografici *neh-gOH-tsee-oh dee ahr-tEE-koh-lee foh-toh-grAH-fee-chee*

camping campeggio *kahm-pAY-jee-oh*

272 • ENGLISH-ITALIAN DICTIONARY

Canadian canadese *kah-nah-dAY-seh*

cancel cancellare *kahn-chehl-lAH-reh*

candle candela *kahn-dAY-lah*

candy dolci *dOHl-chee;* caramelle *kah-rah-mEHl-leh*

cane bastone *bah-stOH-neh*

capon cappone *kahp-pOH-neh*

car (auto) auto *AH-oo-toh;* **(train)** carrozza *kahr-rOH-tsah;* vagone *vah-gOH-neh;* **dining car** vagone ristorante *vah-gOH-neh rees-toh-rAHn-teh*

car service servizio noleggio *sehr-vEE-tsee-oh noh-lAY-jee-oh*

carburetor carburatore *kahr-boo-rah-tOH-reh*

card (identification card) carta d'identità *kAHr-tah dee-dEHn-tee-tAH;* **(playing) cards** carte da gioco *kAHr-teh dah jee-OH-koh;* **(deck of) cards** mazzo di carte *mAH-tsoh dee kAHr-teh*

careful attento *aht-tEHn-toh;* **be careful!** stia attento! *stEE-ah aht-tEHn-toh*

carrot carota *kah-rOH-tah*

to carry portare *pohr-tAH-reh*

carton of cigarettes stecca di sigarette *stAY-kah dee see-gah-rAYt-teh*

carved intagliato *een-tah-ly-ee-AH-toh*

cashier cassa *kAHs-sah;* cassiere *kahs-see-AY-reh*

to catch prendere *prAYn-day-reh*

cathedral cattedrale *kaht-tay-drAH-leh*

Catholic cattolico *kaht-tOH-lee-koh*

cavity carie *kAH-ree-eh*

centimeter centimetro *chayn-tEE-meh-troh*

center centrale *chayn-trAH-leh*

ceramics ceramiche *chay-rAH-mee-keh*

cereals cereali *cheh-reh-AH-lee*

chain (gold) catenina *kah-tay-nEE-nah*

chair sedia *sEH-dee-ah;* **chaise longue** sedia a sdraio *sEH-dee-ah ah sdrAH-ee-oh*

chambermaid cameriera *kah-meh-ree-AY-rah*

to change cambiare *kahm-bee-AH-reh*

change (money) resto *rEHs-toh;* **small change** spiccioli *spEE-chee-oh-lee*

character personaggio *pehr-soh-nAH-jee-oh*

charm ciondolo *chee-OHn-doh-loh*

chart cartellino *kahr-tehl-lEE-noh*

cheap a buon mercato *ah boo-OHn mehr-kAH-toh;* **cheaper** più a buon mercato *pee-OO ah boo-OHn mehr-kAH-toh*

check (chess game) scacco *skAH-koh;* **(money)** assegno *ahs-sAY-ny-oh;* **checkmate** scaccomatto *skAH-koh-mAHt-toh*

checkers dama *dAH-mah*

checkroom guardaroba *goo-AHr-dah-rOH-bah*

cheek guancia *goo-AHn-chee-ah*

cheers! salute! *sah-lOO-teh*

cheese formaggio *fohr-mAH-jee-oh*

chess scacchi *skAH-key;* **chessboard** scacchiera *skah-key-AY-rah*

chest petto *pEHt-toh;* **a chest cold** un colpo d'aria al petto *oon kOHl-poh dAH-ree-ah ahl pEHt-toh*

chestnuts castagne *kahs-tAH-ny-eh*

to chew masticare *mahs-tee-kAH-reh;* **chewing gum** gomma masticante *gOHm-mah mahs-tee-kAHn-teh*

chicken pollo *pOHl-loh*

chiffon chiffon *sheef-fOHn*

child bambino *bahm-bEE-noh*

Chilean cileno *chee-lAY-noh*

chill brivido *brEE-vee-doh*

chin mento *mEHn-toh*

Chinese cinese *chee-nAY-seh*

chocolate cioccolato *chee-oh-kOH-lah-toh*

chop (meat) cotoletta *koh-toh-lAYt-tah*

Christmas Natale *nah-tAH-leh*

church chiesa *key-AY-sah*

cider sidro *sEE-droh*

cigar sigaro *sEE-gah-roh;* **cigar store** tabaccaio *tah-bah-kAH-ee-oh;* tabaccheria *tah-bah-kEH-ree-ah*

cigarette sigaretta *see-gah-rAYt-tah;* **cigarette lighter** accendino *ah-chayn-dEE-noh*

cinema cinema *chEE-neh-mah*

city città *cheet-tAH*

class classe *klAHs-seh*

to clean pulire *poo-lEE-reh*

clear chiaro *key-AH-roh*

clerk impiegato *eem-pee-ay-gAH-toh*

to climb salire *sah-lEE-reh*

to close chiudere *key-OO-deh-reh;* **may I close?** posso chiudere? *pOHs-soh key-OO-deh-reh;* **closed** chiuso *key-OO-soh*

cloth panno *pAHn-noh*

clothing vestiti *vays-tEE-tee;* **evening clothes** abiti da sera *AH-bee-tee dah sAY-rah*

club club *klOOb;* **nightclub** night club *nAH-eet klOOb;* **golf clubs** mazze da golf *mAH-tseh dah gOHlf*

clutch frizione *free-tsee-OH-neh*

coat cappotto *kahp-pOHt-toh*

cocktail cocktail *kOHk-tayl*

coconut noce di cocco *nOH-cheh dee kOH-koh*

codfish merluzzo *mehr-lOO-tsoh*

coffee caffè *kahf-fEH*

cold freddo *frAYd-doh;* **I have a cold** ho il raffreddore *OH eel rahf-frayd-dOH-reh*

cold cuts affettati *ahf-fayt-tAH-tee;* salumi *sah-lOO-mee*

color colore *koh-lOH-reh;* **light color** color chiaro *koh-lOHr key-AH-roh*

comb pettine *pEHt-tee-neh*

to come in venire *vay-nEE-reh;* **come in!** entri! *AYn-tree* avanti! *ah-vAHn-tee*

comedy commedia *kohm-mEH-dee-ah*

commercial commerciale *kohm-mehr-chee-AH-leh*

compartment compartimento *kohm-pahr-tee-mEHn-toh*

concert concerto *kohn-chEHr-toh;* **concert hall** sala da concerti *sAH-lah dah kohn-chEHr-tee*

to confirm confermare *kohn-fayr-mAH-reh*

consommé consommé *kohn-sohm-mAY*

constipation stitichezza *stee-tee-kAY-tsah*

consulate consolato *kohn-soh-lAH-toh*

to contact contattare *kohn-taht-tAH-reh*

contact lenses lenti a contatto *lEHn-tee ah kohn-tAHt-toh*

contagious contagioso *kohn-tah-jee-OH-soh*

to continue continuare *kohn-tee-noo-AH-reh*

contraceptive contraccettivo *kohn-trah-cheht-tEE-voh*

cooked cotto *kOHt-toh*

cookies dolci *dOHl-chee*

cool fresco *frAYs-koh*

copy copia *kOH-pee-ah*

coral corallo *koh-rAHl-loh*

corn plaster callifugo *kahl-lEE-foo-goh*

corner angolo *AHn-goh-loh;* **at the corner** all'angolo *ahl-lAHn-goh-loh*

correct corretto *kohr-rEHt-toh*

cosmetic cosmetico *kohs-mEH-tee-koh*

to cost costare *kohs-tAH-reh*

cottage villino *veel-lEE-noh*

cotton cotone *koh-tOH-neh*

cough tosse *tOHs-seh;* **cough drops** pasticche per la tosse *pahs-tEE-keh pehr lah tOHs-seh*

countryside campagna *kahm-pAH-ny-ah*

course (golf course) campo di golf *kAHm-poh dee gOHlf;* **of course** naturalmente *nah-too-rahl-mEHn-teh;* **(of meals)** portata *pohr-tAH-tah*

courtyard cortile *kohr-tEE-leh*

crabs granchi *grAHn-key*

cramps crampi *krAHm-pee;* **stomach cramps** crampi allo stomaco *krAHm-pee AHl-loh stOH-mah-koh*

cream crema *krEH-mah*

credit credito *krEH-dee-toh;* **credit card** carta di credito *kAHr-tah dee krEH-dee-toh*

croissant cornetto *kohr-nAYt-toh*

crossroad incrocio *een-krOH-chee-oh*

crossing traversata *trah-vehr-sAH-tah;* passaggio a livello *pahs-sAH-jee-oh ah lee-vEHl-loh*

crown corona *koh-rOH-nah*

to crush calpestare *kahl-pehs-tAH-reh*

crust crosta *krOHs-tah*

crutch stampella *stahm-pEHl-lah*

crystal cristallo *krees-tAHl-loh*

Cuban cubano *koo-bAH-noh*

cucumber cetriolo *chay-tree-OH-loh*

cup tazza *tAH-tsah*

curls riccioli *rEE-chee-oh-lee*

currency valuta *vah-lOO-tah*

current corrente *kohr-rEHn-teh*

curse maledizione *mah-lay-dee-tsee-OH-neh*

curve (road) curva *kOOr-vah*

customs dogana *doh-gAH-nah*

to cut tagliare *tah-ly-ee-AH-reh;* **to cut cards** tagliare il mazzo *tah-ly-ee-AH-reh eel mAH-tsoh*

cut taglio *tAH-ly-ee-oh;* **a haircut** un taglio di capelli *oon tAH-ly-ee-oh dee kah-pAYl-lee;* **a shortcut** un'accorciatoia *oo-nah-kOHr-chee-ah-tOH-ee-ah*

cutlet cotoletta *koh-toh-lAYt-tah;* **veal cutlet** cotoletta di vitello *koh-toh-lAYt-tah dee vee-tEHl-loh*

Czech cecoslovacco *chay-kohs-loh-vAH-koh*

D

daily quotidiano *koo-oh-tee-dee-AH-noh*

to dance ballare *bahl-lAH-reh*

dance floor pista di ballo *pEEs-tah dee bAHl-loh*

danger pericolo *peh-rEE-koh-loh;* **dangerous** pericoloso *peh-ree-koh-lOH-soh*

Danish danese *dah-nAY-seh*

dark scuro *skOO-roh*

darn it! maledizione! *mah-leh-dee-tsee-OH-neh*

date data *dAH-tah;* **what's today's date?** che data è oggi? *kay dAH-tah EH OH-jee*

dates (fruit) datteri *dAHt-teh-ree*

daughter figlia *fEE-ly-ee-ah*

day giorno *jee-OHr-noh;* **good morning** buon giorno *boo-OHn jee-OHr-noh*

to deal the cards dare le carte *dAH-reh leh kAHr-teh*

decayed (tooth) cariato *kah-ree-AH-toh*

December dicembre *dee-chEHm-breh*

to declare dichiarare *dee-key-ah-rAH-reh*

deer cervo *chEHr-voh*

delay ritardo *ree-tAHr-doh*

to deliver consegnare *kohn-say-ny-AH-reh*

dental dentale *dehn-tAH-leh;* **dental prosthesis** protesi dentale *prOH-teh-see daynt-tAH-leh*

dentist dentista *dehn-tEEs-tah*

deodorant deodorante *day-oh-doh-rAHn-teh*

to depart partire *pahr-tEE-reh*

department store magazzino *mah-gah-tsEE-noh*

to desire desiderare *day-see-day-rAH-reh*

detective stories gialli *jee-AHl-lee*

detergent detersivo *day-tayr-sEE-voh*

detour (road) deviazione *day-vee-ah-tsee-OH-neh*

to develop sviluppare *svee-loop-pAH-reh*

devil diavolo *dee-AH-voh-loh;* **what the devil do you want?** ma che diavolo vuole? *mah kay dee-AH-voh-loh voo-OH-leh?*

diabetes diabete *dee-ah-bEH-teh*

diamond diamante *dee-ah-mAHn-teh*

diarrhea diarrea *dee-ahr-rEH-ah*

dictionary dizionario *dee-tsee-oh-nAH-ree-oh*

to dine pranzare *prahn-tsAH-reh*

dining room sala da pranzo *sAH-lah dah prAHn-tsoh*

dinner pranzo *prAHn-tsoh*

to direct indicare *een-dee-kAH-reh*

direction direzione *dee-ray-tsee-OH-neh;* **direction indicator (car)** freccia *frAY-chee-ah*

director direttore *dee-reht-tOH-reh*

dirty sporco *spOHr-koh*

discotheque discoteca *dees-koh-tEH-kah*

discount sconto *skOHn-toh*

dish piatto *pee-AHt-toh*

disk disco *dEEs-koh*

to dislike detestare *day-tehs-tAH-reh*

to disturb disturbare *dees-toor-bAH-reh*

dizzy: I feel dizzy mi gira la testa *mee jEE-rah lah tEHs-tah*

to do fare *fAH-reh*

doctor dottore *doht-tOH-reh;* **doctor's office** ambulatorio *ahm-boo-lah-tOH-ree-oh*

document documento *doh-koo-mEHn-toh*

doll bambola *bAHm-boh-lah*

dollar dollaro *dOHl-lah-roh*

dominoes (game) domino *dOH-mee-noh*

door porta *pOHr-tah;* **doorknob** maniglia *mah-nEE-ly-ee-ah*

dot puntino *poon-tEE-noh;* **dots** pallini *pahl-lEE-nee*

doubt dubbio *dOOb-bee-oh*

down giù *jee-OO*

dozen dozzina *doh-tsEE-nah*

drama dramma *drAHm-mah*

to dress vestire *vays-tEE-reh;* **get dressed!** si vesta! *see vEHs-tah*

dress (garment) abito *AH-bee-toh*

dress (woman's) vestito *vays-tEE-toh*

to drink bere *bAY-reh*

drink (beverage) bibita *bEE-bee-tah;* **drinking glass** bicchiere *bee-key-AY-reh*

drinkable potabile *poh-tAH-bee-leh*

to drive guidare *goo-ee-dAH-reh;* **driver's license** patente di guida *pah-tEHn-teh dee goo-EE-dah*

to drown affogare *ahf-foh-gAHr-eh*

drugstore farmacia *fahr-mah-chEE-ah*

dry secco *sAY-koh*

to dry-clean lavare a secco *lah-vAH-reh ah sAY-koh;* **dry cleaner** tintoria *teen-toh-rEE-ah*

duck (bird) anatra *AH-nah-trah*

during durante *door-AHn-teh*

dust polvere *pOHl-vay-reh*

duty (customs) dogana *doh-gAH-nah*

dye tintura *teen-tOO-rah*

dysentery dissenteria *dEEs-sehn-toh rEE-ah*

E

each ogni *OH-ny-ee*

ear orecchio *oh-rAY-key-oh*

early presto *prEHs-toh*

earrings orecchini *oh-ray-kEY-nee*

earth terra *tEHr-rah*

east est *ehst*

easy facile *FAH-chee-leh*

to eat mangiare *mahn-jee-AH-reh*

eel anguilla *ahn-goo-EEl-lah*

egg uovo *oo-OH-voh;* **hard-cooked eggs** uova sode *oo-OH-vah sOH-deh;* **scrambled eggs** uova strapazzate *oo-OH-vah strah-pah-tsAH-teh;* **soft-boiled eggs** uova alla coque *oo-OH-vah AHl-lah kOHk*

eggplant melanzana *may-lahn-tsAH-nah*

eight otto *OHt-toh;* **eight hundred** ottocento *OHt-toh-chEHn-toh*

eighteen diciotto *dee-chee-OHt-toh*

eighth ottavo *oht-tAH-voh*

eighty ottanta *oht-tAHn-tah*

elbow gomito *gOH-mee-toh*

electric elettrico *ay-lEHt-tree-koh;* **electricity** elettricità *ay-leht-tree-chee-tAH*

elevator ascensore *ah-shayn-sOH-reh*

eleven undici *OOn-dee-chee*

emerald smeraldo *smeh-rAHl-doh*

emergency emergenza *eh-mehr-jEHn-tsah*

emergency room pronto soccorso *prOHn-toh sohk-kOHr-soh*

enamel smalto *smAHl-toh*

to end finire *fee-nEE-reh*

to endorse firmare *feer-mAH-reh*

English inglese *een-glAY-seh*

enlargement ingrandimento *een-grahn-dee-mEHn-toh*

enough abbastanza *ahb-bah-stAHn-tsah;* **that's enough!** basta! *bAHs-tah*

to enter entrare *ayn-trAH-reh*

entrance ingresso *een-grEHs-soh*

envelope busta *bOOs-tah*

epileptic epilettico *eh-pee-lEHt-tee-koh*

equipment equipaggiamento *ay-koo-ee-pah-jee-ah-mEHn-toh*

eraser gomma *gOHm-mah*

escalator scala mobile *skAH-lah mOH-bee-leh*

even pari *pAH-reh*

evening sera *sAY-rah;* **evening gown** abito da sera *AH-bee-toh dah sAY-rah*

every ogni *OH-ny-ee;* **everyone** ognuno *oh-ny-oo-noh;* **everything** tutto *tOOt-toh*

to examine esaminare *ay-sah-mee-nAH-reh*

except eccetto *ay-chEH-toh*

to exchange cambiare *kahm-be-AH-reh;* **the exchange rate** il cambio *eel kAHm-bee-oh;* **exchange office** ufficio di cambio *off-fEE-chee-oh dee kAHm-bee-oh*

excursion escursione *ays-koor-see-OH-neh;* gita *jEE-tah*

to excuse scusare *skoo-sAH-reh;* **excuse me!** mi scusi! *mee skOO-see*

exhaust pipe tubo di scappamento *tOO-boh dee skahp-pah-mEHn-toh*

exit uscita *oo-shEE-tah*

expensive caro *kAH-roh;* costoso *kohs-tOH-soh*

express espresso *ays-prEHs-soh*

to extract estrarre *ays-trAHr-reh*

eye occhio *OH-key-oh;* **eye doctor** oculista *oh-koo-lEEs-tah;* **eyedrops** collirio *kohl-lEE-ree-oh*

eye shadow ombretto *ohm-brAYt-toh*

eyebrows sopracciglia *soh-prah-chEE-ly-ee-ah*

eyeglasses occhiali *oh-key-AH-lee;* **sunglasses** occhiali da sole *oh-key-AH-lee dah sOH-leh*

eyelashes ciglia *chEE-ly-ee-ah*

eyeliner eyeliner

F

to face dare su *dAH-reh soo*

face faccia *fAH-chee-ah*

facial facciale *fah-chee-AH-leh*

to faint svenire *svay-nEE-reh*

fall (autumn) autunno *ah-oo-tOOn-noh*

to fall cadere *kah-dAY-reh*

family famiglia *fah-mEE-ly-ee-ah*

fan ventaglio *vehn-tAH-ly-ee-oh;* ventola *vEHn-toh-lah;* **fan belt** cinghia del ventilatore *chEEn-ghee-ah dayl vehn-tee-lah-tOH-reh*

far lontano *lohn-tAH-noh*

fare corsa *kOHr-sah;* biglietto *bee-ly-ee-AYt-toh*

farm fattoria *faht-toh-rEE-ah*

fast veloce *vay-lOH-cheh;* **faster** più veloce *pee-OO vay-lOH-cheh*

fat grasso *grAHs-soh*

father padre *pAH-dreh*

faucet rubinetto *roo-bee-nAYt-toh*

favor favore *fah-vOH-reh*

February febbraio *fayb-brAH-ee-oh*

to feel sentire *sayn-tEE-reh;* **I don't feel well** non mi sento bene *nohn mee sEHn-toh bEH-neh*

felt (cloth) feltro *fAYl-troh*

fender parafango *pah-rah-fAHn-goh*

fever febbre *fEHb-breh*

few alcuni *ahl-kOO-nee;* **a few** qualche *koo-AHl-keh*

field campo *kAHm-poh*

fifteen quindici *koo-EEn-dee-chee*

fifth quinto *koo-EEn-toh*

fifty cinquanta *cheen-koo-AHn-tah*

fig fico *fEE-koh*

file (nail) limetta *lee-mAYt-tah*

Flowers fiori

to fill, to fill out riempire *ree-ehm-pEE-reh*

filling (tooth) otturazione *oht-too-rah-tsee-OH-neh*

film film; pellicola *pehl-lEE-koh-lah*

filter filtro *fEEl-troh*

to find trovare *troh-vAH-reh*

finger dito *dEE-toh*; **fingers** dita *dEE-tah*

to finish finire *fee-nEE-reh*

fire fuoco *foo-OH-koh*; **fire!** al fuoco! *ahl foo-OH-koh*

first primo *prEE-moh*; **first class** prima classe *prEE-mah clAHs-seh*; **first aid** pronto soccorso *prOHn-toh soh-kKOHr-soh*

fish pesce *pAY-sheh*

five cinque *chEEn-koo-eh*; **five hundred** cinquecento *chEEn-koo-eh-chEHn-toh*

to fix aggiustare *ah-jee-oos-tAH-reh*; riparare *ree-pah-rAH-reh*

flannel flanella *flah-nEHl-lah*

flashlight lampadina tascabile *lahm-pah-dEE-nah tahs-kAH-bee-leh*

flat tire gomma bucata *gOHm-mah boo-kAH-tah*

flight volo *vOH-loh*

flint pietrina *pee-ay-trEE-nah*

florist fioraio *fee-oh-rAH-ee-oh*

flour semola *sAY-moh-lah*; farina *fah-rEE-nah*

flu influenza *een-floo-EHn-tsah*

fluid (for cigarette lighters) benzina *baym-tsEE-nah*

folklore folklore *fohl-klOH-ray*; **folkloric** folkloristico *fohl-kloh-rEEs-tee-koh*

to follow seguire *say-goo-EE-reh*

foot piede *pee-EH-deh*; **to go on foot, walk** andare a piedi *ahn-dAH-reh ah pee-EH-dee*

for per *pehr*

forbidden vietato *vee-ay-tAH-toh*

forehead fronte *frOHn-teh*

forest bosco *bOHs-koh*; foresta *foh-rEHs-tah*

to forget dimenticare *dee-mehn-tee-kAH-reh*

fork forchetta *fohr-kAYt-tah*

form modulo *mOH-doo-loh*

fortune fortuna *fohr-tOO-nah*

forty quaranta *koo-ah-rAHn-tah*

to forward spedire *spay-dEE-reh*; **forward (direction)** avanti *ah-vAHn-tee*

fountain fontana *fohn-tAH-nah*

four quattro *koo-AHt-troh*; **four hundred** quattrocento *koo-AHt-troh-chEHn-toh*

fourteen quattordici *koo-aht-tOHr-dee-chee*

fourth quarto *koo-AHr-toh*

fracture frattura *fraht-tOO-rah*

frame montatura *mohn-tah-tOO-rah*

free libero *lEE-beh-roh*

French francese *frahn-chAY-seh*

fresh fresco *frAYs-koh*

Friday venerdì *veh-nehr-dEE*

fried fritto *frEEt-toh*

friend amico *ah-mEE-koh*

from da *dah*

front davanti *dah-vAHn-tee*

fruit frutta *frOOt-tah*; **fresh-fruit salad** macedonia *mah-chay-dOH-nee-ah*

fuel pump pompa della benzina *pOHm-pah dAYl-lah baym-tsEE-nah*

fuel tank serbatoio *sehr-bah-tOH-ee-oh*

full pieno *pee-AY-noh*

fullback (sport) terzino *tehr-tsEE-noh*

furnished ammobiliato *ahm-moh-bee-lee-AH-toh*

G

game (sports) partita *pahr-tEE-tah*; **(birds)** selvaggina *sayl-vah-jEE-nah*

garage autorimessa *AH-oo-toh-ree-mAYs-sah*

garden aiuola *ah-ee-oo-OH-lah*; giardino *jee-ahr-dEE-noh*

garlic aglio *AH-ly-ee-oh*

garnish contorno *kohn-tOHr-noh*

gasoline benzina *bayn-tsEE-nah*

gate porta *pOHr-tah*; cancello *kahn-chAYl-loh*; uscita *oo-shEE-tah*

gears ingranaggi *een-grah-nAH-jee*

general delivery fermo posta *fAYr-moh pOHs-tah*

gentleman signore *see-ny-OH-reh*

German tedesco *tay-dAYs-koh*

to get ottenere *oht-teh-nAY-reh*; **to get back (to return)** ritornare *ree-tohr-nAH-reh*; **to get dressed** vestirsi *vays-tEEr-see*; **to get off** scendere *shAYn-day-reh*; **to get on** montare *mohn-tAH-ray*; **to get up** alzarsi *ahl-tzAHr-tsee*

gift regalo *ray-gAH-loh*

girl ragazza *rah-gAH-tsah*

to give dare *dAH-reh*; **to give back** ridare *ree-dAH-reh*

glands ghiandole *ghee-AHn-doh-leh*

glass vetro *vAY-troh*; **blown glass** vetro soffiato *vAY-troh sohf-fEE-ah-toh*

glue colla *kOHl-lah*

goat (kid) capra *kAH-prah*; capretto *kah-prAYt-toh*

to go andare *ahn-dAH-reh*; **let's go!** andiamo! *ahn-dee-AH-moh*; **go!** forza! *fOHr-*

tsah; **to go back** ritornare *ree-tohr-nAH-reh*; **to go down** scendere *shAYn-day-reh*; **to go home** andare a casa *ahn-dAH-reh ah kAH-sah*; **to go in** entrare *ayn-trAH-reh*; **to go out** uscire *oo-shEE-reh*; **to go shopping** andare a fare la spesa *ahn-dAH-reh ah fAH-reh lah spAY-sah*; **to go up** salire *sah-lEE-rah*

gold oro *OH-roh*; **solid gold** oro massiccio *OH-roh mahs-sEE-chee-oh*; **gold plated** oro placcato *OH-roh plah-kAH-toh*

good buono *boo-OH-noh*

good-bye arrivederci *ahr-rEE-veh-dAYr-chee*; **(friendly)** ciao *chee-AH-oh*

goose oca *OH-kah*

gram grammo *grAHm-moh*

grapefruit pompelmo *pohm-pAYl-moh*

grass erba *EHr-bah*

gray grigio *grEE-jee-oh*

to grease lubrificare *loo-bree-fee-kAH-reh*

great! magnifico! *mah-ny-EE-fee-koh*

Greek greco *grEH-koh*

green verde *vAYr-deh*

greetings saluti *sah-lOO-tee*

guide, guidebook guida *goo-EE-dah*

gums (teeth) gengive *jayn-jEE-veh*

H

hair capelli *kah-pAYl-lee*; **hair bleach** tintura per capelli *teen-tOO-rah pehr kah-pAYl-lee*; **hair dryer** asciugacapelli *ah-shee-OO-gah-kah-pAYl-lee*; fono *fOH-noh*; **hair lotion** frizione *free-tsee-OH-neh;* brillantina *breel-lahn-tEE-nah;* **hair rinse** cachet *kah-shEH;* **hair spray** lacca *lAH-kah*

haircut taglio di capelli *tAH-ly-ee-oh dee kah-pAYl-lee*

hairdresser parrucchiere per signore *pahr-roo-key-EH-reh pehr see-ny-OH-reh*

hairpin forcina *fohr-chEE-nah*

hake (fish) nasello *nah-sehl-loh*

half mezzo *mEH-tsoh*

ham (cured) prosciutto *proh-shee-OOt-toh*

hamburger hamburger

hammer martello *mahr-tEHl-loh*

hand mano *mAH-noh;* **give me a hand** mi dia una mano *mee dEE-ah OO-nah mAH-noh*

handbag borsetta *bohr-sAYt-tah*

handicapped disabile *dee-sAH-bee-leh*

handkerchief fazzoletto *fah-tsoh-lAYt-toh*

handmade fatto a mano *fAHt-toh ah mAH-noh*

hanger grucce *grOO-cheh;* attaccapanni *aht-tAH-kah-pAHn-nee*

to happen succedere *soo-chEH-deh-reh;* **what's happening?** ma che cosa succede? *mah kay kOH-sah soo-chEH-deh*

happy lieto *lee-AY-toh*

harbor porto *pOHr-toh*

hard duro *dOO-roh*

hardware store ferramenta *fehr-rah-mEHn-tah*

hare lepre *lEH-preh*

hat cappello *kahp-pEHl-loh*

to have avere *ah-vAY-reh;* **to have to** dovere *doh-vAY-reh*

hay fever febbre del fieno *fEHb-breh dayl fee-AY-noh*

hazelnuts noccioline *noh-chee-lEE-neh*

he egli *AY-ly-ee;* lui *lOO-ee*

head capo *kAH-poh;* **headache** mal di testa *mAHl dee tEHs-tah*

headlights fari abbaglianti *fAH-ree ahb-bah-ly-ee-AHn-tee*

health salute *sah-lOO-teh*

to hear sentire *sayn-tEE-reh*

hearing aid apparecchio acustico per l'udito *ahp-pah-rAY-key-oh ah-kOO-stee-koh pehr loo-dEE-toh*

heart cuore *koo-OH-reh;* **heart attack** attacco cardiaco *aht-tAHk-koh kahr-dEE-ah-koh*

heat calore *kah-lOH-reh*

heaven cielo *chee-EH-loh*

heavy pesante *pay-sAHn-teh*

hectogram ettogrammo *eht-toh-grAHm-moh*

heel (foot) tallone *tahl-lOH-neh;* **(shoe)** tacco *tAH-koh*

hello! (telephone) pronto! *prOHn-toh*

to help aiutare *ah-ee-oo-tAH-reh;* assistere *ahs-sEEs-tay-reh;* **help!** aiuto! *ah-ee-OO-toh*

her lei *lEH-ee;* la *lah;* le *lay*

here qui *koo-EE;* qua *koo-AH;* **here is** ecco *EHk-koh*

herring aringa *ah-rEEn-gah*

high alto *AHl-toh*

highway autostrada *ah-oo-toh-strAH-dah*

hill collina *kohl-lEE-nah*

him lui *lOO-ee;* lo *loh*

hip anca *AHn-kah*

to hold tenere *tay-nAY-reh*

home casa *kAH-sah*

hood (car) cofano *kOH-fah-noh*

horn (car) clacson *klAH-ksohn*

hors d'oeuvre antipasto *ahn-tee-pAHs-toh*

horse cavallo *kah-vAHl-loh*

hostel (youth) ostello della gioventù *ohs-tEHl-loh dAYl-lah jee-oh-vehn-tOO*

hot caldo *kAHl-doh*

hotel hotel; albergo *ahl-bEHr-goh*

hour ora *OH-rah;* **at what time?** a che ora? *ah kay OH-rah*

house casa *kAH-sah* **(to make) house calls** visitare i pazienti in casa *vee-see-tAH-reh ee pah-tzee-EHn-tee een kAH-sah*

how come *kOH-meh;* **how are you?** come sta? *kOH-meh stAH;* **how far is it?** quanto dista? *koo-AHn-toh dEEs-tah;* **how long does it take to get there?** quanto tempo ci vuole per andarci? *koo-AHn-toh tEHm-poh chee voo-OH-leh pehr ahn-dAHr-chee;* **how much is it?** quanto costa? *koo-AHn-toh kOHs-tah*

however però *peh-rOH*

hundred cento *chEHn-toh*

hunger fame *fAH-meh;* **I'm hungry** ho fame *OH fAH-meh*

to hurry sbrigarsi *sbree-gAHr-see;* **hurry up!** si sbrighi! *see sbrEE-ghee*

to hurt dolere *doh-lAY-reh;* far male *fahr mAH-leh*

husband marito *mah-rEE-toh*

hygienic igienico *ee-jee-AY-nee-koh*

if se *seh*

ignition accensione *ah-chehn-see-OH-neh*

illness malattia *mah-laht-tEE-ah*

imagination fantasia *fahn-tah-sEE-ah*

important importante *eem-pohr-tAHn-teh*

impossible impossibile *eem-pohs-sEE-bee-leh*

in in *een*

included incluso *een-klOO-soh*

infection infezione *een-feh-tsee-OH-neh*

inn trattoria *traht-toh-rEE-ah*

innocent innocente *een-noh-chEHn-teh*

inside dentro *dAYn-troh*

insomnia insonnia *een-sOHn-nee-ah*

instead invece *een-vAY-cheh*

insulin insulina *een-soo-lEE-nah*

insurance assicurazione *ahs-see-koo-rah-tsee-OH-neh*

international internazionale *een-tehr-nAH-tsee-oh-nAH-leh*

interesting interessante *een-teh-rehs-sAHn-teh*

interpreter interprete *een-TEHR-preh-teh*

intersection incrocio *een-krOH-chee-oh*

into in *een*

iodine iodio *ee-OH-dee-oh*

iron ferro *fEHr-roh*

it esso *AYs-soh;* essa *AYs-sah;* lo *loh;* la *lah*

Italian italiano *ee-tah-lee-AH-noh*

I

I io *EE-oh*

ice ghiaccio *ghee-AH-chee-oh;* **ice cream** gelato *jeh-lAH-toh;* **ice cubes** cubetti di ghiaccio *koo-bAYt-tee dee ghee-AH-chee-oh;* **ice water** acqua ghiacciata *AH-koo-ah ghee-ah-chee-AH-tah*

identification card carta d'identità *kAHr-tah dee-dehn-tee-tAH*

J

jack (car) cricco *krEE-koh;* **(cards)** cavallo *kah-vAHl-loh*

jacket giacca *jee-AH-kah*

jade giada *jee-AH-dah*
jam marmellata *mahr-mehl-lAH-tah*
January gennaio *jehn-nAH-ee-oh*
Japanese giapponese *jee-ahp-poh-nAY-seh*
jar vasetto *vah-sAYt-toh*
jewel gioiello *jee-oh-ee-EHl-loh;* **jeweler** gioielliere *jee-oh-ee-EHl-lee-EH-reh;* **jewelry shop** gioielleria *jee-oh-ee-EHl-leh-rEE-ah*
Jewish ebreo *ay-brEH-oh;* israeliano *ees-rah-eh-lee-AH-noh*
juice succo *sOO-koh*
July luglio *lOO-ly-ee-oh*
June giugno *jee-OO-ny-oh*

K

to keep tenere *tay-nAY-reh;* **keep off the grass** non calpestare le aiuole *nohn kahl-pays-tAH-reh leh ah-ee-oo-OH-leh*
key chiave *key-AH-veh*
kick calcio *kAHl-chee-oh;* **kickoff** calcio d'inizio *kAHl-chee-oh dee-nEE-tsee-oh*
kidney rognone *roh-ny-OH-neh*
kilogram chilo *kEE-loh;* chilogrammo *key-loh-grAHm-moh*
kilometer chilometro *key-lOH-meh-troh*
king re *ray*
to kiss baciare *bah-chee-AH-reh*
kiss bacio *bAH-chee-oh*
kitchen cucina *koo-chEE-nah*
knee ginocchio *jee-nOH-key-oh*
knife coltello *kohl-tEHl-loh*
knight (chess) alfiere *ahl-fee-EH-reh*
to know (facts) sapere *sah-pAY-reh;* **to know (people)** conoscere *koh-nOH-shay-reh*

L

lace merletto *mehr-lEHt-toh;* pizzo *pEE-tsoh*
laces (shoe) lacci *lAH-chee*
lady signora *see-ny-OH-rah;* **ladies' room** bagno per signora *bAH-ny-oh pehr see-ny-OH-rah*
lake lago *lAH-goh*
lamb agnello *ah-ny-EHl-loh*
lamp lampada *lAHm-pah-dah*
land terra *tEHr-rah*
landscape panorama *pah-noh-rAH-mah*
language lingua *lEEn-goo-ah*
large grande *grAHn-deh;* **larger** più grande *pee-OO grAHn-deh*
to last durare *doo-rAH-reh*
last ultimo *OOl-tee-moh*
late tardi *tAHr-dee;* **the train is late** il treno è in ritardo *eel trEH-noh EH een ree-tAHr-doh;* **later** più tardi *pee-OO tAHr-dee;* **at the latest** al più tardi *ahl pee-OO tAHr-dee*
lateness ritardo *ree-tAHr-doh*
to laugh ridere *rEE-deh-reh*
laundry biancheria *bee-AHn-keh-rEE-ah*
lawyer avvocato *ahv-voh-kAH-toh*
laxative lassativo *lahs-sah-tEE-voh*
to leak perdere acqua *pEHr-deh-reh AH-koo-ah*
to learn apprendere *ahp-prAYn-deh-reh*
leather pelle *pEHl-leh*
to leave lasciare *lah-shee-AH-reh;* partire *pahr-tEE-reh*
left sinistro *see-nEEs-troh;* **to the left** a sinistra *ah see-nEEs-trah*
leg gamba *gAHm-bah*
lemon limone *lee-mOH-neh*

lemonade limonata *lee-moh-nAH-tah*

lens lente *lEHn-teh;* **contact lenses** lenti a contatto *lEHn-tee ah kohn-tAHt-toh*

lentils lenticchie *lehn-tEE-key-eh*

letter lettera *lAYt-teh-rah;* **airmail** via aerea *vEE-ah ah-EH-reh-ah;* **insured** assicurata *ahs-see-koo-rAH-tah;* **registered** raccomandata *rAH-koh-mahn-dAH-tah;* **special delivery** espresso *ehs-prehs-soh;* **with return receipt** con ricevuta di ritorno *kohn ree-chay-vOO-tah dee ree-tOHr-noh*

lettuce lattuga *laht-tOO-gah*

library biblioteca *bee-blee-oh-tEH-kah*

to lie down sdraiarsi *sdrah-eeAHr-see;* **lie down!** si sdrai! *see sdrAH-ee*

life vita *vEE-tah*

lifeguard bagnino *bah-ny-EE-noh*

to lift alzare *ahl-tsAH-reh*

light (color) chiaro *key-AH-roh;* **(electric)** luce *lOO-cheh;* **(weight)** leggero *lay-jEH-roh*

lighter (cigarette) accendino *ah-chayn-dEE-noh*

to like piacere *pee-ah-chAY-reh;* **I like it** mi piace *mee pee-AH-cheh*

lime cedro *chAY-droh*

line linea *lEE-neh-ah*

linen biancheria *bee-AHn-keh-rEE-ah;* lino *lEE-noh*

lips labbra *lAHb-brah*

lipstick lipstick; rossetto *rohs-sAYt-toh*

liqueur liquore *lee-koo-OH-reh*

list elenco *eh-lEHn-koh;* lista *lEEs-tah*

to listen ascoltare *ah-skohl-tAH-reh*

liter litro *lEE-troh*

little piccolo *pEE-koh-loh*

to live abitare *ah-bee-tAH-reh*

liver fegato *fAY-gah-toh*

to load caricare *kah-ree-kAH-reh*

loaf (of bread) filone di pane *fee-lOH-neh dee pAH-neh*

loan prestito *prEHs-tee-toh*

lobster aragosta *ah-rah-gOHs-tah*

local (train) locale *loh-kAH-leh*

long lungo *lOOn-goh*

to look guardare *goo-AHr-dAH-reh;* **to take a look** dare un'occhiata *dAH-reh oo-noh-key-AH-tah;* **to look for** cercare *chayr-kAH-reh*

to lose perdere *pEHr-deh-reh*

lotion lozione *loh-tsee-OH-neh;* **suntan lotion** lozione per l'abbronzatura solare *loh-tsee-OH-neh pehr lahb-brohn-tsah-tOO-rah soh-lAH-reh*

lots of molto *mOHl-toh*

loud forte *fOHr-teh*

love amore *ah-mOH-reh*

low basso *bAHs-soh*

lubricate lubrificare *loo-bree-fee-kAH-reh*

luck fortuna *fohr-tOO-nah;* **good luck!** buona fortuna! *boo-OH-nah fohr-tOO-nah*

luggage bagaglio *bah-gAH-ly-oh;* **luggage rack** portabagagli *pohr-tah-bah-gAH-ly-ee*

lump (swelling) gonfiore *gohn-fee-OH-reh*

lunch pranzo *prAHn-tsoh*

lung polmone *pohl-mOH-neh*

M

machine macchina *mAH-key-nah*

mad pazzo *pAH-tsoh*

maid cameriera *kah-meh-ree-AY-rah*

mail posta *pOHs-tah;* **mailbox** cassetta postale *kas-sAYt-tah pohs-tAH-leh*

main principale *preen-chee-pAH-leh*

magazine rivista *ree-vEEs-tah*

magnetic phone card scheda magnetica *skEH-dah mah-nyEH-tee-kah*

major maggiore *mah-jee-OH-reh*

to make fare *fAH-reh*

malt malto *mAHl-toh*

man uomo *oo-OH-moh*

manager direttore *dee-reht-tOH-reh*

mango mango *mAHn-goh*

manicure manicure *mah-nee-kOO-reh*

many molti *mOHl-tee*

map cartina *kahr-tEE-nah*

March marzo *mAHr-tsoh*

margarine margarina *mahr-gah-rEE-nah*

market mercato *mehr-kAH-toh*

married sposato *spoh-sAH-toh*

Mass Messa *mAYs-sah*

massage massaggio *mahs-sAH-jee-oh;* (hair) frizione *free-tsee-OH-neh*

match fiammifero *fee-ahm-mEE-feh-roh*

to matter importare *eem-pohr-tAH-reh;* **what's the matter with you?** ma che cos'ha? *mah kay koh-sAH*

mattress materasso *mah-teh-rAHs-soh*

May maggio *mAH-jee-oh*

maybe forse *fOHr-seh*

me me *may*

meal pasto *pAHs-toh*

to mean significare *see-ny-ee-fee-kAH-reh;* **what does this mean?** che cosa significa questo? *kay kOH-sah see-ny-EE-fee-kah koo-AYs-toh*

means mezzo *mEH-tsoh*

measurements misura *mee-sOO-rah*

meat carne *kAHr-neh*

meatball polpetta *pohl-pAYt-tah*

mechanic meccanico *meh-kAH-nee-koh*

medical medico *mEH-dee-koh*

medicine medicina *meh-dee-chEE-nah*

to meet incontrare *een-kohn-trAH-reh*

melon melone *may-lOH-neh*

men uomini *oo-OH-mee-nee;* **men's room** bagno per uomini (signore) *bAH-ny-oh pehr oo-OH-mee-nee (see-ny-OH-reh);* gabinetto *gah-bee-nAYt-toh*

to mend rammendare *rahm-mehn-dAH-reh*

menu menu *meh-nOO*

message messaggio *mehs-sAH-jee-oh*

meter (length) metro *mEH-troh*

Mexican messicano *mehs-see-kAH-noh*

middle mezzo *mEH-tsoh*

midnight mezzanotte *mEH-tsah-nOHt-teh*

mileage chilometraggio *key-loh-meh-trAH-jee-oh;* **unlimited mileage** chilometraggio illimitato *key-loh-meh-trAH-jee-oh EEl-lee-mee-tAH-toh*

mild leggero *lay-jEH-roh*

milk latte *lAHt-teh*

million milione *mee-lee-OH-neh*

mind mente *mEHn-teh;* **do you mind?** le dispiace? *lay dees-pee-AH-cheh*

mineral water acqua minerale *AH-koo-ah mee-neh-rAH-leh*

minister ministro *mee-nEEs-troh*

minute minuto *mee-nOO-toh*

mirror specchio *spEH-key-oh*

Miss signorina *see-ny-oh-rEE-nah*

to miss mancare *mahn-kAH-reh;* **I miss you** mi manchi *mee mAHn-key*

mistake sbaglio *sbAH-ly-ee-oh*

moment momento *moh-mEHn-toh*

Monday lunedì *loo-nay-dEE*

money denaro *day-nAH-roh;* soldi *sOHl-dee;* **money order** vaglia *vAH-ly-ee-ah*

month mese *mAY-seh*

moped motorino *moh-toh-rEE-noh*

more più *pee-OO*

morning mattino *maht-tEE-noh*

mosque moschea *mohs-kEH-ah*

mother madre *mAH-dreh*

motor motore *moh-tOH-reh;* **motor coach** autopullman *AHoo-toh-pOOl-mahn;* **motor scooter** lambretta *lahm-brAYt-tah;* vespa *vEHs-pah*

motorcycle moto *mOH-toh*

mountain montagna *mohn-tAH-ny-ah*

moustache baffi *bAHf-fee*

mouth bocca *bOH-kah;* **mouthwash** disinfettante per la bocca *dee-seen-feht-tAHn-teh pehr lah bOH-kah*

to move muovere *moo-OH-vay-reh*

movie cinema *chEE-neh-mah;* **movie camera** cinepresa *chee-neh-prAY-sah*

Mr. signore *see-ny-OH-reh*

Mrs. signora *see-ny-OH-rah*

much molto *mOHl-toh;* **how much is it?** quanto costa? *koo-AHn-toh kOHs-tah*

museum museo *moo-sEH-oh*

mussels cozze *kOH-tseh*

music musica *mOO-see-kah*

must dovere *doh-vAY-reh;* **I must go** debbo andarmene *dAYb-boh ahn-dAHr-meh-neh*

mustard senape *sEH-nah-peh;* mostarda *moh-stAHr-dah*

mutton montone *mohn-tOH-neh*

my mio *mEE-oh;* miei *mee-AY-ee;* mia *mEE-ah;* mie *mEE-eh*

mystery mistero *mees-tEH-roh;* **it's a mystery!** è un giallo! *EH oon jee-AHl-loh*

N

nail unghia *OOn-ghee-ah;* **nail clippers** tagliaunghie *tAH-ly-ee-ah-OOn-ghee-eh;* **nail polish** smalto per le unghie *smAHl-toh pehr leh OOn-ghee-eh;* **nail polish remover** acetone *ah-chay-tOH-neh*

name nome *nOH-meh;* **last name** cognome *koh-ny-OH-meh;* **my name is . . .** mi chiamo . . . *mee key-AH-moh*

napkin tovagliolo *toh-vah-ly-ee-OH-loh;* **sanitary napkins** assorbenti igienici *ahs-sohr-bEHn-tee ee-jee-EH-nee-chee*

nationality nazionalità *nah-tsee-oh-nah-lee-tAH*

near accanto *ah-kAHn-toh*

necessary necessario *neh-chehs-sAH-ree-oh*

necklace catenina *kah-tay-nEE-nah;* collana *kohl-lAH-nah;* monile *moh-nEE-leh*

necktie cravatta *krah-vAHt-tah*

to need avere bisogno di *ah-vAY-reh bee-sOH-ny-oh dee;* **I need help** ho bisogno d'aiuto *oh bee-sOH-ny-oh dah-eeOO-toh*

needle ago *AH-goh*

new nuovo *noo-OH-voh*

newspaper giornale *jee-ohr-nAH-leh*

newsstand edicola *ay-dEE-koh-lah;* giornalaio *jee-ohr-nah-lAH-ee-oh*

next to accanto *ah-kAHn-toh*
nightclub night club *nAH-eet klOOb*
nine nove *nOH-veh*
nineteen diciannove *dee-chee-ahn-nOH-veh*
ninety novanta *noh-vAHn-tah*
ninth nono *nOH-noh*
nonsense! sciocchezze! *shee-oh-kAY-tseh*; ma che! *mah kAY*
noon mezzogiorno *mEH-tsoh-jee-OHr-noh*
normal normale *nohr-mAH-leh*
north nord *nord*
nose naso *nAH-soh*
not non *nohn*
notebook taccuino *tah-koo-EE-noh*; block-notes *blOHk-nOH-tays*
nothing niente *nee-EHn-tay*
now adesso *ah-dEHs-soh*; ora *OH-rah*
nuisance seccatura *say-kah-tOO-rah*
number numero *nOO-meh-roh*; **numbered** numerato *noo-meh-rAH-toh*
nut (fruit) noce *nOH-chay*; **(mechanical)** dado *dAH-doh*
nylon nylon *nAH-ee-lohn*

O

to observe osservare *ohs-sehr-vAH-reh*
to obstruct ostruire *ohs-troo-EE-reh*
to obtain ottenere *oht-tay-nAY-reh*
occupied occupato *oh-koo-pAH-toh*
ocean oceano *oh-chEH-ah-noh*
October ottobre *oht-tOH-breh*
octopus polipo *pOH-lee-poh*

oculist oculista *oh-koo-lEEs-tah*
of di *dee*
office ufficio *oof-fEE-chee-oh*
often spesso *spAYs-soh*
oil olio *OH-lee-oh*
omelet frittata *freet-tAH-tah*
on sopra *sOH-prah*; su *soo*
once una volta *OO-nah vOHl-tah*
one un *oon*; uno *OO-noh*; una *OO-nah*; un' *oon*; **one way** senso unico *sEHn-soh OO-nee-koh*
onion cipolla *chee-pOHl-lah*
only solamente *soh-lah-mEHn-teh*
onyx onice *OH-nee-cheh*
to open aprire *ah-prEE-reh*
open aperto *ah-pEHr-toh*
opera opera *OH-peh-rah*; **operetta** operetta *oh-peh-rAYt-tah*
opposite contrario *kohn-trAH-ree-oh*
optician ottico *OHt-tee-koh*
or o *oh*
orange (fruit) arancia *ah-rAHn-chee-ah*; **(tree)** arancio *ah-rAHn-chee-oh*
orangeade aranciata *ah-rahn-chee-AH-tah*
orchestra orchestra *ohr-kEHs-trah*; **(group) section** platea *plah-tEH-ah*
to order ordinare *ohr-dee-nAH-reh*
other altro *AHl-troh*
ouch! ahi! *AHee*
outcome risultato *ree-sool-tAH-toh*
outside fuori *foo-OH-ree*
oven forno *fOHr-noh*
overcoat soprabito *soh-prAH-bee-toh*
to overheat surriscaldare *soor-rEEs-kahl-dAH-reh*
own proprio *prOH-pree-oh*
oyster ostrica *OHs-tree-kah*

P

package pacchetto *pah-kAYt-toh*

pair paio *pAH-ee-oh*

palace palazzo *pah-lAH-tsoh*

panorama panorama *pah-noh-rAH-mah*

panties mutandine *moo-tahn-dEE-neh*

pants pantaloni *pahn-tah-lOH-nee*

panty hose collant *kOHl-lahnt*

paper carta *kAHr-tah*

parcel pacco *pAH-koh*

to park parcheggiare *pahr-kay-jee-AH-reh;* **no parking** divieto di sosta *dee-vee-AYt-oh dee sOHs-tah*

park (garden) parco *pAHr-koh*

partridge pernice *payr-nEE-cheh*

parts (car) pezzi di ricambio *pEH-tsee dee ree-kAHm-bee-oh*

to pass passare *pahs-sAH-reh*

passport passaporto *pahs-sah-pOHr-toh*

pastry pasticceria *pahs-tee-cheh-rEE-ah*

pathway sentiero *sayn-tee-AY-roh*

to pay pagare *pah-gAH-reh*

peas piselli *pee-sEHl-lee*

peach pesca *pAYs-kah*

pear pera *pAY-rah*

pedestrian pedone *peh-dOH-neh*

pen penna *pAYn-nah;* **ballpoint pen** penna a sfera *pAYh-nah ah sfEH-rah*

pencil matita *mah-tEE-tah;* **pencil sharpener** temperamatite *tEHm-peh-rah-mah-tEE-teh*

penicillin penicillina *pay-nee-cheel-lEE-nah*

perfume profumo *proh-fOO-moh*

perhaps forse *fOHr-seh*

period periodo *payr-EEoh-doh*

to permit permettere *pehr-mEHt-teh-reh*

permit (license) patente *pah-tEHn-teh*

pharmacy farmacia *fahr-mah-chEE-ah*

pheasant fagiano *fah-jee-AH-noh*

to photograph fotografare *foh-toh-grah-fAH-reh*

photograph (picture) fotografia *foh-toh-grah-fEE-ah*

piece pezzo *pEH-tsoh*

pig (pork) maiale *mah-ee-AH-leh*

pill pillola *pEEl-loh-lah*

pillow cuscino *koo-shEE-noh*

pin spilla *spEEl-lah*

pineapple ananasso *ah-nah-nAHs-soh*

place posto *pOHs-toh;* località *loh-kah-lee-tAH*

plate piatto *pee-AHt-toh*

plant pianta *pee-AHn-tah*

plastic plastica *plAHs-tee-kah*

platform piattaforma *pee-AHt-tah-fOHr-mah*

platinum platino *plAH-tee-noh*

to play giocare *jee-OH-kAH-reh*

playground zona giochi *tsOH-nah jee-OH-key*

please per favore *pehr fah-vOH-reh;* per piacere *pehr pee-ah-chAY-reh*

pliers pinze *pEEn-tseh*

plug (electric) spina per la corrente *spEE-nah pehr lah kohr-rEHn-teh;* **spark plug** candela *kahn-dAY-lah*

plum susina *soo-sEE-nah;* prugna *prOO-ny-ah*

poker poker *pOH-kehr*

police polizia *poh-lee-tsEE-ah;* **police station** stazione di polizia *stah-tsee-OH-neh dee poh-lee-tsEE-ah;*

Commissariato *kOHm-mees-sah-ree-AH-toh;* caserma dei carabinieri *kah-sEHr-mah dAY-ee kah-rah-bee-nee-AY-ree*

Polish polacco *poh-lAH-koh*

pond stagno *stAH-ny-oh*

pork maiale *mah-ee-AH-leh*

portable portatile *pohr-tAH-tee-leh*

porter portabagagli *pOHr-tah-bah-gAH-ly-ee*

portion porzione *pohr-tsee-OH-nay*

Portuguese portoghese *pohr-toh-ghAY-say*

possible possibile *pohs-sEE-bee-leh*

post office ufficio postale *oof-fEE-chee-oh pohs-tAH-leh*

postage affrancatura *ahf-frahn-kah-tOO-rah*

postcard cartolina postale *kahr-toh-lEE-nah pohs-tAH-leh;* **picture postcard** cartolina illustrata *kahr-toh-lEE-nah EEl-loos-trAH-tah*

poster poster; manifesto *mah-nee-fEHs-toh*

potable potabile *poh-tAH-bee-leh*

potato patata *pah-tAH-tah*

prayer preghiera *pray-ghee-EH-rah*

to prefer preferire *preh-fay-rEE-reh*

pregnant incinta *een-chEEn-tah*

to prepare preparare *preh-pah-rAH-reh*

prescription ricetta *ree-chEHt-tah*

to present presentare *preh-sayn-tAH-reh*

present (gift) regalo *ray-gAH-loh*

price prezzo *prEH-tsoh*

priest prete *prEH-teh*

print (photo) copia *kOH-pee-ah*

private privato *pree-vAH-toh*

profession professione *proh-fehs-see-OH-neh*

prophylactics profilattici *proh-fee-lAHt-tee-chee;* preservativi *preh-sehr-vah-tEE-vee*

program programma *proh-grAHm-mah*

progressive lenses lenti progressive *lEHn-tee proh-grehs-sEE-veh*

Protestant protestante *proh-teh-stAHn-teh*

to prove provare *pro-vAH-reh*

pudding budino *boo-dEE-noh*

to pull tirare *tee-rAH-reh*

pump pompa *pOHm-pah;* **fuel pump** pompa della benzina *pOHm-pah dAYl-lah behn-tsEE-nah*

to purchase comprare *kohm-prAH-reh*

purse borsetta *bohr-sAYt-tah*

to push spingere *spEEn-jay-reh*

to put mettere *mAYt-tay-reh*

Q

quarter quarto *koo-AHr-toh*

queen (cards) donna *dOHn-nah*

question domanda *doh-mAHn-dah*

quick presto *prEHs-toh*

R

rabbi rabbino *rahb-bEE-noh*

rabbit coniglio *koh-nEE-ly-ee-oh*

racetrack ippodromo *eep-pOH-droh-moh*

racquet racchetta *rah-kAYt-tah*

radiator (car) radiatore *rah-dee-ah-tOH-reh*

radish ravanello *rah-vah-nEHl-loh*

railroad ferrovia *fehr-roh-vEE-ah;* **railroad station** stazione ferroviaria *stah-tsee-OH-neh fEHr-ro-vee-AH-ree-ah*

to rain piovere *pee-OH-veh-reh*

raincoat impermeabile *eem-pehr-may-AH-bee-leh*

ramp rampa *rAHm-pah*

raspberry lampone *lahm-pOH-neh*

rate tariffa *tah-rEEf-fah*

razor rasoio *rah-sOH-ee-oh;* **razor blades** lamette *lah-mAYt-teh*

to reach raggiungere *rah-jee-OOn-jay-reh;* arrivare *ahr-ree-vAH-reh*

to read leggere *lEH-jeh-reh*

ready pronto *prOHn-toh*

receipt ricevuta *ree-chay-vOO-tah*

to receive ricevere *ree-chAY-vay-reh*

receiver (telephone) destinatario *days-tee-nah-tAH-ree-oh*

to recommend consigliare *kohn-see-ly-ee-AH-reh;* raccomandare *rAH-koh-mahn-dAH-reh*

record (phonograph) disco *dEEs-koh;* **record player** giradischi *jEE-rah-dEEs-kee*

reduced ridotto *ree-dOHt-toh*

red rosso *rOHs-soh*

referee arbitro *AHr-bee-troh*

refund rimborso *reem-bOHr-soh*

religious religioso *ray-lee-jee-OH-soh*

to remain restare *rays-tAH-reh*

to rent (car) noleggiare *noh-lay-jee-AH-reh;* **(house)** affittare *ahf-feet-tAH-reh*

to repair aggiustare *ah-jee-oos-tAH-reh;* riparare *ree-pah-rAH-reh*

repair shop officina meccanica *ohf-fee-chEE-nah may-kAH-nee-kah*

to repeat ripetere *ree-pEH-teh-reh*

reservation prenotazione *preh-noh-tah-tsee-OH-neh*

reserved riservato *ree-sehr-vAH-toh;* prenotato *preh-noh-tAH-toh*

to reside risiedere *ree-see-AY-deh-reh*

to rest riposare *ree-poh-sAH-reh*

restroom gabinetto *gah-bee-nAYt-toh;* bagno *bAH-ny-oh;* toilette *too-AH-lEHt*

restaurant ristorante *rEEs-toh-rAHn-teh*

result risultato *ree-sool-tAH-toh*

to return ritornare *ree-tohr-nAH-reh*

rice riso *rEE-soh*

refund rimborso *reem-bOHr-soh*

right destro *dEHs-troh;* **that's all right** va bene *vah bEH-neh;* **right away** subito *sOO-bee-toh*

ring anello *ah-nEHl-loh*

river fiume *fee-OO-meh*

road via *vEE-ah;* strada *strAH-dah;* **road map** cartina stradale *kahr-tEE-nah strah-dAH-leh*

roast arrosto *ahr-rOHs-toh*

robe accappatoio *ah-kAHp-pah-tOH-ee-oh*

roll (film) rullino *rool-lEE-noh*

room camera *kAH-meh-rah;* **bedroom** camera da letto *kAH-meh-rah dah lEHt-toh*

rose rosa *rOH-sah*

rouge rossetto *rohs-sAYt-toh*

row (theater) fila *fEE-lah*

ruler riga *rEE-gah*

Rumanian rumeno *roo-mAY-noh*

to run   correre *kOHr-ray-reh;* **running water**   acqua corrente *ah-koo-ah kohr-rEHn-tay*

Russian   russo *rOOs-soh*

rye   segala *sAY-gah-lah*

S

saccharin   saccarina *sah-kah-rEE-nah;* dolcificante *dohl-chee-fee-kAHn-teh*

salad   insalata *een-sah-lAH-tah*

salami   salame *sah-lAH-meh*

sale   svendita *svAYn-dee-tah*

salmon   salmone *sahl-mOH-neh*

salt   sale *sAH-leh;* **salty**   salato *sah-lAH-toh*

same   stesso *stAYs-soh*

sand   sabbia *sAHb-bee-ah*

sandwich   panino (imbottito) *pah-nEE-noh (eem-boht-tEE-toh)*

sapphire   zaffiro *tsahf-fEE-roh*

sardine   sardina *sahr-dEE-nah*

Saturday   sabato *sAH-bah-toh*

sauce   salsa *sAHl-sah*

saucer   piattino *pee-aht-tEE-noh*

to say   dire *dEE-reh*

schedule   orario *oh-rAH-ree-oh;* **on schedule**   in orario *een oh-rAH-ree oh*

science fiction   fantascienza *fAHn-tah-shee-EHn-tsah*

scissors   forbici *fOHr-bee-chee*

score   punteggio *poon-tAY-jee-oh*

Scotch tape   nastro adesivo *nAHs-troh ah-day-sEE-voh*

scram!   si tolga dai piedi! *see tOH-lgah dAHee pee-EH-dee*

screw   vite *vEE-teh*

sea   mare *mAH-reh*

seafood   frutti di mare *frOOt-tee dee mAH-reh*

seasickness   mal di mare *mAHl dee mAH-reh*

second   secondo *say-kOHn-doh*

sedative   sedativo *say-dah-tEE-voh*

to see   vedere *vay-dAY-reh*

seeing-eye dog   cane da guida *kAH-neh dah goo-EE-da*

selection   selezione *say-leh-tsee-OH-neh*

to sell   vendere *vAYn-day-reh*

to send   mandare *mahn-dAH-reh;* spedire *spay-dEE-reh*

September   settembre *seht-tEHm-breh*

series   serie *sEH-ree-eh*

to serve   servire *sayr-vEE-reh*

service   servizio *sehr-vEE-tsee-oh*

seven   sette *sEHt-teh;* **seven hundred**   settecento *sEHt-teh-chEHn-toh*

seventeen   diciassette *dEE-chee-ahs-sEHt-teh*

seventh   settimo *sEHt-tee-moh*

seventy   settanta *sEHt-tAHn-tah*

to sew   cucire *koo-chEE-reh*

shade   ombra *OHm-brah;* **(window)**   tendina *tehn-dEE-nah*

shampoo   shampoo *shAHm-poh*

to shave oneself   farsi la barba *fAHr-see lah bAHr-bah;* **aftershave**   dopobarba *dOH-poh-bAHr-bah*

shaving cream   crema per la barba *krEH-mah pehr lah bAHr-bah*

she   lei *lEH-ee;* ella *AYl-lah;* essa *AYs-sah*

sherry   sherry

to shine shoes   lucidare le scarpe *loo-chee-dAH-reh leh skAHr-peh*

ship   nave *nAH-veh*

shirt   camicia *kah-mEE-chee-ah;* **man's shirt**   camicia da uomo *kah-mEE-chee-ah dah oo-OH-moh*

shoe scarpa *skAHr-pah;* **shoe store** calzaturificio *kahl-tsah-too-ree-fEE-chee-oh*

shoelaces lacci per le scarpe *lAH-chee pehr leh skAHr-peh*

shoemaker calzolaio *kahl-tsoh-lAH-ee-oh*

shop negozio *neh-gOH-tsee-oh;* **shop window** vetrina *vay-trEE-nah*

short corto *kOHr-toh;* **(person)** basso(a) *bAHs-soh(ah);* **short story** novella *noh-vEHl-lah*

shorts pantaloncini *pahn-tah-lohn-chEE-nee*

shoulder spalla *spAHl-lah*

to show indicare *een-dee-kAH-reh*

shower doccia *dOH-chee-ah*

shrimps gamberetti *gahm-bay-rAYt-tee*

to shuffle mischiare *mees-key-AH-reh*

shut up! zitto! *tsEEt-toh*

sick malato *mah-lAH-toh*

side (body) fianco *fee-AHn-koh*

sidewalk marciapiede *mAHr-chee-ah-pee-EH-deh*

to sign firmare *feer-mAH-reh*

signature firma *fEEr-mah*

silence silenzio *see-lEHn-tsee-oh*

silk seta *sAY-tah*

silly sciocco *shee-OH-koh;* **silliness** sciocchezza *shee-oh-kAH-tsah*

silver argento *ahr-jEHn-toh*

sin peccato *peh-kAH-toh*

since siccome *see-kOHm-eh*

to sing cantare *kahn-tAH-reh*

single (room) camera a un letto *kAH-may-rah ah oon lEHt-toh*

sister sorella *soh-rEHl-lah*

to sit sedersi *say-dAYr-see*

site località *loh-kah-lee-tAH*

six sei *sEH-ee;* **six hundred** seicento *sEH-ee-chEHn-toh*

sixteen sedici *sAY-dee-chee*

sixth sesto *sEHs-toh*

sixty sessanta *says-sAHn-tah*

size misura *mee-sOO-rah;* taglia *tAH-ly-ee-ah*

to ski sciare *shee-AH-reh*

ski (boots) scarponi da sci *skahr-pOH-nee dah shEE;* **(lifts)** sciovie *shee-oh-vEE-eh;* **(slopes)** piste (per sciare) *pEEs-teh (pehr shee-AH-reh)*

skiing (water) sci acquatico *shEE ah-koo-AH-tee-koh*

skin pelle *pEHl-leh*

skirt gonna *gOHn-nah*

to sleep dormire *dohr-mEE-reh*

sleeping car (train) vagone letto *vah-gOH-neh lEHt-toh*

sleeve manica *mAH-nee-kah*

slice fetta *fAYt-tah;* **sliced** affettato *ahf-fayt-tAH-toh*

slip sottoveste *soht-toh-vEHs-teh*

slippers pantofole *pahn-tOH-foh-leh;* ciabatte *chee-ah-bAHt-teh*

slowly lentamente *laym-tah-mEHn-teh;* piano *pee-AH-noh*

small piccolo *pEE-koh-loh;* **smaller** più piccolo *pee-OO pEE-koh-loh*

to smile sorridere *sohr-rEE-day-reh;* fare un sorriso *fAH-reh oon sohr-rEE-soh;* **smile!** sorrida! *sohr-rEE-dah*

to smoke fumare *foo-mAH-reh;* **no smoking** vietato fumare *vee-ay-tAH-toh foo-mAH-reh*

smoker fumatore *foo-mah-tOH-reh*

to snatch scippare *sheep-pAH-reh*

to snow nevicare *nay-vee-kAH-reh*

snow neve *nAY-veh*

so così *koh-sEE*

soap sapone *sah-pOH-neh;* saponetta *sah-poh-nAYt-tah*
soccer calcio *kAHl-chee-oh;* **soccer game** partita di calcio *pahr-tEE-tah dee kAHl-chee-oh*
socks calzini *kahl-tsEE-nee;* calzettini *kahl-tsayt-tEE-nee*
soft drink bibita analcolica *bEE-bee-tah ah-nahl-koh-lEE-kah*
sole (fish) sogliola *sOH-ly-ee-oh-lah*
soles (shoes) suole *soo-OH-leh;* **half-soles** mezze suole *mEH-tseh soo-OH-leh*
solid color tinta unita *tEEn-tah oo-nEE-tah*
some alcuni *ahl-kOO-nee;* qualche *koo-AHl-keh;* **someone** qualcuno *koo-ahl-kOO-noh;* **something** qualche cosa *koo-AHl-keh kOH-sah;* **sometimes** qualche volta *koo-AHl-keh vOHl-tah*
son figlio *fEE-ly-ee-oh*
soon presto *prEHs-toh;* **as soon as possible** appena possibile *ahp-pAY-nah pohs-sEE-bee-leh*
soprano soprano
sorry (to be sorry) dispiacere *dees-pee-ah-chAY-reh;* **I'm sorry** mi dispiace *mee dees-pee-AH-cheh*
soup minestra *mee-nEHs-trah*
south sud *sood*
spades (cards) picche *pEE-keh*
Spanish spagnolo *spah-ny-OH-loh*
spare tire la ruota di scorta *lah roo-OH-tah dee skOHr-tah*
spark plug candela *kahn-dAY-lah*
sparkling wine spumante *spoo-mAHn-teh*
to speak parlare *pahr-lAH-reh*

special speciale *spay-chee-AH-leh*
specialty specialità *spEH-chee-ah-lee-tAH*
to spend (money) spendere *spEHn-deh-reh;* **(time)** passare *pahs-sAH-reh*
spicy piccante *peek-kAHn-teh*
spinach spinaci *spee-nAH-chee*
sponge spugna *spOO-ny-ah*
spoon cucchiaio *koo-key-AH-ee-oh;* **teaspoon** cucchiaino *koo-key-ah-EE-noh*
sports car macchina sportiva *mAH-key-nah spohr-tEE-vah*
spot posto *pOHs-toh*
to sprain slogare *sloh-gAH-reh*
sprain (injury) slogatura *sloh-gah-tOO-rah*
spring molla *mOHl-lah;* **(season)** primavera *pree-mah-vEH-rah*
squab (pigeon) piccioncino *pEE-chee-ohn-chEE-noh*
square piazza *pee-AH-tsah*
squid calamari *kah-lah-mAH-ree*
stadium stadio *stAH-dee-oh*
stairs scale *skAH-leh*
stamp francobollo *frahn-koh-bOHl-loh*
to stand stare in piedi *stAH-reh een poo EH dee*
to start cominciare *koh-meen-chee-AH-reh;* **(car)** avviare *ahv-vee-AH-reh*
station stazione *stah-tsee-OHn-neh*
to steal rubare *roo-bAH-reh*
steel acciaio *ah-chee-AH-ee-oh;* **stainless steel** acciaio inossidabile *ah-chee-AH-ee-oh een-OHs-see-dAH-bee-lah*
steering wheel volante *voh-lAHn-teh*
still ancora *ahn-kOH-rah*
stocking calza *kAHl-tsah*
stomach stomaco *stOH-mah-coh*

stone pietra *pee-EH-trah;*
 precious stone pietra
  preziosa *pee-EH-trah pray-*
  tsee-OH-sah
to stop fermare *fayr-mAH-reh*
stop fermata *fayr-mAH-tah;*
 bus stop fermata del bus
  fayr-mAH-tah dayl-boos
store negozio *neh-gOH-tsee-oh*
stories racconti *rah-kOHn-tee;*
  storie *stOH-ree-eh*
straight diritto *dee-rEEt-toh*
stream ruscello *roo-shEHl-loh*
street strada *strAH-dah;* via
  vEE-ah
streetcar tram *trAHm;* tranvai
  trahn-vAH-ee
string beans fagiolini *fah-jee-*
  oh-lEE-nee
strong forte *fOHr-teh;* **stronger**
  più forte *pee-OO fOHr-teh*
stuck bloccato *bloh-kAH-toh*
stupid stupido *stOO-pee-doh;*
 don't be stupid non fare lo
  stupido *nohn fAH-reh loh*
  stOO-pee-doh
subtitle sottotitolo *sOHt-toh-*
  tEE-toh-loh
subway metropolitana *mEH-*
  troh-poh-lee-tAH-nah
suede (leather) renna *rAYn-*
  nah; pelle scamosciata *pEHl-*
  lay skah-moh-shee-AH-tah
sugar zucchero *tsOO-keh-roh;*
 sugar substitute dolcificante
  dohl-chee-fee kAHn-teh
suit abito *AH-bee-toh;* vestito
  vays-tEE-toh
suitcase valigia *vah-lEE-jee-ah*
summer estate *ehs-tAH-teh*
sun sole *sOH-leh*
sunburn scottatura solare
  skoht-tah-tOO-rah soh-lAH-
  reh
Sunday domenica *doh-mAY-*
  nee-kah
sunglasses occhiali da sole *oh-*
  key-AH-lee dah sOH-leh

supermarket supermercato
  sOO-pehr-mehr-kAH-toh
supper cena *chAY-nah;* **to**
 have supper cenare *chay-*
  nAH-reh
sweater maglia *mAH-ly-ah*
Swedish svedese *svay-dAY-say*
sweet dolce *dOHl-cheh*
swelling gonfiore *gohn-fee-*
  OH-reh
to swim nuotare *nOO-oh-tAH-*
  reh
swimming pool piscina *pee-*
  shEE-nah; **(indoor)** piscina
  coperta *pee-shEE-nah koh-*
  pEHr-tah; **(outdoor)**
  piscina scoperta *pee-shEE-*
  nah skoh-pEHr-tah
Swiss svizzero *svEE-tsay-roh*
switch interruttore *een-tehr-*
  root-tOH-reh
swollen gonfio *gOHn-fee-oh*
synagogue sinagoga *see-nah-*
  gOH-gah
synthetic poliestere *poh-lee-*
  EHs-tay-reh; sintetico *seen-*
  tEH-tee-koh
syrup sciroppo *shee-rOHp-poh*
system sistema *sees-tEH-mah*

T

table tavola *tAH-voh-lah*
tablecloth tovaglia *toh-vAH-*
  ly-ee-ah
tablet pasticca *pahs-tEE-kah*
tag cartellino *kahr-tayl-lEE-noh*
tailor sarto *sAHr-toh*
to take prendere *prayn-dAY-*
  reh; **(to a place)** portare
  pohr-tAH-reh; **to take off**
 (airplane) decollare *day-*
  kohl-lAH-reh
taken (occupied) occupato
  oh-koo-pAH-toh
talcum powder talco *tAHl-koh*
tall alto *AHl-toh*
to talk parlare *pahr-lAH-reh*

tampons tamponi igienici *tahm-pOH-nee EE-jee-EH-nee-chee*

tangerine mandarino *mahn-dah-rEE-noh*

tariff tariffa *tah-rEEf-fah*

tavern trattoria *traht-toh-rEE-ah*

tax tassa *tAHs-sah;* imposta *eem-pOH-stah*

taxi tassì *tahs-sEE*

tea tè *tEH*

team squadra *skoo-AH-drah*

telegram telegramma *teh-leh-grAHm-mah*

to telephone telefonare *teh-leh-foh-nAH-reh;* **I want to make a phone call** voglio fare una telefonata *vOH-ly-ee-oh fAH-reh OO-nah teh-leh-foh-nAH-tah;* **local call** urbana *oor-bAH-nah;* **long-distance** in teleselezione, *een teh-leh-say-leh-tsee-OH-neh;* interurbana *een-tayr-oor-bAH-nah;* **person-to-person** con preavviso *kohn prEH-ahv-vEE-soh;* **reverse-charge** riversibile *ree-vehr-sEE-bee-leh*

telephone telefono *teh-lEH-foh-noh;* **public telephone** telefono pubblico *teh-lEH-foh-noh pOOb-blee-koh*

television televisione *teh-leh-vee-see-OH-neh*

to tell dire *dEE-reh;* **tell me** mi dica *mee dEE-kah*

temperature temperature *tehm-peh-rah-tOO-rah*

temporarily provvisoriamente *prohv-vee-sOH-ree-ah-mEHn-teh*

ten dieci *dee-EH-chee*

tennis tennis *tEHn-nees*

tenor tenore *teh-nOH-reh*

tenth decimo *dEH-chee-moh*

terminal (bus, tram, auto) capolinea *kah-poh-lEE-neh-ah*

terrace terrazza *tehr-rAH-tsah*

terrible terribile *tehr-rEE-bee-leh*

thanks grazie *grAH-tsee-eh;* **thank you very much** molte grazie *mOHl-teh grAH-tsee-eh*

that che *kay;* **that one** quello *koo-AYl-loh*

the il *eel;* lo *loh;* la *lah;* i *ee;* gli *ly-ee;* le *leh*

theater teatro *teh-AH-troh*

their loro *lOH-roh*

them li *lee;* le *lay;* loro *lOH-roh*

there lì *lEE;* là *LAH;* **there are** ci sono *chee sOH-noh;* **there is** c'è *chEH*

thermometer termometro *tehr-mOH-meh-troh*

these questi *koo-AYs-tee;* queste *koo-AYs-teh*

they essi *AYs-see;* esse *AYs-say;* loro *lOH-roh*

thief ladro *lAH-droh*

thigh coscia *kOH-shee-ah*

thin sottile *soht-tEE-leh*

thing cosa *kOH-sah*

to think pensare *pehn-sAH-reh*

third terzo *tEHr-tsoh*

thirsty assetato *ahs-say-tAH-toh*

thirteen tredici *trAY-dee-chee*

thirty trenta *trEHn-tah*

this questo *koo-AYs-toh;* questa *koo-AYs-tah*

those quelli *koo-AYl-lee;* quelle *koo-AYl-leh*

thousand mille *mEEl-leh*

thread filo *fEE-loh*

three tre *tray*

throat gola *gOH-lah*

thumb pollice *pOHl-lee-cheh*

Thursday giovedì *jee-oh-vay-dEE*

ticket biglietto *bee-ly-ee-AYt-toh;* **a one-way ticket** un biglietto di andata *oon bee-ly-ee-AYt-toh dee ahn-dAH-tah;* **a round-trip ticket** un

biglietto di andata e ritorno *oon bee-ly-ee-AYt-toh dee ahn-dAH-tah ay ree-tOHr-noh;*
ticket office biglietteria *bee-ly-ee-AYt-tay-rEE-ah*

to tighten stringere *strEEn-jay-reh*

time tempo *tEHm-poh;*
timetable orario *oh-rAH-ree-oh*

tip mancia *mAHn-chee-ah*

tire pneumatico *pneh-oo-mAH-tee-koh;* **flat tire** gomma bucata *gOHm-mah boo-kAH-tah*

tired stanco *stAHn-koh*

to a *ah*

to toast (drink) brindare *breen-dAH-reh*

tobacco tabacco *tah-bAH-koh;* **tobacco shop** tabaccheria *tah-bAH-kay-rEE-ah;* **snuff tobacco** tabacco da fiuto *tah-bAH-koh dah fee-OO-toh*

today oggi *OH-jee*

toe alluce *AHl-loo-cheh*

together insieme *een-see-EH-meh*

toilet gabinetto *gah-bee-nAYt-toh;* toilette *too-ah-lEHt;* bagno *bAH-ny-oh;* **toilet paper** carta igienica *kAHr-tah ee-jee-EH-nee-kah*

token gettone *jayt-tOH-nay*

tomato pomodoro *poh-moh-dOH-roh*

tomorrow domani *doh-mAH-nee;* **the day after tomorrow** dopodomani *dOH-poh-doh-mAH-nee;* **see you tomorrow** a domani *ah doh-mAH-nee*

tonic tonico *tOH-nee-koh*

tonight stasera *stah-sAY-rah*

tonsils tonsille *tohn-sEEl-leh*

too anche *AHn-keh*

tools attrezzi *aht-trAY-tsee*

tooth dente *dEHn-tay;*
toothache mal di denti *mAHl dee dEHn-tee;*
toothbrush spazzolino per i denti *spah-tsoh-lEE-noh pehr ee dEHn-tee;* **toothpaste** dentifricio *dehn-tee-frEE-chee-oh*

top cima *chEE-mah*

topaz topazio *toh-pAH-tsee-oh*

to touch toccare *toh-kAH-reh*

tourist (for tourists) turistico *too-rEEs-tee-koh*

tow truck carroattrezzi *kAHr-roh-aht-trAY-tsee*

towel asciugamano *ah-shee-OO-gah-mAH-noh*

toy store negozio di giocattoli *neh-gOH-tsee-oh dee jee-oh-kAHt-toh-lee*

track (train) binario *bee-nAH-ree-oh*

traffic light semaforo *seh-mAH-foh-roh*

train treno *trEH-noh*

training allenamento *ahl-lay-nah-mEHn-toh*

transit transito *trAHn-see-toh*

transition lenses lenti fotocromatiche *lEHn-tee foh-toh-kroh-mAH-tee-keh*

travel viaggio *vee-AH-jee-oh;* **travel agency** agenzia di viaggi *ah-jehn-tsEE-ah dee vee-AH-jee*

traveler's check assegno di viaggiatore *ahs-sAY-ny-oh dee vee-ah-jee-ah-tOR-reh*

tree albero *AHl-beh-roh*

to trim (hair) spuntare *spoon-tAH-reh*

trip viaggio *vee-AH-jee-oh;* gita *jEE-tah*

trouble fastidio *fahs-tEE-dee-oh*

trout trota *trOH-tah*

true vero *vEH-roh*

to try provare *proh-vAH-reh*

Tuesday martedì *mahr-teh-dEE*

tuna tonno *tOHn-noh*

turkey tacchino *tah-kEE-noh*

Turkish turco *tOOr-koh*

to turn girare *jee-rAH-reh;* **it's your turn** tocca a lei *tOH-kah ah lEH-ee*

turquoise turchese *toor-kAY-seh*

tweezers pinzette *peen-tsAYt-teh*

twelve dodici *dOH-dee-chee*

twenty venti *vAYn-tee;* **twenty-one** ventuno *vayn-tOO-noh;* **twenty-two** ventidue *vAYn-tee-dOO-eh*

two due *doo-eh;* **two hundred** duecento *doo-eh-chEHn-toh*

typing paper carta per battere a macchina *kAHr-tah pehr bAHt-teh-reh ah mAH-kee-nah*

U

umbrella ombrello *ohm-brEH-loh*

uncle zio *tsEE-oh*

under sotto *sOHt-toh*

undershirt canottiera *kah-noht-tee-EH-rah*

to understand capire *kah-pEE-reh*

underwear biancheria intima *bee-AHn-kay-rEE-ah EEn-tee-mah*

university università *oo-nee-vayr-see-tAH*

unless a meno che *ah mAY-noh keh*

until fino a *fEE-noh ah*

us ci *chee*

to use usare *oo-sAH-reh*

usher (theater) maschera *mAHs-keh-rah*

V

vegetarian vegetariano *veh-jeh-tah-ree-AH-noh*

very molto *mOHl-toh*

view panorama *pah-noh-rAH-mah*

village villaggio *veel-lAH-jee-oh*

vinegar aceto *ah-chAY-toh*

to visit visitare *vee-see-tAH-reh*

W

to wait aspettare *ahs-peht-tAH-reh*

waiter cameriere *kah-meh-ree-EH-reh*

waitress cameriera *kah-meh-ree-EH-rah*

to wake up svegliare *svay-ly-ee-AH-reh*

to walk camminare *kahm-mee-nAH-reh*

walker il girello *eel jee-rEHl-loh*

to want volere *voh-lAY-reh*

warm caldo *kAHl-doh*

to wash lavare *lah-vAH-reh*

to watch guardare *goo-ahr-dAH-reh*

watch orologio *oh-roh-lOH-jee-oh;* **wristwatch** orologio da polso *oh-roh-lOH-jee-oh dah pOHl-soh;* **watchmaker** orologiaio *oh-roh-loh-jee-AH-ee-oh*

water acqua *AH-koo-ah;* **drinkable water** acqua potabile *AH-koo-ah poh-tAH-bee-leh;* **running water** acqua corrente *AH-koo-ah kohr-rEHn-teh*

waterfall cascata *kahs-kAH-tah*

watermelon cocomero *koh-kOH-may-roh;* anguria *ahn-gOO-ree-ah*

wave onda *OHn-dah*

wavy hair capelli ondulati *kah-pAYl-lee ohn-doo-lAH-tee*

waxing depilazione mediante ceretta *deh-pee-lah-tzee-OH-neh meh-dee-AHn-teh cheh-rAYt-tah*

we noi *nOH-ee*

weak   debole *dAY-boh-leh*

to wear   portare *pohr-tAH-reh;* indossare *een-dohs-sAH-reh*

weather   tempo *tehm-poh*

Wednesday   mercoledì *mehr-koh-lay-dEE*

week   settimana *seht-tee-mAH-nah*

well   bene *bEH-neh*

west   ovest *OH-vehst*

what   che *kay;* che cosa *kay kOH-sah*

wheel   ruota *roo-OH-tah*

wheelchair   sedia a rotelle *sEH-dee-ah ah roh-tEHl-leh*

when   quando *koo-AHn-doh*

where   dove *dOH-veh;* **where is it?**   dov'è? *doh-vEH*

which   quale *koo-AH-leh*

whiskers   baffi *bAHf-fee*

while   mentre *mEHn-treh*

white   bianco *bee-AHn-koh*

who   chi *key;* che *kay*

why   perché *payr-kAY*

wide   largo *lAHr-goh*

wife   moglie *mOH-ly-ee-eh*

to win   vincere *vEEn-chay-reh*

window   finestra *fee-nEHs-trah*

wine   vino *vEE-noh;* **wine shop**   enoteca *AY-noh-teh-kah;* rivendita di vini *ree-vAYn-dee-tah dee vEE-nee*

wing   ala *AH-lah*

winter   inverno *een-vEHr-noh*

to wish   desiderare *day-see-deh-rAH-reh*

with   con *kohn;* **within** dentro *dEHn-troh;* **without** senza *sEHn-tsah*

woman   donna *dOHn-nah*

wonderful   fantastico *fahn-tAH-stee-koh;* stupendo *stoo-pEHn-doh*

wool   lana *lAH-nah*

word   parola *pah-rOH-lah*

to work   lavorare *lah-voh-rAH-reh;* **(machinery)** funzionare *foon-tsee-oh-nAH-reh*

to worship   adorare *ah-doh-rAH-reh*

wound   ferita *fay-rEE-tah*

wow!   eh! *AY*

to wrap   incartare *een-kahr-tAH-reh*

to write   scrivere *skrEE-veh-reh*

writing pad   blocchetto di carta *bloh-kAYt-toh dee kAHr-tah*

Y

yard   iarda *ee-AHr-dah*

year   anno *AHn-noh*

yellow   giallo *jee-AHl-loh*

yes   sì *sEE*

yesterday   ieri *ee-AY-ree*

you   tu *too;* lei *lEH-ee;* voi *vOH-ee;* te *tay;* loro *lOH-roh*

young   giovane *jee-OH-vAH-neh;* **young lady** signorina *see-ny-oh-rEE-nah;* **young man** giovanotto *jee-oh-vah-nOHt-toh*

your   suo *sOO-oh;* sua *sOO-ah;* vostro *vOH-stroh;* loro *lOH-roh;* tuo *tOO-oh;* tua *tOO-ah*

youth   gioventù *jee-oh-vayn-tOO;* **youth hostel** ostello della gioventù *ohs-tEHl-loh dAYl-lah jee-oh-vehn-tOO*

Yugoslav   jugoslavo *ee-OO-gohs-lAH-voh*

Z

zero   zero *tsEH-roh*

zipper   cerniera *chayr-nee-EH-rah*

zoo   zoo *tsOH-oh*

ITALIAN-ENGLISH DICTIONARY

The following Italian words are presented here with accent marks to aid pronunciation. As there are actually very few accents used in Italian, you will find most of these words without accents when used in context.

A

a to, at, in
abbàcchio lamb, spring lamb
abbagliànti headlights
abbastànza enough
abbronazatúra suntan
abitàre to live
àbito dress, suit; _____ **da séra** evening gown
accànto next to, near
accappatòio robe for man
accèndere to light
accendíno cigarette lighter
accensióne ignition
accettàre to accept
acciàio steel; _____ **inossidàbile** stainless steel
acciúga anchovy
accónto deposit, partial payment
accorciatòia shortcut
acéto vinegar
acetóne nail polish remover
àcqua water; _____ **corrènte** running water; _____ **potàbile** drinkable water
acquamarína aquamarine
adèsso now
adoràre to adore, to worship
aèreo airplane
aeropòrto airport
affàre business
affettàto sliced; **affettàti** cold cuts
affittàre to rent; **si affítta** for rent
affrancatúra postage

agenzía agency; _____ **d'informazioni** information office; _____ **di viaggi** travel agency
aggiustàre to fix, to repair
àglio garlic
àgnèllo lamb
ago needle
agósto August
ahi! ouch!
aiuòla flower bed, garden, grass
aiutàre to help
aiúto help
àla wing
albèrgo hotel, inn
àlbero tree
albicòcca apricot
àlbum album
àlcool alcohol
alcúni a few, some
alfière knight
allenaménto training, practice
allèrgico allergic
àlluce big toe
àlto high
àltro other; **un àltro** another
alzàre to lift, to raise; _____ **il màzzo** to cut cards
amàlgama amalgam
ambulatòrio first-aid station, doctor's office
americàno(a) American
ametísta amethyst
amíco(a) friend
amóre love; **per l'amòr del cièlo!** my goodness!
analcòlico nonalcoholic; **bíbita analcòlica** soft drink

ananàsso pineapple
ancóra still
andàre to go; **andiàmo!** let's go!
andàta one-way trip; _____ **e ritórno** round trip
anèllo ring
àngolo corner; **all'àngolo** at the corner
anguílla eel
angùria watermelon
ànitra duck
ànno year
antiàcido antacid
antibiòtico antibiotic
antícipo advance
antipàsto appetizers, hors d'oeuvre
antisèttico antiseptic
aperitívo aperitif
apèrto open
appartamènto apartment
appéna as soon as
appendicíte appendicitis
apprèndere to learn, to come to know of
appuntaménto appointment
aprile April
apríre to open; **è apèrto?** is it open?
aragósta lobster
aràncio(a) orange tree (fruit)
aranciáta orangeade
àrbitro referee
argènto silver
ària air; _____ **condizionàta** air-conditioning
arínga herring
arrivàre to reach, to get to a place
arrivedérci good-bye
arròsto roast
artícolo item, article
ascensóre elevator (lift)
ascèsso abscess
asciugacapélli hair dryer
asciugamàno towel
ascoltàre to listen
àsma asthma
aspàragi asparagus

aspettàre to wait; **aspètti!** wait!
aspirína aspirin
àsso ace
asségno check
assicurazióne insurance
assístere to assist, to help
assorbènti igiènici sanitary napkins
attàcco cardíaco heart attack
attènto(a) attentive, careful; **attènto!** watch out!
attenzióne attention; **stía attènto(a)!** be careful!
atterràre to land
attórno around, roundabout
attravèrso across, through
attrazióne attraction
attrézzi tools
àuto car; **màl d'àuto** car sickness
autoambulànza ambulance
àutobus bus
automàtico automatic
autopúllman motor coach
autoriméssa garage
autóre author
autostràda highway
autúnno fall
avére to have; **ma che còsa ha?** what's the matter with you?
avànti forward; **avànti!** come in!
avventúra adventure; **avventúre poliziésche** detective stories
avviàre to start
avvocàto lawyer
azzúrro blue

B

baciàre to kiss
bacíno pelvis; basin
bàcio kiss
bàffi moustache
bagníno lifeguard
bàgno bathroom
balcóne balcony

ballàre to dance
ballétto ballet
bàllo dance
bambíno child, kid, baby
bàmbola doll
banàna banana
bànca bank
banconòta banknote
bàrba beard, shave
barbería barbershop
barìtono baritone
bàsso low, short, bass voice
bàsta enough; **bàsta (cosí)!** that's enough!
battería battery
bellézza beauty; **salóne di ___** beauty parlor
bèl, bèllo(a) beautiful, handsome, nice
bène well; **va bène** that's all right
benzína gasoline (petrol)
bére to drink
biancheria linen, laundry; **___ íntima** underwear
biànco(a) white
bíbita drink
bibliotèca library
bicchière drinking glass
biciclétta bicycle
bigliettería ticket office
bigliétto ticket, banknote; **un ___ da mílle líre** a 1000-lire bill; **un ___ di andàta e ritórno** a round-trip ticket
biòndo (chiàro) (light) blond
bírra beer
biscòtto cookie
bisognàre to be necessary, to have to
bisógno need
bistécca beefsteak
bloccàto(a) stuck
blocchétto (di càrta) writing pad
blu blue
blúsa blouse
bócca mouth; **in ___ al lùpo!** good luck!

boccóne bite; **mangiàre un ___** to have a bite
bollíto boiled
bórsa handbag
botànico botanic
botteghíno (theater) box office
bottíglia bottle
bottóne button
bowling bowling
bracciàle armlet, bangle, bracelet
bràccio arm
branzíno bass (fish)
brívido shiver, chills
bròdo broth
bruciàto burnt
brúna dark-haired woman, brunette
budíno pudding
bullóne bolt
bugía lie; **è una ___!** it's a lie!
buòno(a) good
búrro butter
bústa envelope

C

cabína cabin; **___ telefònica** phone booth
cachèt color rinse
cadére to fall; **sono cadùto(a)** I have fallen
caffè coffee; **___ corrètto** with liquor
calamàri squid
càlcio kick, soccer; **il ___ d'inìzio** the kickoff; **una partìta di ___** a soccer game
càldo warm, hot
callìfugo corn plaster
calpestàre to crush underfoot; **è vietàto ___ l'èrba** keep off the grass
càlza stocking
calzaturifício shoe store
calzíni socks
calzolàio shoemaker

cambiàre to change, to exchange

càmbio change; **l'ufficio di _____** (money) exchange office

càmera room; **_____ da lètto** bedroom

camerièra maid, waitress

camerière waiter

camícia shirt; **_____ da uòmo** man's shirt

campàgna countryside

campéggio camping

càmpo field; **_____ di golf** golf course

cancellàre to erase

candéla spark plug, candle

canottièra man's undershirt

cantàre to sing

capélli hair; **un tàglio di _____** a haircut

capíre to understand; **io capísco** I understand

càpo head

capolínea (bus) terminal

cappèllo hat

càpperi! man alive!

cappóne capon

caprétto baby goat

caramèlla candy

carburatóre carburetor

cariàto decayed; rotten

caricàre to load

càrne meat

caròta carrot

carroattrézzi tow truck

carròzza railroad car; **in _____!** all aboard!; **_____ ristorànte** dining car

càrta paper, map; **_____ di crèdito** credit card; **_____ d'identità** identification card; **_____ stradàle** road map; **_____ da giuòco** playing card; **_____ igiènica** toilet paper; **_____ da imballàggio** wrapping paper; **_____ per bàttere a màcchina** typing paper

cartellíno chart, tag

cartolína card; **_____ illustràta** picture postcard; **_____ postàle** postcard

cartúccia cartridge

càsa house

cascàta waterfall

che who, that; **_____ còsa?** what?

chi who; **_____ è?** who is it?

chiamàre to call; **mi chiàmo** my name is

chiàro clear, light-colored

chiàve key

chièsa church

chíffon chiffon

chílo kilogram

chilòmetro kilometer; **a chilometràggio illimitàto** unlimited mileage

chiúdere to close; **pòsso _____?** may I close?

chiúso closed

céci chickpeas

cetriólo cucumber

ciabàtte slippers

ciào hi, hello, bye

cièlo heaven, sky; **per l'amór del _____!** my goodness!

cíglia eyelash

ciliègia cherry

cínema cinema, movie house

cineprésa movie camera

cinquànta fifty

cínque five

cinquecènto five hundred

cintúra belt

cioccolàta chocolate

ciòndolo charm

cipólla onion

città city

clàcson (car) horn

clàsse class

cocktail cocktail

cocómero watermelon

còfano hood

cognóme last name

colazióne breakfast

cólla glue
còllant panty hose
collína hill
collírio eyedrops
cólpo d'aria (al pètto) (chest) cold
coltèllo knife
cóme as, how; _____ **sta?** how are you?
cominciàre to begin
commèdia comedy
commerciàle commercial
commissariàto police station
compartiménto compartment
compràre to buy
complèto complete, full
compréso included
con with
concèrto concert; **sàla da concèrti** concert hall
confermàre to confirm
coníglio rabbit
conòscere to know
consegnàre to deliver
consèrva (di pomodòro) (tomato) sauce
consigliàre to recommend, to suggest
consolàto consulate
consommè consommé
contagiòso contagious
continuàre to continue, to keep (doing something)
cònto bill, check; **cònti separàti** separate checks
contòrno garnish; **càrne con contòrno** meat and vegetables
contracettívo contraceptive
contusiòne bruise
copèrta blanket
còpia copy, print
coràllo coral
coròna crown
còrpo body
corrènte current, running
corrètto correct; **caffè** _____ coffee with liquor
corridòio aisle
còrsa fare

cortìle courtyard
còrto(a) short
còsa thing; **che** _____? what?
così so, this way; **bàsta** _____! that's enough!
cosmètico cosmetic
costàta rib
costàre to cost; **quànto còsta?** how much is it?
costóso expensive; **méno** _____ cheaper
costúme da bàgno bathing suit
cotolétta cutlet
cotóne cotton
còtto cooked; **ben còtto** well-done
còzze mussels
cràmpi cramps
cravàtta necktie
crèdito credit; **càrta di** _____ credit card
crèma cream
crícco jack (car)
cristàllo crystal
cròcchia bun
croissànt croissant
cròsta crust
cuccétta berth
cucchiàio spoon
cucchiaíno teaspoon
cucína kitchen, cooking
cucíre to sew
cuòre heart
cúrva curve
cuscíno pillow

D

da from, by, to, at the house of, since
dàdo nut
dàma checkers
dàre to give; **mi sta dàndo** he (she) is giving me; **dàre le càrte** to deal
dàta date; **qual è la dàta di òggi?** what is today's date?

dàtteri dates (fruit)

davànti before, in front of

débole weak

dècimo tenth

decollàre to take off

denàro money

dènte tooth; **mal di dènti** toothache

dentifrício toothpaste

dentísta dentist

deodorànte deodorant

depòsito deposit

desideràre to desire

dessert dessert

destinatàrio receiver; **a càrico del destinatàrio** collect call

deviazióne detour

diabète diabetes

dèstro right; **a dèstra** to the right

detergènte detergent

diamànte diamond

diapositíve slides

diarrèa diarrhea

diàvolo devil; **ma che diàvolo vuòle?** what the devil do you want?

dicèmbre December

dichiaràre to declare

diciannòve nineteen

diciassètte seventeen

diciòtto eighteen

dièci ten

diètro in back of, after

díre to say; **mi díca** tell me; **ha détto** he (she) has said

dirètto direct, express train

direttóre conductor, director, manager

direzióne direction; **in che direzióne?** which way?

dirítto straight; **avànti dirítto** straight ahead

dísco disk, record

discotèca discotheque

disinfettànte (per la bócca) mouthwash

dispiacére to dislike; **mi dispiàce** I'm sorry; **le dispiàce?** do you mind?

dissenterìa dysentery

disturbàre to disturb

dito finger

dóccia shower; **fàre la dóccia** to take a shower

documénto document

dódici twelve

dogàna customs; **pagàr dogàna** to pay duty

dólci sweets

dolcificànte sugar substitute

dolére to hurt; **mi duòle** it hurts

dòllaro dollar

domàni tomorrow; **a domàni** see you tomorrow

doménica Sunday

dòmino dominoes

dònna woman; queen (card games)

dopobàrba aftershave lotion

dopodomàni the day after tomorrow

dormìre to sleep

dottóre doctor

dóve where; **dov'è?** where is it?

dovére to have to, to owe; **quànto le devo?** how much do I owe you?

dràmma drama

drìtto straight

dùbbio doubt; **sènza dúbbio** without fail

dùe two

duecènto two hundred

durànte during

duràre to last

E

e and

ècco here is (are), there is (are)

edìcola newsstand

eh! wow!

égli he
elènco list
elettricità electricity
elèttrico electric
élla she
emergènza emergency
entràre to enter; **éntri!** come in!
equipaggiaménto equipment
èrba grass
esprèsso espresso (coffee), express train, special delivery
èssere to be
estàte summer
estràrre to extract, to pull out
ètto, ettogràmmo 100 grams, hectogram

F

fàccia face
facciàle facial; **massàggio facciàle** facial massage
fagiàno pheasant
fagiòlo bean
fagiolíno green bean
fàme hunger; **ho fàme** I'm hungry
famìglia family
fanalíni (tail)lights
fantasciènza science fiction
fantasìa imagination
fantàstico imaginary, fantastic, wonderful
fàre to do, to make; **mi fàccio il bàgno** I'm taking a bath; **fa fréddo** it is cold; **fa càldo** it is warm; **fàre la fíla** to stand in line
farmacìa pharmacy, drugstore
fàscia bandage
fastìdio trouble, nuisance
fattorìa farm
favóre favor; **per favóre** please
fazzolétto handkerchief; **fazzolétto di carta** paper handkerchief, "tissue"

febbràio February
febbre fever, temperature; **la fébbre del fièno** hay fever
fégato liver
féltro felt
ferìta wound, cut
fermàglio brooch
fermàre to stop
fermàta stop (bus stop, etc.)
férmo (pòsta) general delivery
ferraménta hardware store
ferrovìa railroad
fétta slice
fiammìfero match
fíco (fíchi) fig(s)
fíglia daughter
fíglio son
fíla line, row
fílo thread, wire
film film
filóne long loaf
fíltro filter
finèstra window
finestrìno (train) window
fioràio florist
fióre flower; **fióri** clubs (cards)
fìrma signature
firmàre to sign, to endorse
fiùme river
flanèlla flannel
folclorìstico folkloric
fontàna fountain
fòrbici scissors
forchétta fork
forcìna hairpin
forèsta forest
formàggio cheese
fórno oven; **al fórno** baked
fórse perhaps, maybe
fòrte strong; **più fòrte!** faster!
fortúna fortune; **buòna fortúna!** good luck!
fòrza! go!
fotografìa photograph
fòto-òttica camera store
fra between, among
fràgole strawberries

francobòllo postage stamp

fràngia bang(s)

fratèllo brother

frattúra fracture

fréccia direction indicator

fréddo cold

fréno brake

frésco cool, fresh

frétta hurry; **ho frétta** I'm in a hurry

frittàta omelet

frítto fried; **frítto místo** fish fry

frizióne tonic, massage, clutch

frónte front, forehead

frullàto (di làtte) (milk) shake

frullatóre blender

frútto(a) fruit

fumàre to smoke

fumatóre smoker

fúngo mushroom, fungus

funzionàre to work

fuòco fire; **al fuoco!** fire!

fuòri outside; **fuòri!** get out!

G

gabardíne gabardine

gabinétto toilet, rest room

gàmba leg

gàmberi prawns, shrimp

gas gas

gassàta with gas; **àcqua gassàta** carbonated water

gelateria ice-cream store

gelàto ice cream

gengíve gums

gennàio January

gettóne token

ghiacciàto iced; **àcqua ghiacciàta** ice water

ghiàccio ice; **cubétti di ghiàccio** ice cubes

ghiàndole glands

giàcca jacket

giàda jade

giàllo yellow; **è un giàllo** it's a mystery

giàra jar

ginòcchio knee

giocattolería toy store

gioiellería jewelry store

giornàle newspaper

giórno day; **buòn giórno** good morning

giovanòtto young man

giovedì Thursday

gioventù youth

giradíschi record player

giràre to turn; **giràre un asségno** to endorse a check; **mi gíra la tèsta** I'm dizzy

gíta trip, tour

giúgno June

giocàre to play (games)

gli the, to him

góla throat; **mal di góla** sore throat

gómito elbow

gómma eraser; **gómma bucáta** flat tire

gónfio swollen

gonfiòre swelling, lump

gónna skirt

gràmmo gram

grànchio crab

grànde large, big; **più grànde** larger

gràzie thanks; **mólte gràzie** thank you very much

grígio gray

grúcce dress hangers

guància cheek

guànto glove

guardàre to look at, to watch

guardaròba checkroom

guàsto breakdown, trouble

guàva guava

guída guide, guidebook

guidàre to drive

H

hambúrger hamburger

hotèl hotel

I

identità identity; **càrta d'identità** identification card
iàrda yard
ièri yesterday
igiénico hygienic; **un ròtolo di càrta igiènica** a roll of toilet paper
impaccàre to wrap up, to pack
impermeàbile raincoat
impiegàto clerk
importàre to matter; **non impòrta** it doesn't matter
importànte important
impossíbile impossible
impòsta tax
in into, in
incartàre to wrap in paper
incínta pregnant
inclúso(a) included
incominciàre to start
incontràre to meet
incrócio crossing, crossroad
indicàre to show, to point out
indiètro back, backward(s)
indirízzo address
indossàre to wear
infezióne infection
influènza flu
inglèse English
ingranàggio (del càmbio) gearshift
ingrèsso entrance
iniziàre to start
innamoràto(a) lover, sweetheart (girlfriend)
innocènte innocent
insalàta salad
insième together
insònnia insomnia
insulína insulin
intagliàto carved
interessànte interesting
internazionàle international
interpretàre to interpret
intèrprete interpreter
interròmpere to cut off (telephone)

interruttóre (electric light) switch
interurbàna long-distance call
intórno around
invéce instead
investito(a) run over (by a car)
inviàre to send
io I; **io stésso** myself
iòdio iodine
ippòdromo racetrack

L

la the, her, you
là there
làbbra lips
làcca hair spray
làcci (da scàrpe) shoelaces
làdro thief
làgo lake
lamétta blade
lambrétta motor scooter
làmpada lamp
lampóne raspberry
làna wool
lancétta hand (of a watch)
lasciàre to leave; **mi làsci in pàce!** don't bother me!
lassatívo laxative
làto side
làtte milk
lattúga lettuce
lavàggio wash; **lavàggio a sécco** dry cleaner
lavàre to wash; **lavàre a sécco** to dry-clean
le the, them, to her, to you
leggèro light, mild
lèi she, her, you
lentaménte slowly
lènte lens; **lènte a contàtto** contact lens
lentícchie lentils
lèpre hare
lèttera letter; **per vía aèra** airmail; **assicuràta** insured; **raccomandàta** registered; **esprèsso** special delivery;

con ricevùta di ritórno
with return receipt
lètto bed
li them
lì there
líbero free, not occupied; **il líbero** halfback (soccer player)
librería bookstore
líbro book
lièto happy
limétta (per le únghie) (nail) file
limóne lemon
línea line
língua tongue
líno linen
liquóre liqueur
lísta list
lítro liter
locàle place
località site, place
lontàno distant, far away
lóro their, theirs; **a lóro** to them
lozióne lotion; **lozióne per l'abbronzatùra** suntan lotion
lubrificàre to lubricate, to grease, to oil
lúce light
lucidàre to shine (shoes)
lùglio July
lùi he, him
lunedì Monday
lúngo long

M

ma but, yet, however; **ma che!** nonsense!
màcchina machine, automobile
macedònia fresh-fruit salad
macellería butcher shop
màdre mother
magazzíno department store
màggio May
màglia sweater

magnífico great
maiàle pig
màle ill, sick; **màl d'àuto** car sickness; **màl di mare** seasickness
maledizióne malediction, curse; **maledizióne!** darn it!
màlto malt
mancàre to be lacking, to be missing; **tu mi mànchi** I miss you
mància tip
mandàre to send
mandaríno tangerine
màndorle almonds
mangiàre to eat
màngo mango
mànica sleeve
manicúra manicure
manifésto poster
maníglia doorknob
màno hand; **mi día una màno** give me a hand
mànzo beef
màrca brand
màrcia gear (car)
marciapiède sidewalk
màre sea; **che dà sul màre** facing the sea
margarína margarine
maríto husband
marróne brown
martedí Tuesday
martèllo hammer
màrzo March
màschera usher (theater)
masticàre to chew
materàsso mattress
matíta pencil
màzze (da golf) (golf) clubs
màzzo (di càrte) deck (of cards)
me me
meccànico mechanic
medicína medicine
mèdico doctor
mèglio better
méla apple

melanzàna eggplant (aubergine)
melóne melon
menù menu
meraviglióso wonderful
mercàto market; **a buòn mercàto** cheap
mercoledì Wednesday
merlétto lace
merlúzzo codfish
mése month
Méssa Mass
messàggio message
metà half
mètro meter
metropolitàna subway
méttere to put
mezzanótte midnight
mèzzo half, means
mezzogiórno midday, noon
mía my
mi me
miéi my
miglióre better; **il miglióre** the best
milióne million
mílle one thousand
mineràle mineral
minéstra soup
mínimo minimum
minístro minister
minúto minute
mío my
mischiàre to shuffle
misúra measurement, size
mobiliàto furnished
mòdulo blank, form
mòglie wife
mòlla spring
mólto much, a lot
moménto moment
moníle necklace
montàgna mountain
montatúra frame
montóne mutton
moschèa mosque
mostràre to show; **mi mòstri** show me
motociclétta motorcycle

motoríno moped; **motoríno d'avviaménto** starter
muòvere to move
musèo museum
mùsica music; _____ clàssica classical music; _____ modèrna modern music
mutànde shorts, underwear
mutandíne panties

N

nàscita birth; **dàta di nàscita** birth date
nasèllo hake (fish)
nàso nose
nàstro (adesívo) Scotch tape
Natàle Christmas
naturalménte! of course!
nàve ship
nazionalità nationality
ne of (something)
necessàrio necessary
negòzio store; **negòzio d'abbigliamènto** clothing store
néro black
néve snow
nevicàre to snow
niènte nothing
night club nightclub
no no
nocciolíne hazelnuts
nóce (di còcco) (coco)nut
nói we, us
noleggiàre to rent
nóme name
non not
nòno ninth
normàle normal
nòstro(a) our, ours
nòtte night; **buòna nòtte** good night
novànta ninety
nòve nine
novecènto nine hundred
novèlla short story
novèmbre November

núlla nothing
numeràto numbered
número number
nuotàre to swim
nuòvo new
nylon nylon

O

o or
òca goose
occhiàli eyeglasses; **occhiàli da sóle** sunglasses
occhiàta look; **dàre un'occhiàta** to take a look
òcchio eye
occórrere to be necessary; **mi occórrono** I need (them)
occupàto taken, busy
ocèano ocean
oculísta oculist, eye doctor
officína meccànica repair shop
oggètti preziósi jewelry
òggi today
òlio oil
òmbra shade
ombrétto eye shadow
ónda wave
ondulàto wavy; **capélli onduláti** wavy hair
ònice onyx
òpera opera
operétta operetta
óra hour, now; **a che óra?** at what time?
oràrio timetable; **in oràrio** on schedule
ordinàre to order
orecchíno earring
òro gold; **d'òro massíccio** solid gold; **d'òro placcàto** gold plated
orologiàio watchmaker
orològio watch, clock; **orològio da pólso** wristwatch
òrzo barley
osservàre to observe, to watch
ostèllo (délla gioventù) (youth) hostel

ostería wine shop, tavern
òstrica oyster
ostruíre to obstruct, to block up
ottànta eighty
ottenére to obtain
òttico optician
òtto eight
ottocènto eight hundred
ottòbre October
otturàre to fill (a tooth)

P

pacchétto packet, small parcel, small package
pàcco package, parcel
pàdre father
paése village, town
pagàre to pay
pàio pair
palàzzo palace
pàlla ball
pallíni dots
pancétta bacon
pàne bread; **pàne tostàto** toasted bread
panettería bakery
paníno roll
pànna cream
pànno cloth
pannolíno linen, cloth diaper, sanitary napkin; **pannolíni ùsa e gètta** disposable diapers
panoràma view, panorama, landscape
pantalóni (a pair of) trousers, slacks, pants
pantòfola slipper
pantaloncíni shorts
paraúrti bumper
parcheggiàre to park
parchéggio parking
pàrco park
paréggio draw, tie (sport)
parlàre to speak, to talk
parrucchière hairdresser

pàrte part, section, area
partíre to depart, to leave
partíta game
passàggio passage, crossing; **diviéto di passàggio** no crossing
passapòrto passport
passàre to pass, to go by
pàsta pasta, pastry
pasticca (per la tósse) (cough) drop
pàsto meal
pastóre pastor
patènte di guída driver's license
pàzzo mad, crazy; **mi sta facèndo uscíre pàzzo** it's driving me crazy
peccàto sin; **che peccàto!** what a shame!
pedóne pedestrian; pawn (chess)
pèlle skin, leather
penicillína penicillin
pénna pen; _____ **a sfèra** ballpoint pen
pensàre to think
pensióne private residence, usually with meals; **pensióne complèta** room with 3 meals a day
pépe pepper
péra pear
per for, through, about
perché why, what, because
pèrdere to lose
perícolo danger; **pericolóso** dangerous
período period
pèrla pearl
permésso permitted, permit; **con permésso!** excuse me!
perméttere to permit, to allow
perníce partridge
personàggio character
personàle personal
pesànte heavy
pèsca peach
pietrína flint

pèttine comb
pèzzo piece; _____ **di ricàmbio** spare part
piacére pleasure; **per piacére** please; **con piacére** with pleasure
piacére to please, to like, to be fond of; **mi piàce** I like him/her
piànta plant, tree, map
piàtto plate, dish
piattíno saucer
pícche spades (cards)
picción e (implùme) squab (pigeon)
píccolo small; **più píccolo** smaller
piède foot; **andare a pièdi** to walk
pièno full
piètra preziósa (precious) stone
píllola pill
pínze pliers
pinzétta tweezers
piòvere to rain
piscína swimming pool
pisèlli peas
písta dance floor; **le píste per sciàre** ski slopes
più more
pízzo lace; pointed beard
plàstica plastic
platèa orchestra (theater)
plàtino platinum
pneumàtico tire; **un materassíno pneumàtico** an air mattress
pòco little
pòker poker
polièstere synthetic
pólipo octopus
polizía police; **stazióne di polizía** police station
pòllice thumb, inch
póllo chicken
polmóne lung
polpétta meatball
pólso wrist

pólvere dust, powder

pomeríggio afternoon

pomodòro tomato

pómpa pump; **pómpa della benzína** fuel pump

pompèlmo grapefruit

pónte bridge

pòrta door, gate

portabagàgli luggage rack, porter

portacénere ashtray

portafòglio wallet

portàre to bring; **mi pòrti bring me; dove pòrta quésta stràda?** where does this road lead to?

portàta course (meal)

pòrto port, harbor

porzióne portion

possíbile possible

pòsta mail

postàle postal; **vàglia postàle** money order; **pòste e telègrafi** postal and telegraph services

posteggiàre to park

postéggio parking

pósto place, spot, seat

potàbile potable, drinkable

potére to be able to, can

pranzàre to dine, to have dinner

prànzo dinner, lunch

preferíre to prefer

prefísso area code

preghièra prayer

prègo you're welcome

prèndere to take; **lo (la) prèndo!** I'll take it!

prenotazióne reservation

présa di corrènte electric outlet

presentàre to present

prèstito loan

prèsto early

prète priest

prèzzo price; **a prèzzo fisso** fixed price

primavèra spring

prímo first

principàle main, principal

privàto private

professióne profession

profilàttici prophylactics

profúmo perfume

prónto ready; **prónto soccórso** first aid; **prónto!** hello! (telephone)

pròprio own, private

prosciútto ham

pròssimo near, next

pròtesi dentària dental prosthesis

protestànte protestant

provàre to prove, to try; **pòsso provàrmelo?** may I try it on?

prúgna plum

pulíre to clean

púllman motor coach

punch punch

puntéggio score

puntíno dot; **a puntíno** medium (of meat)

Q

qua here

quàdro picture, painting

quàdri diamonds (cards)

quàlche a few, some, any

qualcúno somebody, someone, anybody

qualità quality

quàndo when

quànto how much; **quànto còsta?** how much is it?

quarànta forty

quàrto fourth, quarter

quattórdici fourteen

quàttro four

quattrocènto four hundred

quéllo that, that one; **che cos'è quéllo?** what's that?

quésto this

qui here

quíndici fifteen

quínto fifth

R

rabbíno rabbi
racchétta racquet; **racchétte da scí** ski poles
raccommandàta registered letter
raccónti stories
ràdio portàtile portable radio
raffreddóre cold
ragàzza girl
ragàzzo boy
raggiúngere to reach, to get to, to arrive at
rammendàre to mend
rasóio razor
rattoppàre to patch up, to mend
ravanèllo radish
re king
recapitàre to deliver
regàlo gift
regalíno little present
reggiséno brassiere, bra
regína queen
registratóre tape recorder
religióso religious
rènna suede
respiràre to breathe
restàre to stay, to remain
rèsto change (from a paid bill)
rètro behind; **sul rètro** in the back
rícciolo curl
ricètta prescription
ricévere to receive
ricevúta receipt
ricreazióne recreation
ridótto reduced; **a taríffa ridótta** half-price ticket
ríga ruler; **con ríghe** with stripes
rigonfiaménto swelling
rimanére to remain, to stay
rimorchiàre to tow
riparàre to repair, to fix
riservàto reserved
risièdere to reside, to live
ríso rice

ristorànte restaurant
risultàto score, result, outcome
ritàrdo delay, lateness
ritornàre to return, to go back
ritórno return; **andàta e ritórno** round trip
rivísta magazine, periodical
rognóne kidney
romànzo love story, novel
ròsa rose, pink
rosétta small round bread, bun
rossétto rouge; _____ **per le làbbra** lipstick
rósso red
roulòtte trailer
rubàre to steal
rubinétto faucet
rubíno ruby
rullíno roll of film
ruòta wheel
ruscèllo brook, small stream

S

sàbato Saturday
sàbbia sand
saccarína saccharin
sacchétto bag
sàla large room; **la sàla da prànzo** dining room
salàto salted, salty
salàme salami
sàle salt
salmóne salmon
salóne di bellezza beauty parlor
salòtto living room
salumería delicatessen
salúte health; **salúte!** cheers!
salúti greetings
sàngue blood; **sto sanguinàndo** I'm bleeding
sapére to know; **lo so!** I know it!
saponétta small bar of soap
sardína sardine
sàrto tailor
sbagliàre to make a mistake, to go wrong in (something);

número sbagliàto wrong number

sbigàrsi to hurry up; **si sbríghi!** hurry up!

scàcchi chess

scacchièra chessboard

scàcco chessman

scaccomàtto checkmate

scamosciàto suede

scàmpi shrimp

scàpolo bachelor

scàrpa shoe

scarpóni da sci ski boots

scàtola box

scattàre una fòto to take a picture

scéndere to go down, to get off

scièna back

scí skiing; **scí acquático** waterskiing

sciàre to ski

sciocchézza silliness; **sciocchèzze!** nonsense!

sciòcco silly, foolish

sciovíe ski lifts

scíppo bag snatching

sciròppo syrup

scottatúra solàre sunburn

scrívere to write

scúro dark

scusàre to excuse; **mi scúsi!** excuse me!

sdraiársi to lie down, to stretch; **si sdrài!** lie down!

seccatúra nuisance; **ma che seccatúra!** what a nuisance!

sécco dry

secóndo second

sèdano celery

sedatívo sedative

sedére to sit, to be sitting; **vòglio sedérmi** I want to sit

sèdia chair; **sèdia a sdràio** chaise longue

sédici sixteen

ségala rye

seguíre to follow

sèi six

seicènto six hundred

selezióne selection; **telefonàta in teleselezióne** long-distance call

selvaggína game

semàforo traffic light

sémola bran; **pàne integràle** whole wheat (whole meal) bread

sentièro path, pathway

sentíre to feel, to hear; **non mi sènto bène** I don't feel well

sènape mustard

sènza without

séppia squid

séra evening, night; **buòna séra** good evening

serbatóio fuel tank

sèrie series; **in série A** major league (sport)

servíre to serve

servízio service; **servízi di traspòrti púbblici** public transportation

sessànta sixty

séte thirst; **ho séte** I'm thirsty

settànta seventy

sètte seven; **sètte e mèzzo** blackjack (card game)

settecènto seven hundred

settimàna week

sèttimo seventh

shampoo shampoo; **shampoo e méssa in pièga** wash and set

sherry sherry

si one, they, people, oneself, himself, herself, themselves

sí yes

sídro cider

sigarétta cigarette

sígaro cigar

significàre to mean, to signify; **che còsa significa quésto?** what does this mean?

signóra lady, wife, Mrs.

signóre gentleman, Mr. (use *signór* when addressing the person); **Signór Róssi, come stà?** Mr. Rossi, how are you?

signorína   young lady, Miss
silènzio   silence
sinagòga   synagogue
sinístro   left, left-hand; **a sinístra**   to the left
sistèma   system
slip   man's briefs, shorts
slogàre   to sprain
smàlto   enamel; **smàlto per le únghie**   nail polish
smeràldo   emerald
soccórso   help, aid; **prónto soccórso**   first aid
sògliola   sole (fish)
sòldi   money
sóle   sun
sólo   alone
sópra   on, upon, upstairs
sopràbito   overcoat
sopràno   soprano
sorèlla   sister
sorrídere   to smile
sósta   stop; **divièto di sósta** no parking
sottotítolo   subtitle
sottovèste   slip, undergarment
souvenir   souvenir
spàlla   shoulder
spàzzola   brush
spazzolíno per i dènti toothbrush
spècchio   mirror
specialità   specialty
spedíre   to send, to mail
spésso   often
spettàcolo   show
spiàggia   beach
spíccioli   small change
spílla   brooch
spína per la corrènte   electric plug
spinàci   spinach
spíngere   to push
splèndido   wonderful
spogliàre   to undress; **si spògli!** undress yourself!
spòrco   dirty

sportèllo   window (bank, post office, ticket office)
sportívo   sporting; **una màcchina sportíva** a sports car
sposàto(a)   married
spúgna   sponge
spumànte   sparkling wine
spuntàre   to trim
sputàre   to spit
squàdra   team
stàdio   stadium
stagióne   season
stàgno   pond
stàlla   barn
stànco(a)   tired; **mi sènto stànco**   I'm tired
stàre   to be, to stay, to remain
staséra   this evening
stazióne   station
stécca   carton
sterlíne   pounds (British pound sterling)
stésso   same
stiràre   to iron; **che non si stíra**   permanent press
stitichézza   constipation
stivàle   boot
stòmaco   stomach
stórto   twisted
stràda   street, road
strétto   tight, narrow
stríngere   to tighten
stupèndo(a)   wonderful
stúpido(a)   stupid; **non èssere stúpido!**   don't be stupid!
stuzzicadènti   toothpicks
su   on, upon, up, upstairs
súbito   at once, right away
succèdere   to happen; **che còsa succède?**   what's up?
suòle   soles (shoes)
supermercàto   supermarket
surf (tàvola da surf)   surf
surriscaldàre   to overheat
susína   plum

T

svéndita sale
svegliàre to wake up
sveníre to faint
sviluppàre to develop

tabacchería tobacco shop
tabàcco tobacco; ____ **da fiúto** snuff tobacco
tacchíno turkey
tàcchi heels (shoes)
taccuíno notebook
tàglia size
tagliàre to cut; **un tàglio di capélli** a haircut
tagliaúnghie nail clippers
tàlco talcum powder
tampóni igiènici sanitary tampons
tànto a lot, much
tàrdi late; **a più tàrdi** see you later; **al più tàrdi** at the latest
taríffa tariff, rate, fare
tàxi taxi
tàvola table
tàzza cup
tè tea
teàtro theater
telefonàre to telephone
telefonàta phone call; **in teleselezióne** long-distance; **interurbàna** long-distance; **urbàna** local; **con prevvíso** person-to-person; **riversíbile** reverse-charge
telèfono telephone; **cabína telefónica** telephone booth; **elènco telefónico** telephone directory
telegràmma telegram
televisióne television
temperamatíte pencil sharpener
temperatúra temperature
tèmpo time, weather
temporaneamènte temporarily

tènnis tennis
tenóre tenor
tergicristàllo windshield wiper
termòmetro thermometer
tèrra earth, land
terràzza terrace
terríbile terrible
terzíno fullback (sport)
tèrzo third
tèssera card, ticket, pass, identification card
tèsta head
ti you, yourself
tínta uníta solid color
tintoría dry cleaner
tintúra dye; **tintúra di iódio** tincture of iodine
títolo title
toccàre to touch
toilette rest room
tònico tonic
tonsílle tonsils
tónno tuna
topàzio topaz
tornàre to return, to come back
tórta cake, pie
tósse cough
tossíre to cough
tour trip, excursion
tovàglia tablecloth
tovagliòlo napkin
trànsito transit; **divièto di trànsito** no entrance
tranvài streetcar
trascórrere to spend, to pass
trasmissióne transmission
trattoría inn, tavern
traversàta crossing
tre three
trecènto three hundred
trédici thirteen
trèno train
trènta thirty
trentúno thirty-one
trentadúe thirty-two
tròta trout
trúcco makeup
tu you

turchése turquoise
túbo di scappaménto exhaust pipe
turístico for tourists
tútto(a) all, everything; **tútta l'estáte** all summer

U

uccèllo bird
uff! phew!
ufficio office; **ufficio postàle** post office
uh! ugh!
último(a) last
úndici eleven
università university
un, úno, úna, un' a, a, one
uòvo egg; **uòva sode** hard-cooked eggs; _____ **strapazzàte** scrambled eggs; _____ **alla coque** soft-boiled eggs
urbàno urban
uscíre to go out; **èsca!** get out!
uscíta exit, gate
ustióne burn

V

vacànza vacation
vàglia money order
vagóne railroad car; **vagóne lètto** sleeping car
valígia suitcase
vallàta valley
valúta currency
vaníglia vanilla
vedére to see
vellúto velvet
velóce fast; **più velóce** faster
véndere to sell
venerdì Friday
vénti twenty
ventidúe twenty-two
ventimíla twenty thousand
vènto wind; **tíra vènto** it's windy

ventàglio fan
ventúno twenty-one
vérde green
vèro true, real
vèspa motor scooter
vestàglia robe
vèste dress
vestírsi to get dressed; **si vèsta!** get dressed!
vestíto dress, suit
vetrína shop window
vétro glass; **vétro soffiàto** blown glass
vía street, way; **vía aèrea** airmail
viàggio trip
vicíno near, next to
vietàto forbidden; **vietàto sputàre** no spitting
villàggio village
villíno cottage
víncere to win
víno wine
vísita visit
vitamína vitamin
víte screw
vitèllo calf; **cotolétte di vitèllo** veal cutlets
volànte steering wheel
volére to want, to wish; **vorrèi** I'd like
vólo flight
vòlta time; **úna vòlta** once
vóngole clams

Z

zàffiro sapphire
zèro zero
zía aunt
zío uncle
zítto! shut up!
zóna zone, area
zòo zoo; **giardíno zoològico** zoological garden
zúcchero sugar

INDEX

Longo

Anticaglia   Apostoli

Firenze Corso
Meridionale

Tribunali

Via Duomo

Colletta

Piazza
Garibaldi

Corso Garibaldi

Via Cosmo

Corso Lucci

Corso Umberto

Piazza
Mercato

Via Nuova Marina

Via C. Colombo

Port de Plaisance

M e d i t e r r a n e a n

BOLOGNA

N

Viale P. Pietramellara

Via C. Boldrini

Via Amendola

Viale Angelo Masini

Viale Stalingrado

Viale Carlo

Via Milazzo

Via Serra

Via Galliera

Via dei Mille

La Piazzola

Mura P. ta Galliena

Piazza dei Martiri

Via del Pallone

Via Capo di Lucca

Via del Borgo S. Pietro

Via Mascarella

Via Marconi

Via del Porto

Parco della Montagnola

Via dei Mille

Piazza Otto Agosto

Via Menotti

Via Irnerio

Pinacoteca Nazionale

Via Riva di Ren

Via A. Righi

Via de Castagnoli

Centrotrecento

Via Belle Arti

Via Zamboni

Via Nazario Sauro

Via S. Giorgio

Via Marsala

Via Goito

Basilica di San Martino

Teatro Comunale

Chiesa Metropolitana di S. Pietro

Altabella

Piazza Verdi

Via Ugo Bassi

Via Rizzoli

Piazza Porta

Via San Vitale

Palazzo Comunale

Piazza Maggiore

Due Torri

Chiesa di S. Salvatore

Basilica di San Petronio

Strada

Maggiore

Via Broccaindosso

Chiesa di S.G. Battista Oratorio

Archiginnasio

Via Farini

Basilica di S. Stefano

Via Guerrazzi

Basilica di S. Maria dei Servi

Via Fondazza

Via Tagliapietre

Chiesa di San Procolo

Via Castiglione

Via Rialto

Via Santo Stefano

Via de Coltelli

Via Tovaglie

Piazza San Domenico

Viale XII Giugno

Via Arienti

Via Orfeo

Viale E. Panzacchi

Viale G. Gozzadini

Santuario della Mad. del Baraccano

0	2.5 km.	5 km.
0	1.5 mi.	3 mi.